MW01002424

ALL YESTERDAYS' PARTIES

Also by CLINTON HEYLIN

Despite the System:
Orson Welles Versus the Hollywood Studios

Can You Feel the Silence?:
Van Morrison, a New Biography

Bootleg! The Rise and Fall of the
Secret Recording Industry (2nd Edition)

Bob Dylan:
Behind the Shades Revisited (2nd Edition)

No More Sad Refrains:
The Life and Times of Sandy Denny

Dylan's Dœmon Lover:
The Tangled Tale of a 450-Year-Old Pop Ballad

Never Mind the Bollocks, Here's the Sex Pistols

Bob Dylan:
The Recording Sessions, 1960–1994

Bob Dylan:
A Life in Stolen Moments: Day by Day, 1941–1995

From the Velvets to the Voidoids:
A Pre-Punk History for a Post-Punk World

The Da Capo Book of Rock & Roll Writing (editor)

ALL YESTERDAYS' PARTIES

The Velvet Underground in Print: 1966–1971

Edited by
CLINTON HEYLIN

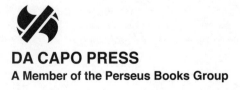

DA CAPO PRESS
A Member of the Perseus Books Group

A list of credits/permissions for all pieces can be found on page 263.

Every effort has been made to contact or trace all copyright holders.
The publishers will be glad to make good any errors or omissions brought
to our attention in future editions.

Designed by Trish Wilkinson
Set in 11.5-point Goudy by the Perseus Books Group

Cataloging-in-Publication data for this book is available from the Library of
Congress

First Da Capo Press edition 2005
ISBN 0-306-81365-3

Published by Da Capo Press
A Member of the Perseus Books Group
http://www.dacapopress.com

Da Capo Press books are available at special discounts for bulk purchases in the
United States by corporations, institutions, and other organizations. For more
information, please contact the Special Markets Department at the Perseus Books
Group, 11 Cambridge Center, Cambridge, MA 02142, or call (800) 255-1514 or
(617) 252-5298, or e-mail special.markets@perseusbooks.com.

1 2 3 4 5 6 7 8 9—08 07 06 05

CONTENTS

1969

1970–71

MB
MACFADDEN
BOOKS

THE VELVET UNDERGROUND

60¢
60-142

Here is an incredible book. It will shock and amaze you. But as a documentary on the sexual corruption of our age, it is a **must** for every thinking adult

BY MICHAEL LEIGH

INTRODUCTION BY LOUIS BERG, M.D.

ACKNOWLEDGMENTS

THANKS TO OLIVIER LANDEMAIN, DAVE KNIGHT, SCOTT CURRAN, AND ANDREW Sclanders for the loan or locating of rare originals. Without them, no book.

And thanks to Da Capo captain of industry, Ben Schafer, for making it happen.

MARCH OF THE WOODEN SOLDIERS
The Velvets and Their Underground Reputation

The Velvets were the first important rock & roll artists who had no real chance of attracting a mass audience. [If] this was paradoxical, . . . the very idea of rock & roll art rests on a contradiction. Its greatest exponents—the Beatles, the Stones, and (especially) the Who—undercut the contradiction by making the surface of the music deceptively casual, then demolished it by reaching millions of kids. But the Velvets' music was too overtly intellectual, stylized, and distanced to be commercial. Like pop art, which was very much a part of the Velvets' world, it was anti-art art made by anti-elite elitists.

ELLEN WILLIS, 1978

WHEN LOU REED, JOHN CALE, AND STERLING MORRISON MADE THEIR FIRST recordings as the Velvet Underground—during July 1965, in the lofty crash-pad of Cale and Reed on Ludlow Street, at the eastern extremity of Manhattan's Lower East Side—they hardly envisioned inhabiting the same realm as their heroes, those exponents of "rock & roll art" Willis cites above. From the start, the band existed on that radical borderline still separating "pop" from serious music (Dylan being days away from dissolving the old order of pop and folk at some tin-poke folk-fest on Rhode Island).

The songs they recorded over the noise of the New York streets that summer afternoon—which now fill the first disc of the Velvets' very own five-CD anthology, *Peel Slowly and See* (1995)—were not merely "too overtly intellectual, stylized, and distanced to be commercial," but their subject matter stood a million miles away from the world of radio play. Sex, drugs, politics, and death collide on "Heroin," "Prominent Men," and "Venus in Furs" (as well as on another, seemingly lost reel where "Black Angel's Death Song" apparently resides, alongside something called "Never Get Emotionally Involved with Man, Woman, Beast, or Child").

There was nothing "pop" about these prototypical recordings, made barely a month after the ramparts were first raised by Dylan's electric marauders on the world's first six-minute pop 45, "Like a Rolling Stone." That Reed was still hiding under Dylan's umbrella is evidenced by "Prominent Men," as well as by the lopsided folkiness of the trio's time signatures. But Reed was already dealing with subject matter at which even an amphetaminized Dylan balked.

Reed had previously been punching the clock (and the wall!) in the Long Island equivalent of the Brill Building, pounding out hit-replicants for the Pickwick label under a variety of necessary disguises. But his final Pickwick recording, "The Ostrich"—leading as it did to that serendipitous rendezvous with Cale—was a *Spitting Image* send-up of this whole sorry factory of pop songsmiths. It was time to get serious.

At the same time, John Cale was looking to embrace a little frivolity. His adoption into one of the more idiot-savant credos among New York's avant-garde—as ongoing member of the Theater of Eternal Music aka Dream Syndicate, an experimental outfit that centered on La Monte Young—certainly made for some challenging evenings bewildering Noo Yawk's arty-sans, even if the warm drones emitting from Young & Co. lent more toward the eternal than the musical.

Upon meeting Lou Reed and hearing him play the likes of "Heroin" and "Waiting for the Man"—"on an acoustic guitar *as if they were folk songs*"—Cale admits that he "was terrifically excited by the possibility of combining what I had been doing with La Monte with what I was doing with Lou, *and finding a commercial outlet*" (my italics). Here comes that dichotomy rearing up again. (And lest we forget, Cale continued his sonic experiments for his own amusement, recording a series of short instrumental pieces like "Loop" and "Noise"—issued in the Velvets' name as part of multimedia packages—as well as more ambitious pieces like the forty-two-minute "Sun Blindness Music," issued in 2000 as the title piece on the first of three archival CDs of Cale's Velvet-era home recordings.)

The kind of contradictions highlighted by Willis were present from day one, inherent in their whole aesthetic. It would center on an in-your-face sonic confrontation, celebrated in the (essentially negative) press quotes proudly emblazoned across the inner sleeve on their debut album. If, at the time, they hoped it might yet prove a selling point, evidence was mounting against them. As soon as they stopped playing to the smart-art crowd and began infiltrating a more pop caucus, they were trying to cry halt on the whole midsixties pop gestalt—with predictable results. Witness Rob Norris's 1979 recollection, in *Kicks*, of the November night the Velvet Underground invaded Summit High School in New Jersey, their first billed performance:

> Nothing could have prepared the kids and parents assembled in the auditorium for what they were about to experience that night. Our only clue was the small crowd of strange-looking people hanging around in front of the stage. When the curtain went up, nobody could believe their eyes! There stood the Velvet Underground—all tall and dressed mostly in black; two of them were wearing sunglasses. One of the guys with the shades had VERY long hair and was wearing silver jewelry. He was holding a large violin. The drummer had a Beatle haircut and was standing at a small oddly arranged drumkit. Was it a boy or a girl? Before we could take it all in, everyone was hit by a screeching surge of sound, with a pounding beat louder than anything we had ever heard.

About a minute into the second song, which the singer introduced as
"Heroin," the music began to get even more intense. It swelled and ac-
celerated like a giant tidal wave which was threatening to engulf us all.
At this point, most of the audience retreated in horror. . . . My friends
and I moved a little closer to the stage, knowing that something special
was happening.

Dylan may have met his nemeses head-on at Newport, and gone on
from strength to strength, but confronting one's audience remained a
tricky business, made trickier for the Velvets by their lack of *any* audience and their expulsion from the Cafés Wha and Bizarre in the West
Village for upsetting the customers. If Captain Beefheart had the
Avalon in San Francisco at which to diddle his "Diddy Wah Diddy,"
and the MC5 had the Grande in Detroit from which to go "Black to
Comm," it took the interest of would-be pop impresario Andy Warhol
before the Velvets found the requisite umbrella under which they
could profit and prosper.

Warhol instinctively realized that if ever there was a rock band designed to be darlings of the underground, it was the Velvets. Save
that, in 1965, there was no pop underground. Nor was there an underground press as such. Whereas, by the end of 1968, when the MC5,
Captain Beefheart, and the Stooges were all signed up, there was at
least the prospect of press for such pop-pariahs.

When the Velvets signed to Verve, in 1966, all bands made their
reputations with singles (something even Dylan recognized after the
Byrds' "Mr. Tambourine Man" introduced him to a whole new demo-
graphic). Most albums comprised two hit singles and a dozen b-sides,
whilst the press still translated the new sounds for an essentially
middle-brow mainstream media. There were no forums for hip young
rock critics, because there were no rock magazines. What passed for the
pop press in America—*Sixteen, Datebook, Teen Scene,* and *Hullabaloo*—
was not merely uncritical, it was wholly nonconfrontational juvenalia
designed to keep teens keen.

It could be argued that the underground rock press came along precisely because the mainstream press maintained a lofty disdain for the more challenging forms of pop music, while the teen mags reduced everything down to favorite sandwich filling. In fact, the Velvet Underground very soon piqued the interest of the dailies, albeit as willing performers in impresario Andy Warhol's latest circus of freaks, first, and musical curios, second.

A typically sardonic *New York Times* review of their first appearance under the Warhol imprimatur—at a psychiatric convention at the Delmonico Hotel on January 10, 1966—provides an exact snapshot of the kind of shock value the band carried as their banner for the longest time: "When 'The Velvet Underground' swung into action the high-decibel sound, aptly described by Dr. Campbell as 'a short-lived torture of cacophony,' was a combination of rock 'n' roll and Egyptian belly-dance music."

A month later they were again to be found in their hometown broadsheet. This time it was their stint at the Cinemateque—playing against a backdrop of mismatched films—that drew the fire of the *Times*' crusty-enough-to-be-a-crustacean critic of film and theater, Bosley Crowther. By the end of the evening, Crowther was clearly beginning to feel that he was getting too old for this. But then, the intent all along was to disturb. As Cale observed in his autobiography, Warhol felt "he had to whip his act into shape and bring the focus and volume to a shattering level. To this end he arranged a week-long engagement in mid-February at the Cinemateque, where underground movies were screened. We were in this tiny little theater playing as loud as possible, just victimizing the audience more than anything."

The whipping—metaphorical and literal—achieved its purpose, and by the spring the Velvets were ready for their first assault on a West Coast state of mind. When they headed west in early May, expecting a long, strange trip, they arrived first at the Whisky A Go Go's short-lived alter ego, the Trip. The band's stint at the Trip, scheduled to last a fortnight, was curtailed by the police, who shut them down after the third night, having viewed the likes of "Venus in Furs" as the pop-song equivalent of one of Lenny Bruce's satirical screeds, and an affront to core values.

As such, the *Los Angeles Times* review, which ran the same day the quartet's First Amendment rights were put on hold, was a prescient piece of writing in its depiction of "a rock group that goes beyond rock." However, it was the "abandoned, frenetic, frenzied dances . . . with leather, ropes and foil, sort of fetishist," that spun the LAPD's wheels. So the Warhol troupe and its court minstrels, the Velvets, fled to the Castle, a mansion in the Hollywood Hills, to await their next engagement and to read an altogether hipper critique in the *Los Angeles Free Press*, courtesy of the awfully well read (it's well known) Paul Jay Robbins. The *Free Press* may not have been a rock fanzine per se, but it counted in the counterculture stakes, continuing to cast the occasional glance at the Velvets throughout their—and its—existence.

Further up the coast, the *San Francisco Chronicle* itself found the Velvets "shatteringly contemporary," though their one and only pop critic, Ralph J. Gleason, gave them the critical cold shoulder after they alienated the overseer of the Fillmore franchise, gruff East European émigré Bill Graham. Gleason never saw the light, even though San Francisco became, in the years to come, the band's second-favorite residence.

The Velvets, seemingly unfazed, returned east via Chicago, where they stopped off at Poor Richard's to perform a couple of shows in their most avant-garde incarnation. Reed had been laid low by some disease of the soul. The show, though, in its Exploding Plastic Inevitability, went on—with Cale as frontman, Mo on bass, and Angus MacLise, the combo's original drummer, beating out time, whilst Ronald Nasser filmed the performance, before dissecting it into some kind of celluloid cut-up for his less-than-representative Exploding Plastic Inevitable (a review of which, from the *Free Press*, appears herein).

Again, opinion was not so much divided as dichotomized within the breezy boroughs of the Second City. Dispatched from the *Tribune* was an uncomprehending Ms. Nelson, determined to prove the whole thing to be one of Warhol's "put-ons," while the *Daily News'* Michaelo Williams found that Warhol's revue "actually vibrates with menace, cynicism and perversion. To experience it is to be brutalized." If the Chicago daily press had entrusted their reactions to the womenfolk, the folkies had also dispatched one of their own to check out what might be happening. It was Larry McCombes, not Mr. Jones, who sent a long, bewildering review to the *Boston Broadside*, a long-standing alternative to New York's *Broadside*, which they duly ran, presumably as a warning to one and all.

If the *Boston Broadside*'s continued interest in more traditional fare—unfazed by Dylan's act of electric apostasy—was about to consign it to the same historical waste-disposal as the *Little Sandy Review*, Minnesota's folkzine (cofounded by Paul Nelson, who *was* converted by Dylan's new sound and would go on to compile VU's double live set, *1969*), it at least concentrated on the musical aspect. In fact, one of its readers had already decided that what was needed was a forum for the more musically furious. In February 1966, a regular subscriber to *Boston Broadside* and a Swarthmore student, Paul Williams, mimeographed the first issue of an ostensibly biweekly review magazine of the latest sounds, fittingly named *Crawdaddy*.

And yet, when the Velvets performed down the road from Swarthmore as part of the Philadelphia Art Festival in December 1966—by which time *Crawdaddy* was printed, not mimeographed, and monthly— it was left to the everyday *Enquirer* to shape public perceptions about this self-proclaimed "mixed-media discotheque." Perhaps the ads for this extravaganza passed Williams by, which temptingly offered a bill that consisted of "first . . . underground films . . . then Andy Warhol, himself, and [then] his rock group, The Velvet Underground And Nico. Then they flash lights on you and everything and turn you into wallpaper. Then you're supposed to go out of your mind. The critics aren't wild about this but only the Arts Council has the nerve to do it."

Williams later admitted, in his mid-1980s rock odyssey *The Map*, that even in 1968 he felt foolish because friends had been telling him

how great the Velvets were for the past two years, "and I wouldn't listen." And yet, to his eternal credit, when he *did* realize the error of his
ways, he ran two seminal critiques of the band in the summer of 1968,
one a review of *White Light/White Heat* by Sandy Pearlman and the
other an iconoclastic demolition of the common perspective in rock
criticism to date (Williams's included) by Wayne McGuire. These appeared in consecutive issues of *Crawdaddy*, which remained under
Williams's tutelage, though it had traveled a long way from its original
mimeographic self.

This pair of think-pieces served as important reminders of the band's
ongoing significance at a time when they had all but fallen off the
commercial cliff. Their initial sprint of newsprint had been exhausted
with and by the end of the Exploding Plastic Inevitable and its "news-
worthy" Warhol association. The message was clear: as long as the Velvets remained Warhol's latest playthings, they could garner column
inches in the drip-dry dailies. It is no coincidence that the last mainstream review of the Velvets in the sixties came from Ann Arbor shows
in April 1967, part of the EPI's final furlough.

At some point during a three-week residency at the New York Gymnasium, which began just three days after their Michigan meeting, the
Velvets—who were billed beneath both Warhol *and* Nico in Gymnasium press ads—jettisoned their imposed prima donna and her artistic
ally. Barely a month after the belated release of their debut album, be-
decked by a pink banana, the Velvets decided to set their own dates
with destiny.

The result, on an artistic level, was a triumph: eighteen months of
white-heat creativity as a live act, during which they reinvented rock
as a performance art (for good). Until September 1968, when their
most versatile contributor, John Cale, was putsched out of the band,
they also inadvertently became modern music's greatest secret. Even
now, when their Import is a given, the only officially available audio
documentation of this eighteen-month period is a recording of two
songs from their final night at the Gymnasium in April 1967 (though

two more songs from an early show at La Cave, in Cleveland, exactly a year later, circulate widely on bootleg).

The studio recordings from this period still highlight the paradoxical nature of the band, combining their most devoutly dissonant statement, *White Light/White Heat*, with the fairground attraction of at least one unissued 45, "Stephanie Says b/w Temptation Inside Your Heart" (both issued on 1985's *VU*). But these recordings from the unnatural confines of four studio walls rarely suggest the dark recesses the band was inclined to explore live—save for "Sister Ray," where the band gambled that the tape would capture the same red-line spirit the song nightly displayed in concert, and it paid off. Serving much the same purpose as the Pink Floyd's "Interstellar Overdrive," which took up far more tape before it was caged on record, "Sister Ray" defined what Cale had hoped the Velvets might become from the very start—before the Warlocks fell on their spikes—"a tapestry behind which [Lou] could set up his words, and we could do anything we wanted. And we would improvise every night, and only record albums live."

The Velvets sat at the forefront of American attempts to turn the four-minute album track into a twelve-minute excursion into extemporization—cock an ear to bootleg recordings of "Run Run Run" from Columbus in November 1966 and the Hillside Festival in August 1969 if you don't believe me—while their true peers lay across the ocean, the Pink Floyd and Fairport Convention being almost as adept at these exercises, albeit minus most of the self-conscious cacophony. As their early producer Joe Boyd once told me, "The Pink Floyd used to do a version of 'Arnold Layne' that went on for ten minutes, but when we recorded it, we did a three-minute version. Most songs were like that. . . . There was definitely a feeling at the time that recordings were supposed to be compact. [So] if you'd heard a track with Richard [Thompson] playing five choruses as a solo, you would then go into the studio and record him compressing . . . those five choruses into one."

Perhaps hoping to capture just such a free-form aesthetic, Cale arranged to record the Velvets' first live foray free of Warholian accoutrements—Nico et al.—at The Gymnasium in New York. It was here that they debuted "Searchin' for My Mainline," aka "Sister Ray," already a seventeen-minute slamfest of vying discordancies, as well as equally punch-drunk paeans like "Guess I'm Falling in Love" and "I'm Not a Young Man Anymore." Sadly, only Lou's anthem to amorous guesswork and the tarmac-stripping takeoff that is "Booker T" have so far been offered (even un)officially to the faithful.

Though the band continued to pound the boards month after month, exponents of audio-vérité go all mute on the eastern front (as do the press) until the Velvets entered Cleveland's La Cave, a year on almost to the day. Here they proceeded to reveal a sound that had fully assimilated the *modus operandi* of Monte Young's Theater of Eternal Music, but to a higher purpose (i.e., musical progression over sonic stasis). Their oft-bootlegged thirty-five-minute "prelude" to "Sister Ray," "Sweet Sister Ray," with which they opened one particular show that April—thankfully captured for posterity by Clevelander Jamie Klimek—shows a band who have welded together elements of "The Nothing Song," "Melody Laughter" (the two long *EPI* improvisations), and "Day of Niagara" (one of Theatre of Eternal Music's last experiments) with broader strokes and a greater dynamic range, riding the subconscious vibes of a sympathetic audience. (Sadly, the "Sister Ray" into which it segues has never circulated and may not even have been recorded).

So what happened to "Sweet Sister Ray"? Compressing its "five choruses into one," the Velvets probably made it an element in a greater whole, as part of a longer, more symphonic "Sister." "Sweet Rock & Roll," aka "Sister Ray, Part 3," is another element/song that seems to have fleetingly transfixed lucky witnesses at a handful of West Coast shows in the summer of 1968. According to the late Sterling Morrison, "Sweet Rock & Roll" was also used as a "preamble" to "Sister Ray": "It kind of just goes along and then hits the chords, which were very heavy." Lester Bangs, more prone to praise, described the song in glowing terms in his Velvets valedictory for Creem in 1971:

The song I remember most particularly was one they did at a strange San Diego concert in 1968. They were on with Quicksilver Messenger Service, and much of the audience was apathetic or put off; they wanted those California acid-vibes instead of what they took for cold New York negativism. . . . In a way it was the ultimate Velvet Underground concert. The audience was terrible; those that weren't downright hostile kept interrupting the announcements between songs to yell out what they wanted to hear, like "How about 'Heroin'!" and even "Play 'Searchin' for My Mainline'!" But right in the middle of all these bad vibes, the Velvets launched into a new song that was one of the most incredible musical experiences of my concert career. Lou announced it as "Sister Ray, Part Two," but it sounded nothing like the previous song. It was built on the most dolorous riff imaginable, just a few scales rising and falling mournfully, somewhat like "Venus in Furs" but less creaky, more deliberate and eloquent. The lyrics, many of which Lou made up as he went along, seemed like some fantasy from an urban inferno: "Sweet Sister Ray went to a movie / The floor was painted red and the walls were green / 'Ooohh,' she cried / 'This is the strangest movie I've ever seen. . . .'" But it was the chorus that was the most moving: "Ohhhh, sweet rock and roll— it'll cleanse your soul. . . ."

The improvised lyric Bangs cites does not appear on any known recording, even those super-slow arrangements from 1969 that have embraced "the most dolorous riff imaginable," but once Sister Ray and her crew took on a life of their own, the song invariably acquired a free-form story line embracing the surreal. The "others" in the band share Cale's belief that Reed frequently adopted an ever-expanding retinue of characters to accompany the sister on her search: "We'd start way off left of field with something totally chaotic and gradually work our way back to the version on the record. Very long, very intense, with Lou becoming a Southern preacher man, telling stories and just inventing these fantastic characters as we played."

Both "Sweet Sister Ray" and "Sweet Rock & Roll" evidently left an indelible mark on some attendees. The latter even warranted a mention in the anonymous single-paragraph review of the July 1968 Shrine show in the *Los Angeles Free Press*. For Lance Loud, though, when describing his own epiphany from a distance of three decades, it was "Sister Ray" who embossed herself on his psyche. He recalled the self-same Shrine performance in considerably greater detail, in a mid-1990s piece in the short-lived *Gadfly*:

> After a moment of complete silence, one of four shadowy figures stepped to the microphone in front. "Good evening Los Angeles. We're the Velvet Underground." Then, turning his back to the audience, Lou Reed counted, "One, two, three. . . ." With a crash, the band slammed into its first song, "White Light/White Heat." Talk about a Wall of Sound. The music's sheer volume, enhanced by massive distortion, multiplied by feedback and then raised to the nth degree by a brutal attack on the instruments, roared like a rhythmic avalanche and crushed the crowd.
>
> At the height of the peace-and-love era, there was very little about this band that suggested flower power. . . . [Reed] introduced "Heroin" sarcastically as "our big hit." Propelled by Cale's viola, the number moved grippingly between dream state and Armageddon.
>
> Apart from Tucker's arresting stage presence, though, the band remained deliberately aloof. Reed rarely looked at the audience, even when he spoke a few mumbled words. But that is not to say that the audience wasn't paying attention. Like bystanders at the scene of a grisly accident, the crowd kept its eyes glued to the stage. . . .
>
> But deep in my memory, the image of that night at the Shrine keeps pounding away. As the band played its final number, "Sister Ray," Cale bent over his electric organ, filling the hall with jagged glissandos, chaotic onslaughts of notes thrown like shards of broken glass into the crowd. And, finally, the audience danced. All the

while, a growing, doomy drone began to envelop and erase the distinct characteristics of the individual instruments, until they all seemed to blend into an ominous rumble that did not stop coming out of the speakers, even after the band left the stage.

Of course, Loud writes here from the other side of the divide. By the time he penned these thoughts, catching the Velvets in their prime had become a badge of honor, and to have been one of the few self-appointees who "got it" only brought further kudos. Ever noticed how everyone who booed Bobby D. at Newport has died off or been rendered mute by the gods? Even Bangs's religious experience in San Diego was imbued with the posthumous glow of notoriety, being recalled when he was trying to bottle the band in his memory bank, knowing that he would not see their kind no more. As the headline to his eight-thousand-word post-Max's essay put it, "Here Lie the Velvets, Underground."

Hence the disproportionate significance of those glaringly few bite-sized reviews the Velvets generated in 1967 and 1968, when the pop world was yet to stir from its self-induced torpor in Pepperland. Just about any contemporary documentation acquires a certain value from its scarcity, and a concomitant paucity of detail as to what really "went down, man." When a letter from October 1968, penned by a gushy Susan Pile to her pen pal Edward Walsh, describes the Velvets at the point of transition from Calean chaos to the Yule school, it becomes an important historical document—if a somewhat scant substitute for audio evidence of the described gig at Whisky A Go Go, where the Velvets were playing for the first time without Cale. In Pile's fevered opinion:

They're sounding better than I can remember them for a long time. The new kid is named Doug(ie)(las)—he's from Boston, plays bass and organ and is really neat-looking (more so—perhaps—from a strictly objective viewpoint—than M. Reed). They have a lot of new material, like one song that ends (in joyous two-part harmony of sufficient unintelligibility) "How does it feel . . . to be dumb?" Plus, things like "Waiting for the Man" slowed to an easy Booker T. Louis doesn't really dominate the group any more—in fact, I would consider Sterling lead guitar. You won't believe how strong they are musically now.

Would that one could bend an ear to the Whisky-infused variant of those precious auditory documents that sporadically revealed how these post-EPI explorations were progressing. One listen to the rendition of "What Goes On" on the official boxed set—uncorked from Jamie Klimek's vintage hoard of La Cave tapes, and presumably a representative sample from what Yule believes to have been his actual live debut in early October 1968—suggests the scale of the loss. Thankfully, it heralded some kind of new age when tape recorders (most, admittedly, attached to cocoa tins by string) began to appear at Velvet Underground gigs, even if they were rarely accompanied by reporters' notebooks.

Those who learned to prefer the not-so-perfect to the note-perfect as long as it remained fresh and vital incorporated a small cabal of Clevelanders, who held on to their faith through the half-yearly intervals in 1968–69 that separated one residency at La Cave from the next. Among those who found reverence, not revulsion, in this dank cavern were Jamie Klimek, later founder of the Cleveland pre-punk combo the Mirrors, who was busy accumulating an archive for personal reference; and an equally callow Peter Laughner, a guitar player already looking for a ride, who concentrated on taking mental notes of the duosonics coming out of Morrison and Reed. Laughner would form a number of Velvet-inspired combos in his hometown, beginning with Cinderella Backstreet, before he took his final ride into the sunset in June 1977, aged just twenty-four. Both lads avidly scanned the few rock-oriented rags for any notes from the Underground.

Also temporarily trapped in the Midwest was another fledgling guitarist for whom the eclectic and the experimental went strap in hand.
Robert Quine was holed up in the Missouri mudflats, awaiting opportunity and working on a law degree, when the Velvets passed through St.
Louis in the spring of 1969. Inspired by a self-made recording of that
show that he played to the brink of death that summer, Quine relo-
cated to the Bay Area that fall, in time for the return of the Velvets to
The Matrix, where another secret society founded on feedback awaited
their ubiquitous shows that fall.

If there were small clubs, non-greedy owners, and loyal punters
enough to fill the band's calendar a month at a time in San Francisco
and its spread-eagled environs, the Velvets still found themselves ex-
cluded from the white boys' club that existed at 746 Brannan Street,
despite its inmates appointing themselves arbiters of all things counterculture in rock. The San Francisco–based *Rolling Stone* had taken
the *Crawdaddy* template but employed a real designer, and despite a
two-year head start, was soon nudging past its more senior rival on the
inside track. Though *Stone* was up and running by the time the Velvets took to the road to promote their second fab waxing, *White
Light/White Heat*, released at the cusp of 1967 and 1968, it failed to
muster even a curt dismissal in the review pages of this not-yet-august
journal—despite Verve stumping up for a full-page ad in issue nine. In
fact, the review editor, John Burks, passed over an unsolicited review
of that album sent in by some shoe salesman from San Diego by the
name of Lester Bangs.

The band's second Verve offering had at least come to the attention
of the not merely august but positively venerable *Melody Maker*, the
oldest pop weekly in the world. Their album reviewer latched on to
the aesthetic right away—as the work of pop Dadaists: "Utterly pretentious, unbelievably monotonous. It even has one track taken up by
a long bit of story-telling." Such was the tone, nay, the extent, of the
band's contemporaneous coverage in the U.K. (A single-paragraph review of the third album was less damning. However, as faint praise

goes, "not sensational, but interesting" hardly encapsulates either *The Velvet Underground* or *White Light/White Heat*.)

Sandy Pearlman, writing in *Crawdaddy*, also found the Velvets' second album pretentious and monotonous, save that on his clipper ship these were terms of praise. Pearlman was hip enough to dig the schtick that "each of the six songs on the album is generated out of its own virtually immutable bass/drum pattern. Repeated over and over. Not even cycled. All sounding mechanistic enough to be mistaken for electronics. 'White Light/White Heat' especially. It fails to be boring 'cause it's got that fascination potential inherent in all mechanically perfect execution (hypnosis)."

The almost total dearth of coverage in the highly competitive British music press hardly suggested the beginning of the kind of groundswell that, twenty-five years later, resulted in the Velvets— with Cale—returning to tour Britain and not the States. Back in October 1969, *Melody Maker*'s Richard Williams—who, in his A&R days at Island would try to sign the Hell-era Television to the label— summed up the tide of apathy in his headline to the one positive review of the Velvets to infiltrate the English music weeklies when the band was still a going concern: "It's a Shame That Nobody Listens."

Lillian Roxon, sweltering in New York and increasingly short of breath, writing in her *Rock Encyclopedia* the same summer (though not being published till the following year), suggested that the media silence stemmed in part from an understandable trepidation about the Velvets and their ostensible message:

> The important thing about the Velvet Underground was that in 1966 and 1967 they were as far away as a group could possibly be from the world of incense and peppermints and lollipops and even earnest teenage protest. Theirs was the dim underworld of drugs and sexual perversion, of heroin addiction and the desperate loss of hope that goes with it. Their concern was with death and violence. They were singing about a world that exists and that they knew. . . . "Heroin" didn't

have to [use] code words to get its meaning across. Musically they were very advanced, using sounds and voices in a way most groups didn't start using until 1968[!]. They were using whips on stage before the Nice and Dave Dee, and with far more sinister intent. Oozing evil and lubricity, they made every other group look like kid stuff, and they made a lot of people nervous. Their records were never played on commercial stations. There is no word for their sound but sometimes it seems as if a presence has taken over, perhaps even His Satanic Majesty himself. You can easily imagine someone performing black masses with the Velvet Underground's albums. Not for the kiddies.

Such was the critical perception of these guys 'n' gal in the summer of 1969. In the wilderness years that separate their residency at The Gymnasium from their triumphant return to Max's Kansas City in 1970, it must have seemed at times like there was but one place where the Velvets had any kind of profile. *Persona non grata* in the city that spawned, then spurned them, the Velvets had in the interim become honorary Bostonians, courtesy of their new manager Steve "Crawling King Snake" Selznick. One of Selznick's side interests was part-ownership of Boston's premier rock venue, The Tea Party, at which the Velvets made their debut at the end of May 1967, barely three weeks after they had cut the purse strings of their pop-art mentor. For two years-plus, there was rarely a season in which the Velvets did not grace the BTP with a residency.

Almost from that first instance, they drew a few moths to their flame, one of whom was the sixteen-year-old Jonathan Richman. He was immediately inspired to articulate his profound experience in print, albeit in the so-far-underground-it-was-invisible pages of Boston's first rockzine, *Vibrations*, where his three-page feature, "New York Art and the Velvet Underground," came complete with a diagram in which Richman predicted the Velvets overtaking everyone save the Beatles, crossing the "made-it line" at some point in 1968, and closing in on God by the end of 1970 (see page xxxv). As Cale later recalled,

"Jonathan would show up persistently with . . . scribbled poems that he had written about this, that and the other, mainly about the band." Evidently, *Vibrations* ran one such scribbling.*

If *Vibrations* existed below just about every radar invented, the next advocate to demand that someone pay attention to these denizens of discordancy was writing in the altogether more snappy-looking *Crawdaddy*. In the summer of 1968, *Crawdaddy* still represented a viable counterpoint to the countinghouse culture already working its poison at *Rolling Stone*. If many of Paul Williams's trusty cabal of rock reactionaries, like Richard Meltzer, Jon Landau, and Sandy Pearlman, were on the verge of jumping ship (as was Williams), he was always looking for fresh perspectives. Along came one in the form of a long, rambling piece by the mysterious Wayne McGuire, ostensibly about something called The Boston Sound. Save that Mr. McGuire did not mean the Hallucinations or the remnants of the Remains, or even that babbling Irish bum who wandered from Cambridge club to Cambridge club claiming to be the author of "Gloria" and "Brown-Eyed Girl." As if.

McGuire was a man on a mission, not merely writing a review of the Velvet Underground, but making it "a review of the end of the world . . . a review of the Antichrist and Christ . . . a review of Life and Death . . . a review of tomorrow and of ever and ever." As for his peers in the music press, he accused them of being "engaged in creating and perpetuating New American Muzak," of being "probably too occupied delving into the subtleties of *Sgt. Pepper*, due to an astigmatism of the mind," to notice the one band that was "musically and mentally two years ahead of its time." Only for the Velvets (and Coltrane) did he reserve words of praise. But what praise: "Put quite simply, the Velvet Underground is the most vital and significant group in the world today." Where did such insights dawn? "At the Boston Tea

*Sadly, Richman refused permission to reproduce the article here, though it can be found on Scorpio bootleg set, *Caught Between the Twisted Stars*.

Party . . . [where] the V.U. brings about an organic fusion of image, light and sound."

So the likes of Richman and McGuire, true evangelists of Velveteen performance-art, *did* exist in towns like Boston. Even here, though, with *Vibrations* as reliable as Errol Flynn on a bender and the fledgling *Fusion* still finding its feet, opportunities to write about the band were as rare as a bad Beatles 45. The cruel historical truth is that much of the self-styled underground press was still searching for an identity when the Velvets were already pinging past their pomp. (By October 1968, Paul Williams, the one editor open enough to publish articles offering a new perspective, even if they came from someone directly attacking his own—as McGuire assuredly did—had quit *Crawdaddy*, retiring to a commune in Mendocino [yes, those were the days!], so even *Crawdaddy* had ceased to document the Velvets, save for one impenetrable interview with frontman Reed in 1970 from some clown who thought it terribly clever to refuse to clarify who was saying what.)

For the moment, *Crawdaddy's* slow crawl to extinction left precious few forums save the pages of the already conformist *Rolling Stone*, where even record reviews were expected to adhere to some vague party line. Reflective of this sorry state of affairs was the fact that even the twenty-one-year-old Lester Bangs, another convert bustin' to write about the band, was obliged to write his first Velvet screed at the behest of *Stone*. That 554-word review of *The Velvet Underground*—that "difficult third album" for the band, but undoubtedly their most accessible offering to date ("Murder Mystery" excepted)—reflected a number of *Stone*-like constraints imposed editorially from above.

At *Rolling Stone*, the prose style of the most original rock critic of his generation was not so much reined in as boxed in and columned up. (Not surprisingly, the album reviewer in question never expected a gold watch for long service, though he penned the odd piece for Wenner's biweekly for the next three years.) As far as *Stone* was concerned, Bangs remained an occasional album reviewer who transmitted his thoughts from the bordertown he inhabited till he was called east by *Creem* and set free. In San Francisco the *Stone* staffers preferred to remain in their ivory townhouse whilst the Velvets launched a sustained assault on all things west in the fall of 1969.

Now, in the twenty-first century, there are five jam-packed CDs of official wares documenting the Velvets' blitzkrieg on the Bay Area in those last months of that monumental decade, including a thirty-eight-minute version of "Sister Ray" from the Matrix one fateful December day that may even have been the specific satanic rite that unleashed the demons who then sped through the Altamont racetrack the self-same evening. *Rolling Stone* devoted half an issue to the events at Altamont, but not even a column inch to the equally apocalyptic events down the street.

1969—a concise enough title for the Mercury double album Paul Nelson compiled in 1974—seemed to provide *prima facie* evidence of a band cutting across every edge going, compiled as it was from November shows at SanFran's very own Matrix and a two-nighter in October 1969 at the End of Cole Avenue in Dallas (though doubts remain as to the provenance of the version of "What Goes On," which came on a reel of its own, and sounds rather Calean to these ears). It certainly prompted a rhapsodic response on its release from punk-poetess Patti Lee Smith, whose *Creeming*-jeans prose still had a place in Detroit's favorite rockzine:

> [The reason] I love this record so much [is that] it goes beyond risk and hovers over like an electric moth. Theres no question no apologizing there is just a trust a bond with time and god their relentlessly relaxed method of getting it on and over the land of strain. Like Rimbaud we rebel baptism but you know man needs water he needs to get clean keep washing over like a Moslem. Well this drowning is eternal and you don't have to track it lambkin you just lay back and let it pour over you. Dig it submit put your hands down your pants and play side C.

However, the contrast between the respective performances at these two venues did not become apparent until the 1991 release of the entire second night at the End of Cole Avenue, Dallas, October 19, 1969, on a quasi-official Italian CD set, when the economics of unauthorized (but kosher in certain places) protection-gap releases made some important archival explorations commercially viable (see my own history of the subject, *Bootleg! The Rise and Fall of the Secret Recording Industry* [Omnibus, 2004]). The Dallas gig, taken from the original master (unlike the four cuts on 1969—"Waiting for the Man," "Femme Fatale," "Pale Blue Eyes," and "I'll Be Your Mirror"—which were from a crude dub given to the Velvets' then-manager), suggested that excursions into extemporization were sometimes the exception rather than the rule.

In fact, Sterling Morrison suggested that the problem was a more general one: the 1969 recordings were "taped in small locations. . . . Generally our sound was bigger. . . . At the Boston Tea Party, a bigger location, the ideal size for us, about 1,200 people, we could really play." The first installment from Dallas suggested Morrison was right. The quartet was certainly playing low and languorous, suffering second-night blues at the End of Cole Avenue and their tether. Even the other then-official document of the Velvets live—Atlantic's twist-my-arm, budget-bootleg, ten-song edit of both sets from their final night at Max's Kansas City in August 1970—seemed to bear out Morrison's prejudice against small shows.

Only when the first night at the End of Cole Avenue, recorded from the back of the hall in authentic cassette-mirk and mire, was given its own protection-gap dispensation in 1993 did the band show it could flex its musical muscles anywhere, anyhow, anyway. The renditions of "I Can't Stand It," "Heroin," and "Sister Ray" (actually already issued on the second-night set as a substitute for the incomplete recording from that night) suggested that place and time had less to do with their flights of fancifulness than whether the attendant few felt the fever. When the main muso at Universal, Bill Levenson, obligingly pulled a ten-minute "Some Kinda Love" from the full Max's tape—Reed's penultimate performance on that farewell farewell—for the *Peel Slowly and See* box, it reinforced the suspicion that they could give pretty much any song "the treatment."

However, it was 2001 before the audio equivalent of a smoking gun was produced—the three-CD *Quine Tapes* (first alluded to in *From the Velvets to the Voidoids* back in 1993). Bob Quine's foresight, and an understanding of the basics of recording from the audience, provided three hours plus of performances from the Matrix and the Family Dog, venues where Morrison's dictums dissolved as familiarity bred extent. Comfortable with their equipment and their audience, the band seemed prepared to bulldoze any preconceptions about song length and direction. Any and all songs could be taken on a journey. Or not. Songs that a month earlier in Dallas barely broke the five-minute barrier here scale double digits in the grandest style imaginable. The ten-minute-plus, extemporized "White Light/White Heat," "Waiting for the Man," and "Ride into the Sun" rank alongside the August 1969 Hillside Festival performances of "Run Run Run" and "What Goes On" as the definitive musical moments of the Yule era.

And then it was a new decade. The band even reached the conclusion that it was high time they made their peace with their hometown, announcing a week-long residency at the fashionably decadent Max's Kansas City in New York City at the end of May 1970 to celebrate a new label (Atlantic) and a new album. (A fourth album's worth of material was recorded for Verve/MGM, but relations were such that the label deemed the results a nonstarter commercially, and the Velvets took their songbag elsewhere, leaving Polygram to rediscover these lost treasures in time for two mid-1980s albums from the archives, *VU* and *Another View*.)

As the one-week residency at Max's became a summerlong homecoming, an unprecedented wave of positive press should have encouraged some Quine-like sage to capture those early performances at Max's that confirmed the promise of the warm-up shows in Philadelphia and Boston, at which the band debuted the likes of "Head

Held High," "Oh Gin," and an eighteen-minute from-hoedown-to-showdown medley of "Train Round the Bend" and "Oh Sweet Nuthin'." Listening to those shows merely affirms how much was sacrificed in the studio to make an album *Loaded* with hits. Nor were the new songs the only ones trimmed to a new cloth. Trusty stalwarts like "Waiting for the Man," given a nine-minute workout in Philly, had been trimmed down to a four-minute afterhours afterthought by the time of *Live at Max's* at the end of August, when Brigid Polk had the wit to lug a tape recorder onto the counter and into the archives. By then, according to Reed, "I couldn't do the songs I wanted to do and I was under a lot of pressure to do things I didn't want to do." Perhaps that final "Some Kinda Love" was intended to be to the Max's residency what the lost rendition of "Black Angel's Death Song" was to the last Café Bizarre gig five years earlier.

But early on at Max's, it would seem, the band still had fire in their fingertips, before a debilitating schedule of simultaneous shows and sessions and the loss of a heavily pregnant Tucker, the timekeeper and peacemaker, finally took its toll on Reed's vocal chords and temper. For the first and last time, it would be the press hounds who were hot on the trail, and the tapers who stayed home, as we once again find ourselves—me and you—obliged to salivate at descriptions by the regular press of how the band's return to their wellspring was an affirmation devoutly to be wished:

> The Velvet Underground plays a hard rock that is powerful and tight as a raised fist; so unified and together that it just rolls itself into a knot and throbs.
>
> —*THE NEW YORK TIMES*

Opening night, of course, was something of an event, a kind of Old Home Week that brought together various elements of the rock/pop hierarchy; plus nostalgia seekers and true believers, most of whom had not seen the Velvets since they exercised at the Gymnasium three years ago. I don't know what they expected to hear, but they certainly weren't disappointed.

—THE VILLAGE VOICE

However, by the summer of 1970 the local scribes from the *New York Times* and the *Village Voice* were having to slum it with the rock hacks from the new journals, for the rock underground was in bloom and oblivious to the flowers of evil they were about to propagate. *Creem* from Detroit, *Fusion* from Boston, *New Times* from New York, *Circus* too, *Friendz* and *Zigzag* from England, all wanted to praise the band just for surviving. Max's afforded them the opportunity:

> They sound something like the old Velvets, the old Who and Cree-dence Clearwater stuck together. Hard rock with the trademark of Lou Reed's Bo Diddley strumming. Maureen Tucker's stethoscopic drumming isn't there, but Doug's bruvver swings a lot more. . . . "White Light White Heat" [is] at pain threshold volume and rocking like fuck. Lou Reed, hand on hip, hand waving, head nodding with a little sneer, makes Jagger look like Val Doonican.
>
> *—FRIENDS*

The reviewers who rhapsodized about the Max's residency continued to hold their heads high when the Velvets' Atlantic debut platter, *Loaded*, appeared at the winter solstice. By then, it was known that *Loaded* was also to be the final proclamation of the band. *Loaded* and Max's had taken too much out of them, being a step too far along the road to commercial acceptance ("Who Loves the Sun," in particular, I find to be a sickly, pale eye-shadow copy of "Ride into the Sun"— whither "Ocean"?). Perhaps it was inevitable that Reed's ambivalent attitude to success would make him prefer "sweet nuthin'" as soon as commercial acceptance mutated into a probability. Equally predictably, now that the Velvets were dead, their legions arose to salute them.

After the fact, the likes of Jonathan Richman, Sandy Pearlman, Peter Laughner, Jamie Klimek, Bob Quine, Lenny Kaye, and Jim Carroll carried the aesthetic with them into their music-making. Meanwhile, Lester Bangs, hamstrung by a patent lack of musicality himself, founded an entire school of rock journalism on the Velvets and all that they had stood for, often taking his prose where Sister Ray led. Soon enough it would be left to others, less fortunate, to write secondhand accounts of the band and its Import, until—like all things once vital and alive—its more mythopoeic elements, in large capital letters, blocked out the truth: that there was a time when the only people taking any of this in were the boys (and girls) in the backroom at the Tea Party, the End of Cole Avenue, the Dom, the Family Dog, or the Whisky.

The glare of hindsight may require some shades. Proceed with caution. As for the Velvets themselves, they continue to linger on, as an influence overarching every worthy successor to their cultish crown.

Clinton Heylin, June 2004

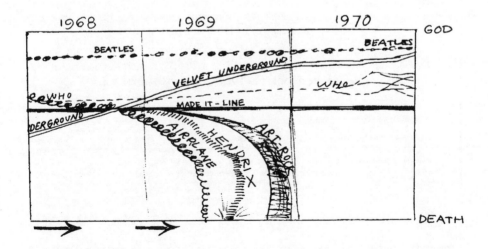

Photo by John E. Lynch

the myddle class

IN CONCERT

Summit High School Auditorium
125 Kent Place Blvd. Summit, N. J.

8 p.m.   December 11, 1965 · Admission: $2.50

Tickets may be purchased in advance at:

Scotti's Record Shop	Adams Haberdashers	Henriksen's Pharmacy
346 Springfield Ave.	1271 Springfield Ave.	415 Springfield Ave.
Summit	New Providence	Berkeley Heights

Tickets may also be purchased in advance by sending a check or money order to
the myddle class, Box 221, Berkeley Heights, N. J.

Also appearing on the program:

The Forty Fingers   The Velvet Underground

1966

BALLOON FARM

ANDY WARHOL'S EXPLODING PLASTIC INEVITABLE RETURNS
THE VELVET UNDERGROUND & NICO
228-2190
23 ST. MARKSPLACE EVERY FRIDAY FRI. AND & SAT. & HOLIDAYS 9 PM TO3 AM

ANDY WARHOL
PRESENTS
Nico

SINGING TO THE SOUNDS OF
The Velvet
Underground
AT THE UNDERGROUND BAR AT
THE NEW
MOD-DOM

23 ST. MARK'S PLACE   777-2210
APPEARING NITELY EXCEPT SUN. & MON.

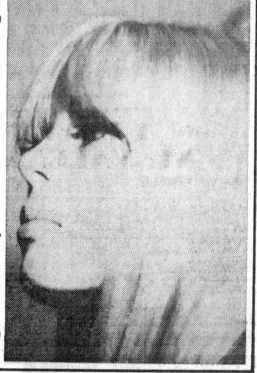

SYNDROMES POP AT DELMONICO'S
Andy Warhol and His Gang Meet the Psychiatrist

Grace Glueck

The New York Times, January 14, 1966

January 13, 1966, Delmonico's Hotel, NYC
Annual Dinner of the New York Society for Clinical Psychiatry

THE NEW YORK SOCIETY FOR CLINICAL PSYCHIATRY SURVIVED AN INVASION last night by Andy Warhol, Edie Sedgwick and a new rock 'n' roll group called "The Velvet Underground."

"The Chic Mystique of Andy Warhol," described by an associate of the painter as "a kind of community action–underground–look at yourself–film project," was billed as the evening's entertainment for the psychiatry society's 43rd annual dinner at Delmonico's Hotel. And until the very last minute, neither group quite believed the other would show up.

But sure enough, as the black-tied psychiatrists and their formally gowned wives began to trickle into Delmonico's lobby at 6:30, there was Andy, and in the evening get-up, too—sunglasses, black tie, dinner jacket and corduroy work pants. And right there with him were some of his "factory" hands—Gerard Malanga, poet; Danny Williams, cameraman; and the "factory" foreman, Billy Lunch.

The "factory," as any Warhol buff knows, is the big, silver-lined loft where he and his coterie make their underground films and help mass-produce Andy's art.

What "The Chic Mystique" was nobody really explained. The Warhol part of the program included a showing of his underground films as background for cocktail conversation and, at dinner, a concert by the rock 'n' roll group. And Warhol and his cameramen moved among the gathering with hand-held cameras, using the psychiatrists as the cast of a forthcoming Warhol movie.

The psychiatrists, who turned out in droves for the dinner, were there to be entertained—but also, in a way, to study Andy. "Creativity and the artist have always held a fascination for the serious student of human behavior," said Dr. Robert Campbell, the program chairman. "And we're fascinated by the mass communications activities of Warhol and his group."

Delmonico's elegant white-and-gold Colonnade and Grand Ballroom had probably never seen such a swinging scene. Edie Sedgwick, the "superstar" of Warhol's movies, was on full blast—chewing gum and sipping a martini.

There was John Cale, leader of "The Velvet Underground," in a black suit with rhinestones on the collar. There was Nico, identified by Warhol as "a famous fashion model and now a singer," in a white slack suit with long blond hair. And there were all those psychiatrists, away from their couches but not really mingling, not letting their hair down at all.

"I suppose you could call this gathering a spontaneous eruption of the id," said Dr. Alfred Lilienthal. "Warhol's message is one of super-reality," said another, "a repetition of the concrete quite akin to the LSD experience." "Why are they exposing us to these nuts?" a third asked. "But don't quote me."

Dr. Arthur Zitrin, director of psychiatry at Bellevue Hospital, was slightly worried. "We've had everyone appear at these annual dinners, from Paul Tillich to Warhol," he said. "I'm program chairman for next year. How the hell are we going to follow this act?"

The act really came into its own midway through the dinner roast beef with stringbeans and small potatoes, when "The Velvet Underground" swung into action. The high-decibel sound, aptly described by Dr. Campbell as "a short-lived torture of cacophony," was a combination of rock 'n' roll and Egyptian belly-dance music.

The evening ended with a short talk by Jonas Mekas, film director and critic. But long before that, guests had begun to stream out. The reaction of the early departees was fairly unanimous. "Put it down as decadent Dada," said one. "It was ridiculous, outrageous, painful," said Dr. Harry Weinstock. "Everything that's new doesn't necessarily have meaning. It seemed like a whole prison ward had escaped."

"You want to do something for mental health?" asked another psychiatrist. "Kill the story."

ANDY WARHOL'S "MORE MILK YVETTE" BOWS

Bosley Crowther

The New York Times, February 9, 1966

February 8, 1966, Film-Makers' Cinematheque, NYC

GIVE ANDY WARHOL ENOUGH ROPE AND SOME LONG ENOUGH SPOOLS OF raw film and he'll succeed in putting "underground" movies right down a hole in the ground. That is the not unpleasant prospect vitalized by Mr. Warhol's latest jape—at least, the latest to be exhibited. It is something called "More Milk Yvette," which was put on last night at the Film-Makers' Cinematheque, the basement theater at 125 West 41st Street. It will be shown each night through Sunday at 8 and 10.

In this little bit of veiled allusion, Mr. Warhol is letting his camera go on a couple of close-up studies that are composed on a split or double screen. In the first study, a bewigged and roughed transvestite does a weary and witless travesty on a movie star (maybe Lana Turner) drinking milk and eating a hamburger and a pear with a bored and listless fellow, while on the other half of the screen there is a tedious pantomime of a phony torture in which a grinning guy is bound and lashed with ropes.

6

This section of the picture may be vaguely and drearily observed (if you want to observe it as something) as a mockery of masculinity.

The second part is a split screen composition of a feminine portraiture. On one side of the screen, a baby-doll blonde type is primped and powdered by a make-up man, while on the other side the same girl eats a long meal in an elegant dining-room. At the end, both panels are used to show the girl with her head in the toilet. It's an appropriate way to finish this film.

Also on the bill is a performance by a group of rock 'n' roll singers called the Velvet Underground. They bang away at their electronic equipment, while random movies are thrown on the screen in back of them.

When will somebody en-noble Mr. Warhol with an above ground movie called "For Crying Out Loud"?

A "HIGH" SCHOOL OF MUSIC AND ART

John Wilcock

The East Village Other, April 15, 1966

ANDY WARHOL AND HIS FOUR-MEMBER POP GROUP, THE VELVET UNDER-
ground, came to the Village last week, settling into the tatty, old Polish National Hall (above the Dom, on St. Mark's Place) for a three
week stay. A slender, white hand-painted banner stretching from the
balcony of the third-floor hall almost to the street was lit by winking
lights diverting the young couples who had almost decided to enter
the ground-floor Dom and listen to Tony Scott.

Upstairs, Warhol (silver hair, shades, leather jacket) watched im-
passively from the balcony as about one-third of the tables in the vast
hall filled up as soon as the ticket office opened. "It's a place for people
who have nothing to do," he said. "They took my paintings as collateral. My pictures are collateral for everything." An ironic thought
from an artist who admits that he himself doesn't even paint most of
his pictures—merely signs them.

(Recently the Dannon yoghurt people invited him to paint their
truck, actually paint it. Of course, everybody tells Andy that he should
collect a fat fee, hire a couple of truck painters and merely sign their
work. Conversely, there's the man uptown who's opening a new discotheque and invited Warhol to design it for him. Andy refused but

8

the man is broadcasting it around that he's hired Warhol and nobody will know the difference anyway unless Andy sues.)

For the first part of the opening night on St. Mark's Place there was some worry about whether the bar could open or not but by half past ten it did (beer 75 cents, cokes 50 cents) and customers were carrying paper plates of 50-cent sandwiches (salami, bologna, Swiss cheese) back to their red and white checkered tablecloths, anxious not to miss any of the gradually expanding action.

Onstage the rear wall was still being painted while the movie "Couch" was being projected on it, giving an interesting three-dimensional effect to the film, and even if there hadn't been a step-ladder in front of the "screen" it still wouldn't have been easy to follow the plot because infrequent bursts of rock and roll would burst through the amplifiers completely drowning out the already garbled soundtrack. Occasionally a couple would get up and dance but most people preferred to sit and watch.

A pair of other projectors up in the balcony went into action beaming two different movies onto the narrow strips of wall beside the stage. A colored spotlight onstage focused onto the mirrored ball that revolved in the ceiling sending pinpoints of light on predictable circuits around the room. A plastic globe glowed in cycles of changing pastel colors.

Somebody was watching the late news on a tiny, portable television set. "Wow!" said Andy. "Wouldn't it be great if we could have one of those on every table?"

The action was hotting up. Colored floodlights stabbed out from the corners, caressing the dancers with beams of green, orange, purple. At one point three loudspeakers were pouring out a cacophony of different sounds; three records played simultaneously. Oddly it all seemed to fit. "Vinyl" was playing on the screen ("We borrowed that story from Anthony Burgess," Andy says. "Hope he doesn't mind. We wanted to buy his book but we couldn't afford it") but it was being obscured by brightly colored slides and patterns from two slide machines operated by Jacki Casson. Slashes of red and blue, squares of black and white, rows of dancing dots covered the walls, the ceiling, the dancers.

Twice during the evening were sets by The Velvet Underground, a group whose howling, throbbing beat is amplified and extended by electronic dial-twiddling. It is a sound hard to describe, even harder to duplicate, but haunting in its uniqueness. And with the Velvets comes the blonde, bland, beautiful Nico, another cooler Dietrich for another cooler generation.

From upfront, by the stage, the hall was a frantic fandango of action: the lights flashing on and off, the fragmented pieces of movies, the colored patterns and slides sweeping the mirrored walls, the steady white beams of balcony projectors, the Sylvania strip lighting writhing on the floor, flashing on and off like a demented snake who's swallowed phosphorus, the foot-long flashlights of Gerard Malanga randomly stabbing the darkened hall as he danced frenetically in front of the group.

When they counted the takings they discovered that more than 400 people had paid the $2.50 to attend. Already Andy Warhol, sometime painter, has been fingerprinted for a cabaret card (which, typically, bears the picture of his assistant, Paul Morrissey). Now there is a talk of unions and agents and long-term contracts. Art has come to the discotheque and it will never be the same again.

A FAR-OUT NIGHT WITH ANDY WARHOL

Kevin Thomas

The Los Angeles Times, May 5, 1966

Wham! BAM! POW!!!

Not since the *Titanic* ran into that iceberg has there been such a collision as when Andy Warhol's Exploding Plastic Inevitable burst upon the audience at the Trip Tuesday. For once a Happening really happened, and it took Warhol to come out from New York to show how it's done.

Andy's new Disco-Flicka-Theque was lights, cameras and action. It was SuperKolossal-Kinetic-Karma.

Out came Nico, the long-haired, deep-voiced German model to sing songs as beautifully banal as herself, and the Velvet Underground, a rock group that goes beyond rock. . . . It was like a searing sound from another planet. Out came Superstars Gerard Malanga, a gypsy type, and Mary Woronov, who looks like Joan Baez—really a beautiful pair—to dance their abandoned, frenetic, frenzied dances. There was lots of stuff with leather, ropes and foil—sort of fetishist, perhaps, but effective.

Films of themselves were projected on three screens behind them as they performed. The whole show took on a ritualistic, incantatory quality. Everybody, but everybody, was turned on except some joker who shouted, "Make Believe Ballroom!" when one of those old-timey spotlighted mirrored spheres began to rotate. (Well, maybe in his way he was right.)

Far-Out Sound

The Velvet Underground is so far out that it makes the tremendous thumping beat of that great, groovy group, the Modern Folk Quartet, which opened the program, sound passe.

After the first set of TVU was finished, the leather-jacketed apostle of Pop himself came over for a chat. "I wasn't being mean, I'm just shy," said Andy Warhol by way of apology for an earlier brush-off—although he had previously agreed to an interview.

While he does seem truly shy, this pale, slight young man—it was too dark to see if he does in fact paint his hair silver—has a genius for publicity greater than Zsa Zsa Gabor and Jayne Mansfield combined.

The arrival of Andy, the hippie's hippie, on the Sunset Strip, the hippie's paradise, makes for the most perfect combination since peanut butter discovered jelly. "I love L.A. I love Hollywood. They're beautiful. Everybody's plastic—but I love plastic. I want to be plastic," says Warhol, of whom it is theorized that as a serious artist he is dedicated to making himself as insensitive as possible.

Speaking of those ladies he has made the pop girls of the year—Baby Jane Holzer in '64, Edie Sedgwick in '65 and Nico, a candidate for '66—Andy feels that "Edie was the best, the greatest. She never understood what I was doing to her. I don't know what's going to happen to her now."

Double-Terrific

"Jane wants to make it so bad and Hollywood could make her terrific. I don't understand why she hasn't made it already." When it was suggested that maybe Jane was so complete a creation that there was nothing left for Hollywood to mold, Warhol disagreed. "That should make her double-terrific."

"Nico could probably make it here tomorrow. She has that ability to be 5 and 50 at the same time. Actually, it's Gerard who wants to be the new pop girl. He tries very hard, and the EVO—that's the *East Village Other*, which is something like your *Free Press*—has already named him Slum Goddess." Asked about the absence of Ingrid Superstar, Andy explained that "we had to leave her home—she talks too much."

Part con man, part prophet, Andy Warhol, whose works are on exhibit at the Ferus Gallery on La Cienega, has got to be the biggest put-on of them all.

ANDY WARHOL AND THE NIGHT ON FIRE

Paul Jay Robbins

The Los Angeles Free Press, May 13, 1966

ANDY WARHOL, A BASICALLY OTHER-MADE MAN, IS THE SPOTLIT MOUTH OF that created creature called Pop. Since 1962, his gratis but lucrative campaign for Campbell's Soup and other cultural negations has propelled him forward if not upwards. If he is significant because he reflects his times, then it is a reflection from a shattered mirror—for he is a victim of his times. Warhol (and I use the word only to describe his products, not his personality) passed from art to advertising to anti-art to anti-film; he has now broken clean on a familiar field of anti-all. His significance is that of those gruesome pictures depicting accidents at which you stare down at the Traffic Bureau.

About a year ago, Warhol became intrigued with rock & roll and collected unto himself an assemblage of musicians called the Velvet Underground. Him, they, a chick name of Nico, a matched pair of morbid dancers, and a clutch of camp-followers, all come together in a show called the Plastic Inevitable. It's all at the Trip on Sunset Strip till May 18.

The show's name is indicative of Warhol's outlook, his motive attitude. If you can surmount your shock at what you see—and if you can keep your smile while others around you are losing theirs—the

inevitable conclusion is that all is plastic . . . , everything Western culture has fermented and eked out is plastic: sterile, mechanistic, anti-
human and transparent. We are synthetic and tasteless. The show
proves it.

Rude sprays and swathes of violent light smash into audience and
performers in colors ranging from striking to ghastly. Three screens vi-
brate unending samples from Warhol's cinematic kindergarten. The
music, flattened, minor-keyed and non-keyed, bassy, trudges into your
ears like a monastic muffle. The dancers entice and highlight the dirty
corners of your soul. Every component builds towards the final ultimate revelation of blackness, the fiery char of your hope, the demolition of stature.

Am I being condemnatory? I hope not. I dig reading Poe like any
morassed romantic, I savor Beardsley like a feather on my privates, I
read Kafka and de Sade in my intimate wine-cellar of fermenting for-
bidden fruit; even Alistair Crowley sits on my book shelf hypnotically
swinging his legs. Such artists may be described as morbid or aberrated
or even simple-sick—but only by way of attitude, not worth. Warhol,
too, has his place.

Before more, however, I should dip into the dry ice of Warhol's
cauldron and give you a sample of the soup he is now serving. . . .

His movies are no longer the innocent surveys and inspections of
the Empire State Bldg. or sleeping persons or even the ingenuous in-
gestion of a banana by someone of suspect sex. They are down-home
bondage freak-out flicks, complete with silver-bossed leather head-
masks, excruciating whips, stiff white rope. Still uncut and plotless,
they retain Warhol's concept of film as a microscope aimed at what we
always look at but never see. In this sense, along with all non-Art, it
has a certain didactic value. The dehumanizing perversions he infers,
are those we all feel but seldom confess. Of course he's right about it; I
have spun out on sado-masochistic reveries in my day and if I confess
them it's only my exhibitionistic writer's way.

The dancers retain the bondage warp and advance on it as only the living presence of flesh can; in fact, much of the footage shown is of the dancers. The male is small, finely featured, has long curly blond hair and dresses floridly; his expression usually is tormented. The female dancer is in black leather, her face strong and bare of frilly make-up, her shoulders broad and her movements bold. Much of their dancing consists of him trying to get away from her or attempting to conquer her; needless to say, she always wins—although both their whips are the same length.

Stroboscopic lights force their images to stagger haltingly in a communicative jut of quivering pain and bewildered ecstasy.

The Velvet Underground has two styles of music. One is a phlegmatic mode which accompanies lyrics which smack of Baudelaire speaking through early-morning Bob Dylan; their other style is centered around a bone-scraping electric violin played by a boy who looks like a girl (their drummer is a girl who looks like a boy). The rumbling terror of their delivery is saved only by the viscous movement of the music: if it moves slowly enough, anything lethal becomes tolerable.

Nico, the chanteuse, mitigates the impending collapse of sanity primarily because of her ineptitude as a singer. Her heavy and diffident voice seems to suggest that perhaps this is all a put-on—and by the time you realize it isn't, you've grown accustomed to the mace. Their sound is so jaded and abstracted that I can only assume they are background music for the visuals.

The lighting end of the production, with its purples and blues, maintains this pressure of fatalism and decadence. Although occasionally broken by truly beautiful patterns of light, their main effect is an assault on the eyes; not unwelcome, but not delightful.

And so it comes together, with Warhol, a slight figure in leather jacket, quietly fidgeting in the background. Nothing exalting or noble or healthy or graceful or humorous is offered—but, by God, everything else is there! Does it all sound unbearable and evil? Perhaps evil, but certainly bearable. As I said, even de Sade can be a kick if you don't depend on him too much.

It all depends on the viewer. Once I shunted aside Warhol's attempted rape on whatever mental health I've accrued, I had a ball. It was a catharsis and an enlightenment. When I left, it was good to breathe the cool night air, sweet to savor laughter. I had come through an intense spatter of nihilism—the peculiar brand of it so fashionable in New York circles—with a renewal of energies. Warhol's show is decadence, clean as a gnawed skull and honest as a crap in the can. For the first time since Warhol's mode of art gained prominence, I realized what it meant and why it is successful—aside from the big money behind it. Put simply, it is only an extrusion of our national disease, our social insensitivity. We are a dying culture and Warhol is holding our failing hand and sketching the carcinoma in our soul.

We love it because we don't know it. "More Lions!" we cry with gumdrops between our teeth from our bleached seats in the arena. We Lionize Warhol because he has the baldness to exemplify all we are pitted against and all that is pitting us. He tells us we are insensitive fools with sewers in our circulatory systems and we urge him forward with cattle prods. That is, MOST of us. And here we find Warhol's blind spot.

The only point Warhol has missed is that a new culture is queuing up backstage. Already the phoenix is preening its pretty feathers in the fire that's hardly begun; even as Warhol bites his belly, the radiant workers are advancing past him on all sides. As he stands in the jaded night snipping off his nerve-endings, glowing figures move across the horizon sowing careful seeds and singing possible songs.

Again, I am only positioning Warhol's effect, not negating its worth. He says No to today—which is a good thing to say. However, he does not say Yes to tomorrow—which is a better thing to say. If you

are honest, you will find much to enjoy in his production at the Trip—
and even more to enjoy when you leave. Warhol has a significance and
validity so powerful that to refuse or blur him on grounds of taste and
humanism is to deny the problem and accept the answer. Besides
which, there are many jollies to get off in a lifetime. . . .

Poor Richard's
— PRESENTS —
ANDY WARHOL AND HIS
EXPLODING PLASTIC
INEVITABLE (SHOW)

★ ★ ★ ★ ★ FEATURING ★ ★ ★ ★ ★

THE NEW SOUND OF THE
VELVET UNDERGROUND

★ ★ ★ ★ ★ ★ WITH ★ ★ ★ ★ ★ ★

★ NICO – Pop Girl of '66

★ ★ ★ ★ ★ ★ ★ ★ ★ ★ ★ ★ ★ ★ ★ ★ ★ ★

JUNE 21 thru JUNE 26

MOVIES, LIGHT, NOISE

Susan Nelson

The Chicago Tribune, June 29, 1966

June 21–26, 1966, held over July 3rd, Poor Richard's, Chicago, Illinois

THE ONLY SENSES WHICH DON'T SURFACE INTENSELY IN POP ARTIST ANDY Warhol's "Exploding Plastics Inevitable" revue are taste and smell. Sights there are, and sounds. For feeling, put yourself in a stable loft surrounded by panicked co-inhabitants.

Ingrid Superstar, who has "attained POP recognition," according to a press release, briefed me after the first show on opening night at Poor Richard's in Old Town. With her short, white hair lying flat and blurred make-up restored, she cooled off in a silver-lame pants suit before the second show started. She was filling in for two dancers—top billed un-Superstars—who hadn't made it for the Chicago opening.

Action had begun with three movies flashing simultaneously on white paper screens. Colored lights were reflected in mirrored balls, and a constant clash of rock 'n' roll music and garbled movie sound tracks accompanied the films. "In one film, a fellow in a rocking chair was just eating," we ventured.

Artist Eats Mushroom

"That is Robert Indiana, the artist," Miss Superstar explained. "He is eating—a big mushroom." For 35 minutes, he is caught in close-up, sometimes with a pet cat, sometimes just masticating.

We tried again. "And on the adjacent wall, did the two films of the same people show someone being tortured?"

"Oh, they must've shown 'Vinyl,'" said Miss Superstar, coming alive. "That's one of Andy's most famous classics. It's shown either one reel at a time or both at once. They're beating up Gerard [Malanga]—the one I was dancing with."

Gerard, clad in black leather pants, red-dotted leg o' mutton–sleeved shirt, leather vest and assorted leather straps at the wrists, joined us. With him was a Chicago poet. (Gerard is a poet, too.)

Film Is Farce

"'Vinyl,'" he explained patiently, "is supposed to be a farce." Actually, it spoofs a sado-masochistic work of literature, as does the bullwhip he uses in his dance with Miss Superstar. Gerard choreographed "Venus in Furs."

"This show is a new phase for Andy," Gerard continued. "It has no message: it's just entertainment." Gerard has been with Warhol four years—thru the Campbell's soup can and Brillo box phase, the underground films, and now the rock 'n' roll.

"Rock 'n' roll?"

"Yes, the films, the lights, the music are all parts—but the main thing is music. Andy is the catalyst for this, but he has no part in the show itself," Gerard said.

Movies, Lights, Noise

During the movie-lights sequence, three speakers pitch out music with intermittent groans from "Vinyl" audible, too. The sounds don't stop, except for the five minutes it takes for the Velvet Underground to set up two big amp guitars, one big amp, viola and assorted percussion pieces.

It's at this point that Gerard and Miss Superstar, and four local "volunteer" dancers, enter the scene. Then stroboscopic lights (the kind that make everything jump) are aimed at dancers gyrating with silver foil in their hands, and the sounds begin again. This time they don't stop until the end of the show, some 30 minutes later.

What makes the show a success? Gerard was asked. "The ideas," he said. What's next for the troupe? Miss Superstar mentioned something about going to London—and continuing the "concert element." They may even make room for readings by famous poets, she posed.

Concerts are usually attended for their entertainment value. But after the novelty of the lights and the big amp shocks of the group wore off, it seemed that most of the audience in the loft of Poor Richard's was bored—and on the verge of heat prostration. To feign comprehension—some tried valiantly—is letting a group which admits its farcicality put you on.

CHICAGO HAPPENINGS

Larry McCombs

Boston Broadside, July 1966

Andy Warhol's EXPLODING PLASTIC INEVITABLE with the
Velvet Underground at Poor Richard's, Chicago, 24 June 1966

IT'S HOT. GODAWFUL, STICKY, SWEATY, MISERABLE HOT. THE PLACE IS JAMMED
and there's hardly room to move. The waitress does her best, but it
takes a while to get your drink and you're dying of thirst.

There's all sorts of mirrors and lights overhead, some of them rotat-
ing. Lights shining and blinking and changing colors. White dots
moving across the walls and ceiling in a complex pattern, up one wall
and along another. Red dots start moving through and around and
among them, in a different pattern (or is it the same?).

Suddenly on the side wall there's a black & white movie, poor quality, like a badly done home movie, of a man eating. He eats slowly, lux-
uriously, savoring each bite, staring blankly off into space. He goes on
eating. Music and noise begins to come from somewhere.

Now on the end wall there's another movie. People moving
around—a girl?—several boys—one tall, well built blonde, lifting
weights, posing, dressed in Levis and open black leather jacket with a
white T-shirt underneath. He moves with a strange combination of

cruelty and sensuous delight. The man on the side wall goes on eating, staring blankly at this scene once in a while. The lights continue to dance over and through the movies. The music gets louder; a voice begins to talk but you can't understand the words; there are shouts and screams occasionally.

There's a man strapped to a chair, stripped to the waist, being whipped. Are those his screams? No, they aren't in time. The man goes on eating. The girl smokes. Is she part of the whipping scene, or has she somehow slipped over from the eating movie? The music is very loud now, with a driving rock and roll beat. The muscular blonde is moving slowly about with a whip which he curls about his body.

Suddenly, he flings himself into a dance in time with the music, a vicious, body-snapping dance, while the whipping goes on behind him. Suddenly that film moves to the top of the screen and below it appears another view of the same scene, earlier or later? The whipping is in the foreground, or is it a dance? Lights, noise, screams—the man on the side wall eats slowly, fondles a cat, stares at the audience.

Various tortures, fights, dances—all mixed together. Inextricable. Lights shining unbearably bright in your eyes. Dancing lights on the wall. Nasty torturous dancing with whips and lighted matches. The man eats, watches, watches you. Louder, faster, noisier.

Suddenly the films end. The noise and music go on. Several people have appeared from somewhere. They stand on a stage in front of the screen, tuning instruments. The noise of their tuning, the electric buzzes and hums, begins to blend with the noise and music from the films. Then they gradually take over. Behind them on the wall are movies of a girl. One, two, several views of her in different movies. Close-up, far away, they begin to zoom in and out in time with the music. Eyes, mouths, noses, she stares, blinks, licks her lips. On stage now is the cruel blonde man, with his whip, dancing with a tall masculine blonde girl in silver lame costume. The lights have become a dim blue flicker, but a flicker that goes faster and slower and pauses now and then, just as your eyes get used to each kind of flicker. Dancers on the floor, with huge strips of silver material that flash above their heads as they dance. Clean-cut, straight looking kids, working hard at dancing to the noise.

Bright green and red spotlights, the dancers silhouetted on the walls in great grimacing poses. The musicians occasionally revealed, sweating over their instruments, grinding out a noise that has music in it somewhere. They're watching the movies, watching each other watching you. Too much happening—it doesn't go together. But sometimes it does—suddenly the beat of the music, the movements of the various films, the pose of the dancers, blend into something meaningful, but before your mind can grab it, it's become random and confusing again. Your head tries to sort something out, make sense of something. The noise is getting to you. You want to scream, or throw yourself about with the dancers, something, anything!

The noise builds to a climax and ends. The dancers pause. Everyone looks a bit weary. The musicians diddle around with their instruments and amplifiers. The lights and films go on. One of the musicians is a girl. Or is it?

They start again. There's an electrified violin making horrible bagpipe sounds against the noisy background. It's grating, terrible, and yet your mind latches onto that bit of tune against all the chaos. It's almost a relief.

The films are doing strange things. The blonde girl becomes a brunette—girl or boy? Showers of colored lights suddenly burst upward from the drums with a crash of cymbals and shoot across the ceiling and walls like a fireworks burst. The dancers on the floor are looking tired and ecstatic and bored, all at once. The music gets noisier, the violin is frantically screaming a tune, higher and higher. On the screens, some of the views of the girl are replaced by films of the blonde boy and silver lame girl, dancing, fighting, torturing each other with the whip. The real pair are there too, making weird shadows on the wall, the boy dancing, but writhing in torment with his hands over his head.

The music is lost in the chaos of noise. Are there children chanting or singing? The amplified violin goes higher and higher, becomes a shriek, a feedback noise, a regular dit-dah-dit of unbearable Morse code screaming above the other noise. It all builds to a tremendous climax. Then it goes on and on and on and on. You wish it would stop. The musicians build wilder and wilder. The drummer hits a shuddering beat that you feel through the floor. It's all coming to an end. But it doesn't. It goes on. The lights flash in your eyes. The noises all blend into one and your mind tries to sort out little bits of rhythm or tune. The screaming Morse message is still there, but you only hear now when you listen for it. The dancers on the floor are sweating, looking like they can't bear any more of it all. But it goes on and on. Finally it all comes to a shuddering screaming end, the music and noise die down, the films flicker out. Only the colored lights still dance across the walls. The musicians and dancers wearily leave, looking wilted. You sit there for a while, finally find your waitress, pay your check, leave. It's hot.

What can you say?

A QUIET NIGHT AT THE BALLOON FARM

Richard Goldstein

New York, October 1966

. . . THE VELVET UNDERGROUND IS NOT A FIRST-CLASS CAR ON THE LONDON transit system, but Andy's rock group. Sometimes they sing, sometimes they just stroke their instruments into a single, hour-long jam. Their sound is a savage series of atonal thrusts and electronic feedback. Their lyrics combine sado-masochistic frenzy with free-association imagery. The whole thing seems to be the product of a secret marriage between Bob Dylan and the Marquis de Sade. It takes a lot to laugh; it takes a train to cry.

Andy says he is through with phosphorescent flowers and cryptic soup cans. Now it's rock. He may finally conquer the world through its soft, teenage underbelly.

"It's ugly," he admits. "It's a very ugly effect when you put it all together. But it's beautiful. You know, you just look at the whole thing—the Velvets playing and Gerard dancing and all the film and light, and it's a beautiful thing. Very Vinyl. Beautiful."

"Yeah, beautiful. There are beautiful sounds in rock. Very lazy, dreamlike noises. You can forget about the lyrics in most songs. Just dig the noise, and you've got our sound. We're putting everything together—lights and film and music—and we're reducing it to its lowest common denominator. We're musical primitives."

That's John Cale, composer, guitarist and resident Welshman for the Velvet Underground. Cale plays a mean, slashing viola. And piano, when he has to. He and Lou Reed once shared a three-room flat on Ludlow Street and a group called the Primitives. Their place was cold (broken crates in a wood-burning fireplace looked very chic but also kept the blood circulating). The group was cold too, bassman Sterling Morrison recalls: "Sometimes we'd do more jumping around in a night than the goddam waitresses. Before Andy saw us at the Cafe Bizarre (which isn't exactly the Copa of McDougal Street) we were busting our balls in work. Up to here. And you can't do anything creative when you're struggling to keep the basic stuff coming. Now it seems we have time to catch our breath. We have more direction—that's where Andy comes in. We eat better, we work less and we've found a new medium for our music. It's one thing to hustle around for odd jobs. But now we're not just another band; we're an act. See, when a band becomes an act, you get billing. You get days off. You don't just work nights—you're like, Engaged."

Nightly at the Balloon Farm the Velvets demonstrate what distinguishes an act from a band. They are special. They even have a chanteuse—Nico, who is half goddess, half icicle. If you say bad things about her singing, she doesn't talk to you. If you say nice things, she doesn't talk to you either. If you say that she sounds like a bellowing moose, she might smile if she digs the sound of that in French. Onstage, she is somewhat less communicative. But she sings in perfect mellow ovals. It sounds something like a cello getting up in the morning. All traces of melody depart early in her solo. The music courses into staccato beats, then slows into syrupy feedback. All this goes on until everyone is satisfied that the point has gotten across.

Oh yeah; the point! John Cale sits dreamily, eyeing a Coke, pushes his hair back from his face to expose a bony nose, and observes: "You can't pin it down." (Granted.) "It's a conglomeration of the senses. What we try to get here is a sense of total involvement." (You mean acid, scoobie-doobie-doo?)

"Coming here on a trip is bound to make a tremendous difference. But we're here to stimulate a different kind of intoxication. The sounds, the visual stuff—all this bombarding of the senses—it can be very heady in itself, if you're geared to it."

John Cale is a classicist. His first composition was "written on a rather large piece of plywood." He studied viola and piano at the London Conservatory of Music and came to the United States as a Leonard Bernstein fellow. His sponsor was Aaron Copland. "We didn't get on very well," John says. "Copland said I couldn't play my work at Tanglewood. It was too destructive, he said. He didn't want his piano wrecked."

Cale pursued his vision with John Cage. On the viola, he would play a single note for as long as two hours. Then he met Lou Reed, and the sound that John calls "controlled distortion" was born.

The Velvets, with Nico and Andy and all that light, began to construct a scene around the title "Exploding Plastic Inevitable." They've done quite a bit of traveling since, and their reviews reflect the ambivalence a quiet evening at the Balloon Farm can produce. Said the *Chicago Daily News*: "The flowers of evil are in full bloom." *Los Angeles* magazine compared the sound to "Berlin in the decadent thirties." Even Cher (of Sonny and Cher) was heard to mutter: "It will replace nothing except suicide."

Dauntless, the troupe returned home. Now they are popping eardrums and brandishing horse-whips on a nightly basis. Their first album sounds a bit restrained (though a long, harrowing cut called "Heroin" isn't exactly calculated to make the radio as a "good guy sure-shot"). But it's still The Sound. And the group is brimming with innovation.

"We want to try an electronic drum," says John. "It would produce sub-sonic sounds, so you could feel it even when you couldn't hear it.

We'd then be able to add it to a piece of music, and it would be like underlining the beat" (in cement).

On-stage, Gerard Malanga motions wildly. They have run out of records, and that means it's time for another set. John puts down his Coke and wraps a black corduroy jacket over his turtleneck. He slides his hair over his face, covering his nose again. Lou tucks his shirt in.

"Young people know where everything is at," he says. "Let 'em sing about going steady on the radio. Let 'em run their hootenannies. But it's in holes like this that the real stuff is being born. The university and the radio kill everything, but around here, it's alive. The kids know that."

The girl in the black stockings is leaning against the stage, watching them warm up. "You can tell this is going to be a very atonal set," she says. "It's something about the way they handle their instruments when they first come on stage."

"Beautiful," sighs her partner, rolling his larynx and his eyes. With a single humming chord, which seems to hang in the air, the Velvet Underground launches into another set. John squints against a purple spotlight. Lou shouts against a groaning amplifier. Gerard writhes languidly to one side. Sterling turns his head to sneeze. And Nico stands there, looking haunted. The noise, the lights, the flickering images all happen. Everybody grooves.

From the balcony, Andy Warhol watches from behind his glasses. "Beautiful," he whispers. Sterling sneezes audibly but it seems to fit. "Beautiful." Gerard hands his partner a bull-whip and the girl in black begins to sway. "Just beautiful."

SEE

● IN PERSON ●

ANDY WARHOL

NICO — Girl of the Year   **GERARD — Superstar**

and the

"VELVET UNDERGROUND"
The World's First
MOD WEDDING HAPPENING

FREAK OUT
NOON TILL 10 P.M.

THE CARNABY STREET FUN FESTIVAL
SUNDAY, NOVEMBER 20
MICHIGAN STATE FAIRGROUNDS

MOTHER'S MOD LAMENT

Linda La Marre

The Detroit News, November 21, 1966

Holy matrimony was replaced by unholy pandemonium in what was billed as a wedding yesterday at the State Fairgrounds Coliseum.

It was marriage in the Mod Tradition. The country's first. And let's hope it's not what's happening, baby.

Wearing a white minigown, eight inches over her knees and white, thigh-high boots, Randy Rossi, 18, became the bride of clothing sales-man Gary Norris, 25, amid a melange of simultaneous "happenings."

Andy Warhol, of soup can painting fame and the "father of Pop art," arrived from New York to give away the bride. With him came his rock & roll group, the Velvet Underground, vocalist Nico, and the Exploding Plastic Inevitable, Warhol's gaudy lighting effects.

Some 4,500 shaggy-haired wedding guests swarmed the arena for the prenuptial rituals. Electronic devices screamed, guitars and drums throbbed and a fiddle added to the din as purple and orange lights splashed dots and squares across the stage.

"Hey, we're really witnessing something, it's history, history!" a young girl shouted.

Huddled on the sidelines were the bride's parents, Mr. and Mrs. John Rossi, of Mt. Clemens, the bridegroom's mother, Mrs. Thelma

Norris, of Taylor, his sister and brother-in-law, the Robert Wionceks, of Dearborn.

"It's not the kind of wedding we had planned for our daughter," Mrs. Rossi said, as eerie screeches emitted from the stage.

"He's old enough to know his own mind," Mrs. Norris added, while Nico, clad in a lavender pantsuit, cupped the mike in both hands and began moaning some song.

After an eternity of noise, a black Rolls-Royce with the bridal couple slowly backed into the arena. The pair wisely chose to stay inside the car a few moments.

Warhol's psychedelic sounds, which seek to create the same illusion as mind-expanding drugs, succeeded.

Gerard [Malanga], the whip dancer, slithered and spun across the darkened stage. Another member of the cast hopped atop a wrecked DeSoto, bashing it with a sledge hammer.

"If I take to love, will I find you gone," groaned Nico. Warhol ascended the platform, paint bucket and catsup bottles in hand. Contents of both containers were carefully applied to a girl wearing a white paper dress throughout the proceedings.

The bride smiled as she marched up the platform steps. The bridegroom wore a gray checked, Beatle-type suit, black boots, green and white flowered tie. He looked sober.

The couple volunteered for the Mod wedding, which concluded the three-day Carnaby Street Fun Festival. Their reward, a free honeymoon in New York and screen test with Warhol.

After giving away the bride Warhol sat serenely upon a box of tomato soup, autographing cans. A color film of Nico's face flickered on and off the back curtains as she read a few appropriate, but indistinguishable sentences from a yellow book.

Another member of the cast paraded with a five-foot Baby Ruth candy bar balloon, Warhol's gift to the newlyweds.

Judge David L. Golden, of Highland Park, conducted the cere-mony to pulsating rhythms from drums and guitars. "You may kiss the bride," he concluded. Vigorous applause followed.

It was over. But things were still happening. The 4,500 skinny, young bodies swayed toward the stage, toward cake, catsup and soup cans.

WARHOL "HAPPENING" HITS LIKE A NOISY BOMB

Judy Altman

The Philadelphia Daily News, December 12, 1966

THEY CAME IN DROVES—THE WASHED, THE UNWASHED, THE OVERDRESSED, the underdressed, the beat, the neat, the elite.

They came because this was it, the "Velvet Underground" right here in Philadelphia, with pop-artist-turned-filmmaker Andy Warhol and his "superstar" Nico, and his cohorts and hangers-on. It was a "Happening," Philadelphia's first, and now they could see it, right down at the YMCA at Broad and Pine Sts.

The city's avant and not so avant garde crammed themselves into the auditorium on Saturday and Sunday night and they spilled out into the hall.

The Underground films were brief, erratic and nerve-wracking, but everyone was waiting for the "Happening." Then suddenly it happened. The lights went out and huge spots of green and purple floated across the walls. The screen, split three ways, came to life—a man wiggled his hips, a girl smoked a cigarette, the camera panned in and out, up and down in huge seasick motions.

Meanwhile, let's not forget the noise. No one else could. Loud drums, electronic screeches, zinged through the room.

"Maybe they're tuning up," said one boy hopefully to a neighbor. "No, that's how it sounds," said his friend.

The Thing—whatever it was—went on and on. People drifted in and out, pressing their hands to their heads. "I'm getting one of my migraines," said a girl.

Periodically one man jumped up from his seat and called, "Author, author," and the people around him laughed.

"This is the best argument against taking LSD I've ever seen, if that is what it's supposed to be like," said a man under his breath. "I think it was sponsored by the narcotics squad," someone answered. "I mean, when you get out of here, you don't want LSD—you want an Excedrin," said the man.

Curled up on a window ledge outside the auditorium, his face practically obscured by hair, was John ("you don't need a last name, do you?"), road manager for the Velvet Underground.

"Over the last few months we've had this show in Washington, Boston, Cincinnati, L.A., San Francisco, Morgantown, West Va.— you name it. I'd say the reaction tonight is pretty good. We've had better. In New York, it's more of a nightclub scene, you know.

"It's not supposed to be psychedelic. The newspapermen just seized on that word and used it to death. Any clown can see that this isn't like taking LSD."

One of the musicians walked out. "This is a great town. People curse at you and throw things. Great town," he said, half-chanting the words.

Superstar Nico appeared, holding a small child. It was blonde, Germanic and beautiful. "Is that your daughter?" someone asked. "No. My son," she said.

It was very hot in the auditorium at Broad and Pine. The Happening had been happening for about three hours now. The lights were still flashing, and the noises were still reverberating, but a lot of people were leaving by now. Practically in droves.

The Velvet Underground, which was born in New York City, has since spread like radioactivity throughout the country. It was bound to hit Philadelphia. Only the private ear-drum could determine whether it was a direct smash or a dull thud.

The moongoddess
Nico will conduct services
nightly at Steve Paul's The
Scene...leading you in all
your splendor with her
liturgical chants.

October 23-
October 30

Dancing for the body
and soul also availa-
ble before and after
the services.

Steve Paul's
The Scene
301 W. 46th St.
JU 2-5760

1967

SO FAR UNDERGROUND,

V/V6-5008

YOU GET THE BENDS!

What happens when the daddy of Pop Art goes Pop Music?
The most underground album of all! It's Andy Warhol's hip
new trip to the current subterranean scene.

Sorry, no home movies. But the album *does* feature Andy's
Velvet Underground (they play funny instruments). Plus his
this year's Pop Girl, Nico (she sings, groovy). Plus an actual
Warhol banana on the front cover (don't smoke it...peel it)!

The Velvet Underground, produced by Andy Warhol, is now
available at record stores across the country. Just bring your
own plain brown wrapper.

Verve

Verve Records is a division of Metro-Goldwyn-Mayer Inc.

INDEX INTERVIEW WITH
THE VELVET UNDERGROUND

Ingrid Superstar

Index, 1967

INGRID SUPERSTAR: Well. I'm supposed to talk about the Velvets' music. Let me see, how can I describe this different, original psychedelic band with their psychedelic pop sounds. Well, my usual word would be trippy. Their songs are very, very nice, quite nice. Their record is simply superb in its sound.

Well, I remember when I was in Chicago there was one last song they did in the show, and they had the feedback from the guitars which sounded like 12 million guitars going at one time with these amplified, intensified screeches that really hurt the eardrums, and it was nothing but a chaotic confusion of noise. You couldn't even make out any distinction or hesitation between the notes, and I wouldn't call it beautiful and I don't know what I'd call it. It's different. And I'm sure the audience readily would agree with me.

And, like—we seldom got any applause, maybe one or two claps here and there and when the audience walked out they just walked out struck in a daze and a trance because they were just so shocked and amazed they didn't know what to think. They didn't know whether they were being put on or being put out or being put in or whatever you want to call it.

I don't really, I don't listen to the words that much, I just dance and try to catch the rhythm of the songs which isn't too easy to do. I don't know. What is "I'm Waiting for the Man" about? And "Heroin" is a . . . I don't know . . . very strange song. It goes slow and then fast and then slow and then fast, and it's all about somebody shooting up heroin in the arm.

VELVET: It's a musical rush. Down and through.

INGRID SUPERSTAR: Down and through. And some of the words that I remember in "Heroin" is "It's my life and it's my wife." So whoever composed this song and I'm not mentioning any names, must have really, really dug this horrible excruciating drug that eats out the inside of your body at one time because of the way he talks, it's my wife and it's my life. He must have really held it very dear to his heart like he couldn't live without it. He had to go uptown to cop, like "I'm Waiting for the Man," so he could live one more day. . . . Right?

VELVET: I don't know. I made it all up from a book I read.

INGRID SUPERSTAR: How does the audience react?

VELVET: How does the audience react? Well, they just sit there and they listen. I remember a couple of times like in Rutgers and in Ann Arbor the audience—part of the audience went a little berserk, especially the young punky kids sitting up in the front rows, especially a couple of guys they rolled on the floor like they were having epileptic fits, when you played there, this was I think last March, and there were a few hecklers in the audience. Like they're all a bunch of immature punks.

Like we have these problems with the audience, like a very enthusiastic audience that yells and screams and throws fits and tantrums and rolls on the floor, usually at colleges and benefits like that for the younger people.

And then I remember at the *Paris Review* downstairs at the Village Gate they had all the lights out and they had on the strobe lights flashing on Gerard and Mary and some of the band, and . . . oh, I remember just before going on stage, John Cale fell flat on his face, and I had to practically lift him up. He couldn't even, you know, see where he was going.

INGRID SUPERSTAR: Why did he fall flat on his face?

VELVET: I don't know, he probably drank too much. So anyway, the effect of the music on the audience is like the audience is just too stunned to think or say anything or give any kind of opinion. But then later, like, I asked a few people in Ann Arbor, Michigan, who had come to see the show a couple of nights in a row, and they formed an opinion slowly, and they said that they thought that the music was very way out and supersonic and fast and intensified, and the effect of sound that it produced just vibrated all through the audience and through the hall that they were playing, and they walked out onto the street and in about 15 minutes . . . for about 15 minutes they still had these vibrations in their ears from this music, especially that last song, called "Nothing Song," which was just noise and feedbacks and screeches and groans from the amplifiers.

INGRID SUPERSTAR: And then there's Maureen Tucker. The only girl in the band. Now, when I . . .

VELVET: (*indistinct*)

INGRID SUPERSTAR: She's got red hair and freckles . . . Maureen's very natural. She doesn't wear any make-up. She told me. I asked her. I even felt her hair. You better watch what you say. And she's got freckles, and she's a cute little Irish girl, very religious, goes to church every Sunday. . . .

VELVET: You know what her favorite expression is?

INGRID SUPERSTAR: Yeehaw.

VELVET: No.

INGRID SUPERSTAR: Ho hum.

VELVET: No.

INGRID SUPERSTAR: What?

VELVET: You pig.

INGRID SUPERSTAR: I thought that was Fazon's expression.

VELVET: No, it's Moe's.

INGRID SUPERSTAR: Now, last but not least, we come to the beautiful, flawless, chanteuse, Nico, who right now is in Giza, Spain, but we hope she will rejoin us here in New York soon. She's got blonde hair, sort of Jane Asher style would you say, or is it more May Britt style, you know bangs and the straight flowing hair about down to her shoulders, sort of like a sandy, a little darker than platinum shade. She's got blue eyes, and she's about 5′9″, 5′10″. A very good photographic model, and actress, and she's got great potential.

Her voice is very bland and calm and low and smooth. Some people mistake it like for a boy's voice. And she sings sort of like in one tone mostly. She doesn't have too much modulation.

WARHOL'S DRUGTIME PHASE
BRINGS EXPLODING INEVITABLE

Andrew Lugg and Larry Kasdan

The Michigan Daily, November 4, 1967

The Velvets' final show as part of the EPI appears to have been in Ann Arbor, Michigan. Their return to this haunt prompted a preview of sorts by Andrew Lugg in The Michigan Daily:

. . . OVER A YEAR AGO, WARHOL AND PART OF THE VELVET (UNDERGROUND) performed at the Film Festival. It is hard to say that the piece has become more "polished" with its long run at the Dom and its more recent outlet at the Gymnasium, both in New York City. The piece has certainly changed, being now much more dynamic and "offhanded"— offhanded in a manner which seems reserved for Warhol alone.

Audiences at Hill tonight will see the last vestiges of dragtime have been dispelled and that the "Plastic Exploding Inevitable" [*sic*] is set squarely in drugtime.

The usual imperatives—blow your mind, strip the peel—are decidedly in order.

When it came to the show itself, Lugg proved to be an enthusiast, even if he constantly refers to the band as "The Velvet":

For the first time since I have been writing for *The Daily* I find I have to review a performance in terms of explaining away the fact that although a large number of the audience walked out and although about 90% of the remaining viewers were hostile to the show, the Warhol Velvet Underground's Exploding Plastic Inevitable was one of the finest "film-pieces" Ann Arbor has witnessed for a long time. . . .

Andy Warhol began his part of the evening with a half-hour excerpt from his new film, *Sin*, which, when assembled, will run twenty-five hours on two screens. . . . *Sin* is a film dealing with love, and the section we saw concerned Judge Ondine pontificating over a group of lovers, some self-conscious, others oblivious to all that is going on. Superimposed on this are scenes of Nico waiting, looking on sadly and attempting to sing a Dowland-like song against background sounds provided by the Velvet Underground. . . .

[And] then Nico and the Velvet appear on stage. Nico takes up the chant from Nico-on-screen. The Velvet begin to produce "sound," and Gerard Malanga lies on the floor listening. *Sin* finishes and a black and white film of Nico and the Velvet is projected together with slides, large patterns filling the stage area. A huge light is shone at the audience and Gerard begins to dance with, and against, the strobes. The Velvet play "Venus [in] Furs," "Run Run Run," "Heroin."

And then it's all over. The "performers" move off and you wonder what sort of performance this has been. Gerard, Nico and the Velvet seemed just there, they seemed to say, "Here we are, superstars, what more do you want?" And this is the first question, namely, "What is the nature of performance?"

People used to say that the superstar bit was a parody of Hollywood. Not at all, they establish a reality which is peculiarly theirs, which requires no explanation; or perhaps all the explanation in the world.

Two hours of their real live time and two hours of yours, too, has been expended. The actual fact that it has been expended is all that matters; not how or why—that is the traditional notion of entertainment. Warhol says, "If the audience can take it for ten minutes, I show it fifteen minutes." What does it mean then, to have an aesthetic of the excruciatingly bad? And how is it that this aesthetic produces such magnificent elegance, as in *Sin*, and such exquisite beauty as in the Nico performance?

However, The Michigan Daily *film critic Larry Kasdan was, er, less of a convert:*

The show is terrible. It goes on and on and on. The [support act] accomplishes the almost impossible task of making Beatle[-type] music sound bad. The light show is mediocre. The movies are long and boring—true Warhol. The Velvet Underground is totally unimpressive. Each one of their songs seems to last about three hours. . . .

1350 AVENUE OF THE AMERICAS, NEW YORK, N.Y. 10019 • 262-3131
A DIVISION OF METRO-GOLDWYN-MAYER INC.

"BANANAS ARE IN SEASON"

THE VELVET UNDERGROUND & NICO

Produced By ANDY WARHOL

V/V6-5008

REVIEW OF
THE VELVET UNDERGROUND AND NICO

Timothy Jacobs

Vibrations, #2

WHILE LISTENING TO THIS ALBUM, IT IS BEST, PERHAPS, TO PUT YOURSELF IN THE frame of mind that you might assume while listening to Indian music, for the Velvet Underground produces a type of music that is distinctly different from American popular music.

The Underground was first introduced as an intrinsic part of Andy Warhol's total environment light show, "The Exploding Plastic Inevitable," a program which was intended as a reflection of our society, and the message was one of perversion, sickness, and turmoil. This message is carried over in this album, with only a few exceptions.

"Venus in Furs" is perhaps the best example of the severity of the music. The texture of the song is pure sado-masochism. The music is remarkable in its expression of this message; the words speak of a life of sheer pain and misery, with frequent mention of Severin, a sadistic monk from *Justine* [sic], by the Marquis de Sade.

The texture is continued in "Heroin" and "I'm Waiting for the Man," which deal with the use of opiate drugs; the latter dealing mainly with the procuring of the drug, while the former concentrates on the physical and psychological effects. In both, the music backs up the words in excellent expression of the message.

The trend is continued in all the other songs (with the exception of "Femme Fatale" and "I'll Be Your Mirror"). These other songs are reflections of society in general, and what is said is not complimentary. The most notable of this group is "European Son to Delmore Schwartz," a song which ends in a seven minute musical freak-out to rival the Mothers' "Return of the Son of the Monster Magnet" and the Fugs' "Virgin Forest."

The music on this band, and indeed, on most of the whole album, is a full-fledged attack on the ears and on the brain. Using devices such as controlled feedback and a shrieking electric viola, the Velvet Underground attacks, grates, screams, and pounds on the eardrums until the mind is virtually reduced to oatmeal.

Then, in marked contrast, comes "Femme Fatale" and "I'll Be Your Mirror." With the beautiful Nico chanting the verses, her haunting, almost ethereal voice lulls you into peaceful escape from the harshness of the rest of the album. Though "Femme Fatale" might be considered to be negative in its message, it is nonetheless a beautiful song. And then there's "I'll Be Your Mirror," no less than a love song in the midst of all the pain and misery of the rest of the album. ("I find it hard to believe you don't know the beauty you are—but if you don't, let me be your eyes—a hand in the dark, so you won't be afraid.")

All in all, for what it is striving to express, this is a good album. It is distinct—not for those who desire to hear the usual popular music, but for those who desire to hear a very unusual, perhaps even experimental type of music, we recommend it highly. A good first album for this group, though in the future we hope that other efforts will not be quite as negative.

1968

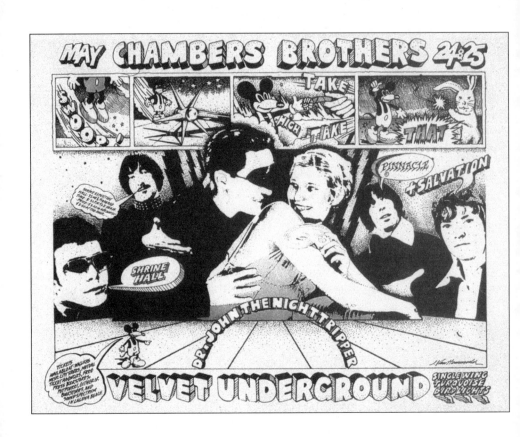

REVIEW OF RONALD NAMETH'S
EXPLODING PLASTIC INEVITABLE

Richard Whitehall

The Los Angeles Free Press, May 1, 1968

THE BEST FILM ON THE CURRENT CINEMATHEQUE 16 PROGRAM IS THE ONE Ronald Nameth made from Andy Warhol's Exploding Plastic Inevitable when that intermedia show was playing Poor Richard's in Chicago.

I say "from" rather than "of" advisedly. Since Nameth's movie exists independently as a work of art in the way that most screen adaptations, regardless of their origins, do not. As a jangle and concord of sound and image, a poetic expression of all the arts of white magick, of the cinema of imagery built around the strobe-light rather than the arc, it is something wonderful and exciting.

From Warhol's intermedia, the sharp cry of pain and desperation which seems to be the heart of all his work, Nameth has employed a pulsation of light and sound to modulate an event into an abstraction. With its stop-framing, sunbursts of light, bloodbursts of color, its mixture of black and white, negative, its dancers moving sinuously through the vortex like memory's white ghosts, its metallic glint of silver and slivers of clashing color, even in its use of the heavily-grained print for aesthetic purposes, it has become dance-animation of a decadent dream.

Near the end, for instance, in one of the few images held to any
length, there's a stop-frame sequence of Gerard Malanga, turning his
head from right to left, a poet sleep-walking through his own dreams.
But which poet? Malanga is a poet. But is this Malanga? The imagery
through most of Nameth's movie is more reminiscent of Rimbaud.
The Rimbaud of *A Season in Hell*. The Rimbaud who believed in all
marvels. Who knew Beauty, found her bitter, and cursed her.

PRESS RELEASE ON THE VELVET UNDERGROUND

Verve Records

April 1968

THEY BEGAN IN 1964 DOING WHAT THEY FELT WOULD NEVER BE COMMERCIAL by AM radio standards. In essence, they played for themselves. In 1965 they managed to get hired at the Café [Bizarre] in New York City's East Village. This date proved fateful. Although it only lasted two nights and they were fired, it was time enough for Andy Warhol (pop artist-film maker) to discover them.

Andy felt the magnitude and force of their music and instantly asked them to join in his total predicament show called "The Exploding Plastic Inevitable," which was the first show incorporating music, dancers, movies, lights, projections and environment people. The show developed more excitement and creativity on all levels than any of the copies which followed.

Being a pacesetter has its moments; however, they're truly shared by few, dubiously by most. The world that saw the show, indeed, was made nervous by its totality. Understanding that the world wasn't ready for that much yet, the "Plastic Inevitable" was dropped.

The Velvet Underground's music is peculiar to most due to a mixture of feelings and some fogginess surrounding their image. Many were of the immediate opinion that they, due to their association with Warhol, were just another put-on—well nothing could be more false. They were, in fact, a group when Andy found them, had that fabulous name already and most of the songs were written before that time. So, as you can see, they were their own identity and so much so that they are now on their own with MGM guiding their ever brightening path.

Music was, is and always will be their major interest. Lou Reed— lead guitar, vocal, songwriter. Educated at Syracuse University. Lou began studying serious music at age five on piano, then guitar. He's one of the finest guitar players on the contemporary merry-go-round now and the tops at writing songs.

John Cale plays organ, viola, bass. Educated at London Royal Academy. Also began classically at a very early age. At eight years of age he appeared on the BBC doing his own composition. John arrived in this country on a Leonard Bernstein Fellowship and played at Tanglewood till it became dreary and encompassing. He met Lou Reed and joined the Velvet Underground.

Sterling Morrison educated at CCNY. He too started out early at age ten. He played classical trumpet, then picked up guitar in late high school. Sterling helps Lou with the writing and they exchange some of the greatest solos and rhythm pieces performed live today.

Moe Tucker went to Ithaca College, dropped out to play in an all girl rock band and work for IBM, both of which she does well. Her symphonic simplicity is like that of a human computer putting emphasis on that which really matters in the time and life of the song— look for no zany drum skiffles but dedicated rhythms to perfection . . . bounce . . . bounce . . . bounce.

THE ABOVE-GROUND SOUND OF THE VELVET UNDERGROUND

Hullabaloo, May–June 1968

The Velvet Underground's velvet, leather, satin, and brass stuff was designed by Betsey Johnson of Paraphernalia.

Photos by Ralph Garcia

We always get a thrill when a great underground rock group finally breaks through the surface to full-fledged popularity. And we get an even bigger thrill when the group in question happens to be the Velvet Underground.

Spurred to semi-fame, underground style, by Andy Warhol in his Dom days, the Velvet Underground have been laboring in the murky depths for far too long. Now, with the advent of their sensational new album, "White Light/White Heat" (Verve), that problem has been solved, once and for all.

Welcome to the hot glare of fame, fortune, and publicity, group! HULLABALOO gives its first happening party in honor of the four valiant Velvets: Lou Reed (vocals, lead guitar, piano), John Cale (vocals, electric viola, bass guitar), Sterling Morrison (vocals, guitar, bass guitar), and Maureen Tucker (drums).

Happy sunshine!

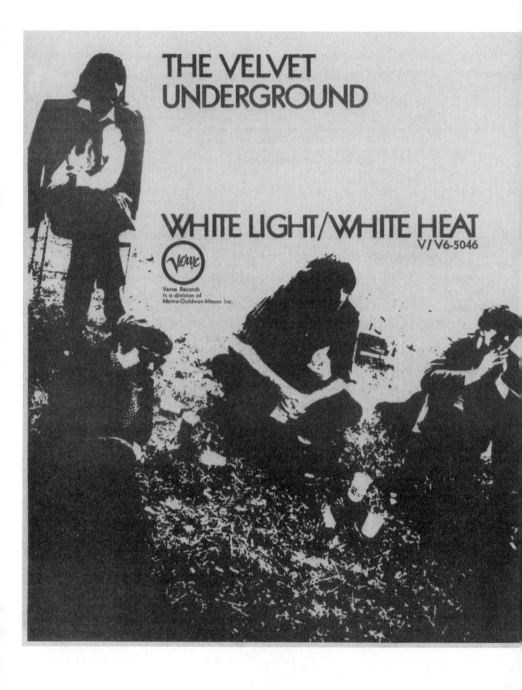

THE VELVET
UNDERGROUND

WHITE LIGHT/WHITE HEAT
V/V6-5046

Verve Records
Is a division of
Metro-Goldwyn-Mayer Inc.

ROUND VELVET UNDERGROUND

Sandy Pearlman

Crawdaddy, #16

SINCE ANDY WARHOL HAS NOT BEEN ENTIRELY UNRELATED TO THE LIFE AND times of the Velvet Underground (Didn't they play as the "house" band for both the fabulous "Exploding Plastic Inevitable" and "his" discotheque the Gymnasium? Wasn't he said to have produced their first "Banana" album? And didn't he do the cover on that Banana album as well as the cover concept on their new one, *White Light/White Heat* Verve V/V6-5046?), isn't it very nice that his reflection on the efficacy of the plethora principle, "When you see a gruesome picture over and over again, it doesn't really have any effect," should go so far toward explaining the albeit-not-hilarious but certainly authentic humor of the newest album from the Velvets?

First of all, this humor is related to the scary. From start to finish there is generated this fantastic specter of doom which consistently and absolutely taints all things. (Traditionally speaking, colleges could certainly treat the Velvet Underground as Black Humorists, couldn't they?) (This could be Lou Reed's big move to recapture the leather championship from Morrison and return it to New York.) For example, side one has: "White Light/White Heat," a doper song rendered nontraditional by these facts: (a) It's about speed! (b) It features the first subordination of the fabulous c/w riff within a dope context. "The Gift," an 8:14 (spoken) short story about unrequited love as it leads to unintentional murder (manslaughter). "Lady Godiva's Operation" sports a truly self-explanatory title. And, "There She Comes Now," a beautiful little love ballad (I mean it. I mean it.) which all those who saw Nico and Jackson Browne at the Dom some 1.3 years ago will doubtless find familiar. As for the flip, it features "Sister Ray," which lasts 17:00 with this line "I'm searching for my mainline" repeated often enough to become indelible. (The Velvet Underground is published by "Three Prong Music.") In mood this LP's most reminiscent of that last ("shoot 'em up") section of *Naked Lunch* wherein Bill Burroughs actually portrays himself (the arch-doper) shooting some narco cop. That's how pretentiously humorous it is. Now this pretentious scene makes its appearance beyond such more-or-less conventional ploys as "The Gift," wherein John Cale's queasy-cultured voice (efficiently dripping the most unimaginable kinds of oil) matter-of-factly divulges its gruesome tale in a way which really taints such details as, "Sheila Klein, her very, very best friend," "Oh, God, it's absolutely maudlin outside," "A bottle of pink and blue vitamins," "The Clarence Darrow Post Office," "That schmuck, said Sheila," and among the best, "She would date occasionally. But merely as amusement." (Such details are presented against a constant background of modernized Bo Diddley–style repetition.) (Counterpoint.) Beyond even the implicitly derisive Wart-Hoglike background grunts that the Velvets make on both "The Gift" and "Lady Godiva's Operation." That is, they move in such a really complex universe of pretension as to go beyond even those who give away "their pretensions through minor-but-telling lapses in detail" (see for example, Morrison's quizzical second of three "now"s on "When the Music's Over"), because the Velvet's big giveaway, the funny part, comes through their seeming absolute dedication. An unrelieved preoccupation with doom makes for an overexposure blatant enough to render doom its very own negation, harkening us right back to Warhol's remarks on the plethora principle and implicating such self-consciousness on their part that we gotta assume they're absolutely distant from what they perform with such dedication: I mean we can question their sincerity. And this question is always there. Always nagging at everything they do. Their cynicism's really so efficient, 'cause all they have to do to be funny is be serious. And with humorous techniques themselves always suffering from overexposure maybe that's the only way. Much of this album's just as funny as Love's "Revelation." And that's a classic.

As for some questions, it's perhaps best to open noting the rumor that Maureen, the Velvet's drummer, used to practice listening to Bo Diddley records when she arrived home from work. And on this record she certainly does groove. Right up there with such strong two-fisters as Buddy Miles (Electric Flag), Tim (Steve Miller) and David Getz (Big Brother). Think of Bo Diddley's "Mona" (done by both the Nashville Teens and the Stones). And you'll realize how far she's into repetition. And so's the whole band. Each of the six songs on the album is generated out of its own virtually immutable bass/drum pattern. Repeated over and over. Not even cycled. All sounding mechanistic enough to be mistaken for electronics. "White Light/White Heat" especially. It fails to be boring 'cause it's got that fascination potential inherent in all mechanically perfect execution (hypnosis). It's a very technological sound. Laden with some more-or-less up-to-date technological blues readymades. The whole album is reminiscent of the Cream/Yardbirds art-rock riff. (And "Sister Ray" is particularly reminiscent of the taut-string readymade offa the Yardbirds' "I'm a Man.") One of the big moves the Velvets make here is to demonstrate that their repetition scene might be the only choice spot for such as the Cream's fuzz-modules. Which the Cream, misguided, used in a variation scene (*Disraeli Gears*). Also, the Velvet's repetition scene makes it hard to tell whether they're playing badly or not (hypnosis plus practice makes perfect), which was an always pressing problem for the Banana album.

THE VELVET UNDERGROUND AT THE SHRINE

Robert Gold

The Los Angeles Free Press, July 26, 1968

THEN: VELVET UNDERGROUND MINUS NICO BUT FEATURING A DRUMMER named Maureen who beats the shit out of the tom-tom and the bass drum. Her heavy, continuous 4/4 outpouring on the drums slams into your bowels and crawls out your asshole. Meanwhile, the rest of the band makes a sound that can only be compared to a railroad shunting yard, metal wheels screeching to a halt on the tracks. It's music to go out of your mind to, if that's your bent. Lead singer Lou Reed, who looks like a teenage Clark Kent, sings original lyrics which can't be understood due to the loudness of the group. [Velvet Underground] did a sour, raucous version of "Sweet Rock & Roll." Velvet indeed!

THE BOSTON SOUND

Wayne McGuire

Crawdaddy, #17

ONE MUST MARVEL AT THE PRESUMPTION OF THE DOORS: BREAK ON Through to the Other Side? Hardly, they are firmly ensconced over here. For to break on through to the other side is a difficult thing to be sure. Probably the only rock group to ever make it through is the Velvet Underground, sons of metallic Burroughs and leather Genet, on "Sister Ray" from *White Light/White Heat* (Verve V6-5046). For to break on through to the other side one must squeeze through that tiny pin hole which connects this dimension of human energies with the jet stream of superhuman energies. Of course, a few American musicians have broken through to that ionosphere, most notably John Coltrane and Pharoah Sanders on *Meditations*. But whereas Coltrane and his disciples are the culmination of New Black Music, the Velvet Underground are prophets of a new age, of breakthrough on an electronic intermedia: total scale. But enough of this pseudo-review style for:

NOW IS THE TIME FOR DISTORTIONS TO BURN. I have, with a heavy heart, silently watched while spiritual dwarves mutilated all that was sacred. But now my resignation has ended and with flaming sword in hand I will clear away those ugly growths which parade as insightful musical criticism.

Probably the most blatant injustice perpetrated by the media on the contemporary music scene has been the virtual black-out on coverage of the Velvet Underground. There have been a few timid stabs at descriptive praise in *Crawdaddy*, *Vibrations* and *Jazz & Pop*, but on the whole reviewers, when confronted with a phenomenon which doesn't conform to any easy slot of reference, choose to turn out reams of material on synthetic groups which have gained mass acceptance. So the Velvet Underground, which is musically and mentally at least two years ahead of its time, goes unrecognized while the Doors, a group which artificially pretends to the chaotic nonentity of which the Velvet Underground are masters, receive torrents of publicity. But eventually, as always, the truth must out and in time the artificial husk will disintegrate and drop away revealing the Velvet Underground firmly at center where they've been all along.

This is a review of the Velvet Underground, this is a review of the end of the world, this is a review of the Antichrist and Christ, this is a review of Life and Death, this is a review of tomorrow and of ever and ever. But first you must come up/down/into here where the airs so heavy/thin but oh so intoxicating. Or as C. S. Lewis once described an important facet of Burroughsian feedback in *That Hideous Strength*:

> Suddenly, like a thing that leaped to him across infinite distances with the speed of light, desire (salt, black, ravenous, unanswerable desire) took him by the throat. The merest hint will convey to those who have felt it the quality of the emotion which now shook him, like a dog shaking a rat; for others, no description will perhaps avail. Many writers speak of it in terms of lust: a description admirably illuminating from within, totally misleading from without. It has nothing to do with the body. But it is in two respects like lust as lust shows itself to be in the deepest and darkest vault of its labyrinthine house. For like lust, it disenchants the whole universe. Everything else that Mark had ever felt—love, hunger, ambition, lust itself—appeared to have been mere milk and water, toys for children, not worth one throb of the

nerves. The infinite attraction of this dark thing sucked all other passions into itself: the rest of the world appeared blenched, etiolated, in-
sipid, a world of white marriages and white masses. . . . These creatures
of which Frost had spoken—and he did not doubt that they were lo-
cally present with him in the cell—breathed death on the human race
and on all joy. Not despite this but because of this, the terrible gravita-
tion sucked and tugged and fascinated him towards them. Never before had he known the fruitful strength of the movement opposite to
Nature which now had him in its grip; the impulse to reverse all reluc-
tances and to draw every circle anti-clockwise. The meaning of certain pictures, of Frost's talk about "objectivity," of the things done by
witches in old times, became clear to him. The image of Wither's face
rose to his memory: and this time he did not merely loathe it. He
noted, with shuddering satisfaction, the signs it bore of a shared experience between them. Wither also knew. Wither understood.

Warhol also knew. Warhol understood. . . . Yet surely this must be
an oversimplification, no? After all, C. S. Lewis was merely an apolo-
gist for a dying Christianity, no?

But why was Bob Zimmerman scared shitless of Warhol? Why did
Zimmerman fear that Warhol wanted to destroy him? It wasn't merely
a case of country boy meets the big city. 'Cause something's happening,
Bob, and . . . ? But enough of this petty sneering criticism. It would be
better to ask why has Bob Zimmerman turned moralist, perhaps even
Christian fundamentalist, on *John Wesley Harding*? Do you remember
before the accident when his lyrics were becoming increasingly schizophrenic, when he cried out in horror that he thought he might be
becoming "evil"? And the accident itself must have presented an ex-
ceedingly intense vision of non-being. So then came Christian conver-
sion? I doubt it. For in case you haven't heard there is a fantastic war
now being waged and our greatest human spirits are either standing or
falling in battle. Most of you out there are still engaged in your petty
pursuits unaware that the roof is about to cave in but wait, I hear a

message from the battlefield: "BULLETIN . . . BULLETIN . . . BUL-
LETIN . . . I—uh—would like to—uh—report a case of circuit overload and—um—many cases—uh—of creeping mindless idiotism . . .
signed A. Warhol."

Yes, so Bob Zimmerman decided to withdraw from the heat of battle for awhile (too much of nothing), it was getting pretty nightmarish
there, and when a *Life* reviewer asserts that Dylan has pulled the plug
out on modern music one must reply wha? For Dylan is no longer at
the vital core and has abdicated his right to significant action or dialogue. He has come full swing from humanism (the protest songs) to
"nihilism" (the schizophrenic surrealistic songs) back to humanism
(the songs with a moral), a more sophisticated humanism than before,
but humanism none-the-less. In the arts today, Tolkien alone has the
Christian perspective honestly, lucidly and poetically wrapped up.

I have before me the February *Crawdaddy* with a pretentious review
by Paul Williams on the Beach Boys, the Rolling Stones and the Jefferson Airplane. The review is a bubble which begs to be pricked, but
why bother. I remember you guys from high school, remember? I tried
to play Coltrane's "Impressions" for you, a heavy piece of music engaged in significant dialogue created by a noble spirit who was risking
all on the battlefield but you were too busy listening to the Beatles
and the Stones and into adolescent masturbation (I can't get no satisfaction; you call this slop a rebellion?), and now you've learned some
musical terms and have taken some speed for insight and are busy fu-
eling the Beatles-Airplane-Doors syndrome or are into ever-so-tired
black blues riffs via Cream, Butterfield, Bloomfield, Canned Heat or
Traffic. Christ, don't you realize that you are engaged in creating and
perpetuating New American Muzak? For instance, Charles Lloyd is
New American Muzak (may God grant Frank Kofsky patience who
has seen Pharoah Sanders verge on transformation into pure spiritual
energy). But the time is coming when you'll be forced to discard your
illusions for as the Buddha once moaned in the throes of a Dionysian
ecstasy: "Intermedia will be the spiritual microcosm of the world, the

tool of a spiritual and political revolution in the West, a manifestation of man's next evolutionary leap in consciousness." Which in translation means: "Ah, to be a media freak plugged into the collective unconscious of the country and ride the electric tidal wave of human history." Which further translated simply means: "Intermedia will be the collective consciousness of the Aquarian Age."

But I digress. Put quite simply, the Velvet Underground is the most vital and significant group in the world today. They are at the fiery center of the twentieth century dilemma, as was Nietzsche. For Nietzsche foresaw that moment in the future when the spiritual citadels of the Judaeo-Christian West would crumble silently to dust. And at that moment our poor human souls will be rent with a pain greater than the heat of a hundred hydrogen bombs. Of course some have anticipated this pain. (For instance, Johnny Jones described to me this dream: It is 1982. John Lennon, master of the Western world, is sitting in the control booth while the yellow barbarians attack the walled western citadel. Lennon, seemingly in control of the situation because of his dynamism and mastery of technology, pokes at some of the myriad of buttons which face him on the control panel causing powerful psychedelic tranquilizers to be shot at the enemy. But still the barbarians charge. Beads of sweat break out on Lennon's brow. He pushes more buttons sending superpowered thought control image barrages at the enemy. But still the barbarians charge and with an inhuman intensity smash through the tired walls. A horrendous shriek pierces the deaf skies as Western Man has his eyeballs gashed out and his body cut up in a slow tortuous death. But goodness, I wouldn't want to invoke the yellow peril threat!) Nietzsche himself fell in battle without compromise as did Van Gogh, Rimbaud, Artaud and maybe Joyce and Beckett. (In our own time those two oracles, Burroughs and Warhol, are still standing. And, of course, Mel.) Many turn to the East but those with integrity know the dilemma facing them to be dimensionally greater than that solution (it being no accident that Hesse wrote *Steppenwolf* after *Siddhartha*). Others explore their Western roots for surcease and again the passionately honest know the roots to be severed and the apparent solution irrelevant to the dilemma (since the Renaissance and Enlightenment were a cashing-in of the assets of our Medieval legacy and now there's nothing left, we're bankrupt). Put in a nutshell, the real question is: how can we control and humanize an increasingly uncontrollable and proliferating technology, an over-poweringly dehumanizing technology, when the value foundation for that attempted humanization is rapidly disintegrating and when the attempt by humans to control such power (who would be the master programmer?) would most certainly be corrupting in the extreme? And if you don't have a solid answer to that question you might as well shut up. Of course, if you're a child of the post-nihilistic era, a part of the emerging crystalline-like growth of humanity, in short, a Crystal Person, faceless and rootless, the question will not have presented itself to your mind, it will appear meaningless. But your ionic solution is now being prepared and when the master seed is dropped you will become the first unwitting victims. Planet Earth, which quakes and trembles, is bathed in a strange light, a demon light electric. All creation groans and strains towards its next evolutionary growth. Or as Confucius recently muttered: "Within the next ten years will be sought and found within Intermedia the Cosmic Haiku, the Apocalyptic Orgasm, which will reverberate throughout planet earth and trigger group mental telepathy." And all this time you probably thought the Velvet Underground was talking about drugs, homosexuality and sadomasochism. Look a bit closer.

But you are probably too occupied delving into the subtleties of *Sgt. Pepper* due to an astigmatism of the mind, a lack of perspective. It is true that the Beatles feel vibrations from the fiery center, but they are weak vibrations manifested in an elegant cynicism seeking escape in a watered down Eastern mysticism. Musically, this piddling spiritual odyssey has resulted in a bag of pretty musical tricks produced primarily by George Martin drawing on superficial characteristics of electronic and Indian music. Jonas Mekas' criticism of USCO, the New York–based mixed media cooperative, is quite applicable to the Beatles:

The USCO show . . . is a search for religious, mystical experience. Whereas in the case of the Plastic Inevitables (the Velvet Underground) the desire for the mystical experience is unconscious, the USCO is going after it in a more conscious way. They have arrived somewhere, and gained a certain peace, certain insights, and now they are beginning to meditate. Nevertheless, often I get the impression that the mystical meditative mood of many of my friends that I meet in psychedelic circles is really not the beginning of the new age or cosmic consciousness, but the sunset peace of the Age of the Fish, of the Christian era—the sunset meditation. At the Plastic Inevitables, however, the dance floor and the stage are charged with the electricity of a dramatic break just before the dawn. If at USCO's show I feel surrounded by the tradition, by the past, by the remnants of the oriental religions—at the Plastic Inevitables it is all Here and Now and the Future.

Spiritually the Velvet Underground's only equivalent is Mel Lyman. It is interesting to note the similar reactions both forces produce in people: uncomprehending indifference, vaguely comprehending hostility and comprehending submission. The first group doesn't have the barest inkling of what's happening since they're dead to the world; the second group feel their small ego base threatened (like the character after the last V.U. performance who, his face distraught and angry, spit out: "They stink!" in much the same way Mel receives letters from pipsqueaks telling him how he's screwed up); the third group understand that the V.U. and Mel are merely vessels through which greater forces are working and they listen attentively.

But what I really want to talk about is the Velvet Underground's music. Essential to that music is drone. Not the pencil-thick drone of Indian music which emanates from spirits and nervous systems which think they've found it and probably have within their limited structure of things, but a drone which is as broad as a house, a drone which is produced by New World Citizen nervous systems plunging into the

Cosmic Whirl. The drone has two levels, high-pitched and low-pitched (corresponding to the drones of the central nervous and the circulatory systems), which are produced by two very heavy nervous systems belonging to Lou Reed and John Cale respectively. The drone is not always heard but rather felt as pure essence and perpetual presence.

The constant feedback is produced by those nervous systems and projected *through* the amps which have been made perfect human extensions; it is organic and comes from the inner recesses of their souls; and their souls are connected to mother earth, their energy is generated from the core of planet earth up through their feet to their heads through their hands and amps to create a wall of sound which is a beautifully intricate and richly textured abstract-expressionist motion picture. The feedback at peak moments is a suspended mystical ecstasy in which spirit is transformed into a negative mirror of itself, in which streams of energy travel into and out of spirit simultaneously at the speed of light. The only other musician to approach such a profound conception of feedback was Jimi Hendrix on *Are You Experienced?* But, as can be heard on *Axis: Bold as Love*, he didn't have enough energy to maintain that powerful conception; and by concentration on such superficial musical aspects as melody and harmonic progression has degenerated to the level of a second-rate jazz musician a la Roland Kirk or Yusef Lateef.

And in case you haven't heard, the new music isn't about notes and pretty structures. It's about spirit, energy, presence and nervous systems. Why is John Cale the heaviest bass player in the country today? Because his nervous system is an aristocrat among nervous systems, because of the deep dark electricity he is able to convey through his bass and viola. And why is Maureen Tucker the perfect drummer for the V.U.? Because of her spirituality and nervous system. No other drummer in the world could play the archetypal 1234 with such perfection, with a weight that verges on religious ritual (not necessarily a Black Mass). And it is that ritualistic quality which is a mainstay of the Underground's powerful stylistic unity, a stylistic element which is immediately recognizable from the initial bar as the driving pulse of a machine-like organism (just listen to one bar of "The Gift"). In essence, she's playing Elvin Jones to Lou Reed's Coltrane or Sonny Murray to Reed's Albert Ayler.

It is no accident that the Velvet Underground was an organic element in Andy Warhol's Exploding Plastic Inevitable. The now defunct Inevitable remains as the strongest and most developed example of intermedia art. Although productions such as Al Rubin's Third World Raspberry have since achieved greater technical dexterity on a visual plane, no one has yet managed to communicate a guiding spirit through the complex form as well as Warhol and the Underground. Again Mekas: "The Inevitable remains the most dramatic expression of the contemporary generation—the place where its needs and desperations are most dramatically split open."

That the Velvet Underground is now the only true intermedia group in the country has been brought out clearly by their appearances at the Boston Tea Party. While all other groups (i.e. Country Joe and the Fish at the Tea Party, the Doors at the Crosstown Bus, the Grateful Dead at the Psychedelic Supermarket, etc.) do their music thing while the "light show" (what an inane phrase) does its thing and never the twain shall meet, the V.U. brings about an organic fusion of image, light and sound. They bring about this fusion by (1) their high energy level, (2) their intense conscious awareness of image and light: "I've got my eyes wide open" attempts to gobble up the light/image flow organism through peripheral vision, (3) their sophisticated use of film projections (for instance, one night while playing "Venus in Furs," Lou Reed focused his vision on a film of his face rhythmically zooming in and out, thus establishing a spiraling feedback connection through himself, the music and light/image flow).

In the beginning I said in so many words that "Sister Ray" made a breakthrough in the gray room. The piece stands as the supreme accomplishment of the rock revolution and a reproach to the musically inorganic patchworks of Sgt. Pepper (an underlying motif does not make an album musically organic), *Their Satanic Majesties Request* and even the Mothers' (bless their hearts) *We're Only in It for the Money*. I know of only five recorded tracks of contemporary American music to match it: "India" and "Impressions" from *Impressions* by John Coltrane, "Bells" from *Bells* by Albert Ayler, "D Trad, That's What" from *Live at the Cafe Montmartre* by Cecil Taylor, and "The Father and the Son and the Holy Ghost" from *Meditations* by Coltrane and Pharoah Sanders (along with hundreds of aborted attempts, Love's "Revelation" being one gross miscarriage among many). "Sister Ray" is much like "Impressions" in that it is a sustained exercise in emotional stamina and modal in the deepest sense: mode as spiritual motif, mode as infinite musical universe. As for organic unity—although the piece shifts gears at least 12 times during the 17 minutes, you will be hard pressed to find any clearly demarcated transition points, each section flows and blends so beautifully into the next.

Devote special attention to Lou Reed's verbal techniques on this track. He molds and bends and stretches and diffracts words and phrases to create effectively complex rhythmic cross-currents in a manner unprecedented in rock. Also notice how Sterling Morrison perfectly performs his usual function by filling in the middle ground between Lou and John Cale.

"Sister Ray" surpasses "Impressions" in its profound textural structure, which is provided by the organ work of John Cale. Cale's architectural conception is remarkably subtle and broad—it is reminiscent of Cecil Taylor's orchestral approach on piano but more effective because of its electronic austerity (fusion and transcendence of Taylor and Stockhausen). Cale is in fact building an awesome granite castle of tonal clusters around Lou, Sterling and Maureen—such an amazing place to live in. And the tidal wave organ drones which inundate the last sections of the piece beginning with the air raid drum explosion— this is the jet stream of superhuman energies, this is the discovered dimension after breakthrough. And remember, "Sister Ray" is not about shooting meth, fellatio or murder. Rather, it is describing the greatest cosmic upheaval in the history of man and you are living in the midst of it. (And I'm not referring to those minor disturbances, the Vietnam War and the racial crisis, inconsequential in the Aquarian Age which will witness the quiet disappearance of all political systems, including communism and capitalist democracy, and its replacement by a universal electronic theocracy.)

"I Heard Her Call My Name" is also a remarkable track simply because it contains the most advanced lead guitar work I think you're going to be able to hear for at least a year or two. I'm talking about Lou Reed's excitingly unpredictable but precisely deliberate phrasing and the tense taut line he walks breathtakingly verging on diffraction of tonality. Compare it to the relative blandness of Hendrix's or Clapton's lines and I think you'll see what I mean. This track also contains one of the most pregnant and highly charged moments I've ever heard in music: a split-second pause of silence after the second "my mind's split open" foreshadowing the following feedback explosion.

The track "White Light/White Heat" best illustrates my earlier contention that John Cale is the heaviest bass player in the country today. While listening to the track on a portable stereo phonograph with the speakers held to each side of the head, notice how profoundly deep and resonant each bass note feels. Most bass players play two-dimensional notes, but John plays three-dimensional granite slabs (it's a question of intonation and density, not volume; it's like the difference between Rauschenberg's two-dimensional Coke bottles and Warhol's three-dimensional Campbell soup cans) which reveal an absolute mastery of his instruments and a penetrating awareness of the most minute details of his music. His body and mind are in perfect tune to the bass range which accounts for his ability to project a bass drone even when playing a simple bass line (a sensibility which was perhaps developed during his stay with LaMonte Young's Theater of Eternal Music). I pointed out this particular quality to LeRoi Jones and he remarked: "So deep, so satisfying. Especially the way it goes thud thud."

Under closer scrutiny, the apparent simplicity of the bass line takes on subtle dimensions. For instance, notice during sections of "White Light/White Heat" how John just barely holds back the beat, subtly altering the rhythmic infrastructure to create a weird tension. This same razor-sharp sensibility was also apparent in the opening of "European Son" on the first album. Notice there how Lou, when entering after John's solo bass opening, slightly but so meaningfully tightens the rhythmic infrastructure.

As for the rest of the album, I'll let you get into it yourself. Forget about hearing it on the radio because even most underground jocks have their heads up their asses. So buy a copy. In a few years it will be recognized as a landmark in the growth of the universal music which is now emerging. But more importantly, hear the V.U. in person. It is absolutely necessary, if you are going to get their complete message, to feel the full visceral impact. And you don't have to worry about getting a watered-down version from the album because the V.U. finds it unnecessary to rely on studio gimmickry.

∽∽∽

As I read back I realize now that I've told you only 50% of the story. For the Velvet Underground possesses more than electronic mastery of that hideous strength and "Sister Ray" (which has been described as "Cakewalk for Frankensteinian Metal Monster") reveals only a part of their nature. They are also creators of a folk music in the deepest sense. Particularly in his latest pieces which are as yet unrecorded ("I'm Waiting for the Man" and "Heroin" have already achieved a certain status as folk classics), Lou Reed is fast becoming an incisive lyricist, creating a folk mythology of New York City and our generation which rings deep and true through the pap of fumbling unfocused artificial surrealistic imagery and facile pseudo-mystical-morality lessons produced by most new groups. They are lyrics which breathe of real life, not empty conjecture, and reveal a very human and loving side, an almost Wagnerian sentimentality (in spite of the crude remark made by one wiseacre regarding John Cale's beautifully mournful viola work on "The Story of My Life": "Even the unjustly persecuted and seemingly insensitive mighty Hulk has feelings, can shed an occasional tear"). The V.U. may well inherit the throne vacated by Dylan as the primary myth-makers of our generation. But that is a subject for a book which no doubt someone will write this summer.

⌒⌒⌒

There has been much nonsense spoken and written recently about the existence or nonexistence and nature of a Boston Sound. It should be quite clear by now that the Boston Sound is the Velvet Underground and Mel Lyman. It is irrelevant that the Velvet Underground first received significant exposure in their home city New York with Andy Warhol's Exploding Plastic Inevitable. It was in Boston, through record sales and Boston Tea Party performances, that they began to find some acceptance and meaningful response (like getting their equipment stolen). It is irrelevant that Mel Lyman's present instrument is Avatar and film, not music. What is relevant is that these two voices best express the character and spirit of the forces at work in Boston, home of the first American Revolution. It is a character and spirit which in the near future will make Boston the center of the second American Revolution, a revolution of the spirit. It is a spirit which reveals its sturdy health and moral purity by rejecting, in the name of truth, false resolutions: the Christian cop-out, the Eastern cop-out, the African cop-out and the Humanist cop-out. The powerful energies which first emerged on the West Coast are finding their focus and direction here. Like Mel Lyman, the Velvet Underground have made their "Declaration of Creation" and translated it into sound:

I am going to burn down the world
I am going to tear down everything that cannot stand alone
I am going to turn ideals to shit
I am going to shove hope up your ass
I am going to reduce everything that stands to rubble
and then I am going to burn the rubble
and then I am going to scatter the ashes
and then maybe SOMEONE will be able to see
SOMETHING as it really is
  WATCH OUT

TWO BRIEF REVIEWS FROM THE WHISKY

The Los Angeles Free Press, November 1968;
Judy Sims, *Disc*, November 30, 1968

Residencies at the Whisky A Go Go, on L.A.'s Sunset thoroughfare, in the fall of 1968 allowed those on the coast to compare the Cale-era combo to its Yule-tied incarnation. An anonymous reviewer in The Los Angeles Free Press *had this to say:*

VELVET UNDERGROUND HAS BEEN IN LOS ANGELES RECORDING THE PAST few weeks, finishing their third album in as many years. (It will be released in January.) While here, they made two appearances at the Whisky. Since their last appearance here, there has been a change in personnel: Doug Yule has joined the group and John Cale has gone to Elektra to "do his own thing." The group did some of the old songs like "Heroin" (the audience wouldn't let them off stage unless they did that one!), "I'm Waiting for My Man" (which they've slowed down and rearranged), and "Sister Ray," but the bulk of their repertoire consisted of new material, including a long number called "[Hey] Mr. Rain" that captivated the sitting listeners and drove the dancers crazy. (The song reaches a point where the only thing that remains constant and consistent is Maureen's drum beat while Lou seems to battle organist Doug with his guitar and Sterling appears to be doing something altogether unrelated on his bass. Lou writes or co-writes all of the group's material, a great deal of which appears to be valid social commentary as well as being musically justified.)

Meanwhile, the one and only U.K. weekly to notice the band as a live entity, Disc, devoted two whole paragraphs of its "Hollywood Scene" section, compiled by Judy Sims, to their activities:

Velvet Underground played the Whisky here twice in the past three weeks; the first time I saw them they were fairly awful, the second time they were fairly great. Doug Yule, new bassist/organist, said they've had exceptional response all over the country, which is surprising because they've never had a hit, and have had only two moderately successful albums (is 199 on the album chart moderate?).

Doug seems to think the world is now ready for them, and he's very enthusiastic about their new album which will be released in January. They're a strange group—the drummer, a girl named Mo Tucker, stands at her drums and flails away; the leader/songwriter/singer, Lou Reed, is into all sorts of weird psychic phenomena like astral projection; the other guitarist, Sterling Somebody, is almost frighteningly outspoken; and Doug is just plain groovy. What's a nice boy like that . . . ?

1969

The Velvet Underground

March 21 & 22   8-12   Dance

The Woodrose Ballroom

Light: **Captain Video**

FORMERLY THE ROAD

Route 5, South Deerfield
(Opp. The Gables Rest.)

FRI.: 18 AND OLDER
SAT.: NO AGE LIMIT

$2.75
Chicks
50c Off

665-3753

THE DAY THE VELVETS MET THE DEAD: TWO REVIEWS

F. D. Williams and Joe Anderson

The Pittsburgh Point, February 8, 1969

Two reviews of the February 7, 1969, appearance of the Velvet Underground with the Grateful Dead and the Fugs at the Stanley Theater appeared in The Pittsburg Point. *The first of these, "The Journey of the Magi" by F. D. Williams, was brief but precise:*

THE VELVET UNDERGROUND WAS MORE VELVET THAN UNDERGROUND— smooth, soft, and sensuous. The juxtaposition of "What Goes on in Your Mind" to a "Merry Melodies" cartoon (starring Bugs, would you believe, Bunny) rearranged our brainwaves in nostalgic patterns.

The Velvet and the audience vibrated in perfect harmony, soothed by music loud enough to reach the inner core of being without shattering the transcendence of community.

"Flesh in the Great Rock Wasteland" by Joe Anderson affirmed the Velvets' ascendancy:

Of course the making of the concert was the tight performance of three Rock groups—the Velvet Underground, the Fugs and the Grateful

Dead. Such a collection of freaks could hardly lead anywhere but up. The Velvet Underground (preceded by Paul Krassner, who got a lot of snickers but really wasn't necessary) opened up the festivities with "Heroin," one of their religious songs. The power of the Velvet Underground has its source in the train-like rhythms of Maureen Tucker, their curly red-haired drummer. Hunched over her drums, flailing the skins like some madwoman, she was quite an impressive sight. Tucker is not a very good drummer by any means, but her primitive, nerve-throb style and her seemingly endless fount of energy make her ideal for the Underground.

I was so fascinated by Tucker's movements as she tortured her drums that I only got around to noticing Lou Reed towards the middle of the lengthy "Sister Ray." The whole time Maureen Tucker was smashing away at the skins, Reed just floated aloof through everything. He only seemed to come around to what was happening when he got into "Sister Ray" with all its sexual narcotic imagery ("She's just suckin' on my ding dong/I'm searchin' for my mainline"). If it's necessary to pick the best group of the evening, then my choice is the Velvet Underground.

The Velvet Underground

PROBLEMS IN URBAN LIVING

Robert Somma

Fusion, April 14, 1969

THE BAND IS STRICTLY NEW YORK. YOU CAN TELL: THEY WORK QUICKLY, ALMOST abruptly, and if you're from out of town, they seem almost spitefully good. Their efficiency and care was once known as professionalism. They used to look hostile, and never said very much. They still do their numbers straight: "This is a song called 'Heroin.'" When it's over, they do another: ". . . thank you. This is a song called 'Sister Ray.'" They don't fuss with their equipment—they spend time tuning. They hardly ever jive with the audience and never with themselves. They sing about the simple items on any New York social calendar: mainlining, balling, hookers, junkies, queens, the usual collection of creeps, freaks and divinely accented characters closer in temperament to the world of Genet than that of the good guys. Everyone seems to know what's going on at the concert: weirdly similar teenagers, dressed in army drag—youthful conscripts of a civilian war; semi-hip, partially-groovy chicks who babble about amphetamizing in the bathroom, wishing they were in a bigger city—paying little attention to the music, a few over-thirties, who watch carefully, and who are, in speech, overly loud as well. The band does its set, says a brief thank you and packs it in. It used to be freak-time in Boston when the Velvets came to town. For a year and more they were the only surviving and functioning rock band to come out of New York intact, and the place to which they brought their music was two hundred miles from the place they put it together.

∾∾∾

The Velvet Underground possesses no characteristic, whether musical or personal, not unique or worthy of investigation. Their drummer is not a chick, she's a girl. Their lead singer, who wrote "Heroin" when the Beatles were holding each other's hand, isn't by profession a doper but a musician. They are not a creation of Andy Warhol, nor still another product of the Factory. From their formation late in 1965 until their one personnel change three years later, they have produced a sound consistent, integral and almost without parallel in rock.

For those three years it was Lou Reed, Sterling Morrison, Maureen Tucker and John Cale. Toward the end of 1968, Doug Yule replaced Cale and the emphasis and personality of the band changed, first imperceptibly, then strikingly. From the beginning they were a gathering-point for hip people. They did the Cafe Bizarre and starved a little. At the film-maker's Cinematheque they played *behind* the screen while Barbara Rubin's *Christmas on Earth* unwound. They were the only rock band to be graced by Warhol's light-show, and made the mixed-media move a scene before the *New York Times* had ever heard of Bill Graham. They toured as part of the Exploding Plastic Inevitable: lights and movies by Warhol, dancing by Gerard Malanga, Nico an occasional "chanteuse." They played the Dom before the Electric Circus moved in, and hosted a party at the Gymnasium. When the Inevitable ended, and the disco scene played out (you could tell: Arthur opened), the Underground retained some well-rehearsed material, a few convictions about the nature of rock and a few suspicions about the hard-nosed realities of promotion, marketing and touring. At that moment they could have withered away.

∾∾∾

The Velvets are unthinkable without New York City. Cale is a Welshman and the others are Long Islanders, but if Manhattan didn't exist,
neither would they. And if the air in New York were unbreathable,
the water potable, the freaks and the perverts avoidable or just not
there—then the Velvets would be laboring cheerfully for IBM,
Sperry-Rand, Discount Records, or who knows, Harper and Row. New
York does for them what Paris did for Baudelaire—provides not an excuse or even a goad, but an existential experience and a justification
for the things they create.

The differences which distinguish the Velvets from all other bands
are primarily ones which resurrect the battle lines between the two
coasts. The eternality of the west coast, its hermetic nourishment and
thalidomide culture, couldn't qualify as even bizarrely noteworthy
back east.

Brought up in Levittown, Brooklyn, Pelham, Peter Cooper Village,
Jamaica or the West Side, one would find it difficult to comprehend a
state of nature such as California proposed. New York is a series of unrequited loves, interrupted trips, false openings and premature closings.
Flower children came to New York to die—their strengths weren't equal
to the exposure. People who hate New York live there for the best reasons: to prevail, triumph, survive. People who love it, leave it for the
worst: anxiety, illusion, doubt. It is the opinion of the Underground that
New York is, at the same time, unfit for human beings and a gift from
heaven. And if a band can express a mentality or a state of mind prevail-
ing among its contemporaries, then the Velvet Underground must be
seen in that light. Everything they have to say, they say about New York.

∾∾∾

There is a reverential air surrounding Andy Warhol which the few
press cliches and publicized truisms of the past five years don't pene-
trate. He is looked upon with a feeling of guarded awe and confidence
one doesn't usually associate with the aggressively self-oriented world

of New York city art. Those who have had close contact with him, as "stars," camp-followers, spear-carriers, professional associates, etc., find him a form of permanency, stability, self-awareness and concern partially or wholly lacking in their own lives. It is almost impossible to convey the sentiment and unconsciously protective attitude many of those around Warhol feel for him, and for the relationship they have with him. It is as though too extensive or probing an investigation would burden those involved beyond endurance.

Warhol was shot the first week of June of 1968 by Valerie Solanis, a tangent on the Warhol circle. She is described, as many of the women around and within that circle, as intelligent, amusing and obviously disturbed. Tension is one of the dynamic motive forces in the group, and Valerie provided her share with her misanthropy, her eccentricity, her terrifying threats. When she walked into the Factory and shot Warhol, she surprised no one, but shocked them all.

But the curious relevant aspect of the Solanis incident is this: as Warhol lay dying, for all practical purposes, the unacknowledged and fascinating attraction of death became frighteningly real to him and to those who knew him. The Velvet Underground, who had explored with Warhol, at one time or another, every deranged evasion of contemporary society—the under-surface of the city, the subterranean conduct of its men and women, their sexual inclinations and dishonesties, their psychological dependencies and experiments—now had come before a reality perhaps more ugly. This time it was no freaked-out head or raging dike who took the trip: it was Andy, who works hard, says little and feeds, as best he can, his sheep. Warhol's intimacy with pain and death, beyond image and speculation, could not fail to be a signal event for the people whose lives touch his at so many common points.

This confrontation with death has existed in the personal life of each of Warhol's associates. His art is not unaware of the method by which the important is made irrelevant in modern life. *Saint Genet* would not have needed to be written if Sartre knew how to draw. He could have merely repeated, endlessly in various colors, the acts of fellatio, the anal penetrations, the petty thefts—all the emblematic moments of Genet's life.

The Velvets, a rock band, are intrinsically related to Warhol. The four people in the group, as a single musical force, and as a collection of individual musicians, couldn't have functioned as Warhol's band had not two conditions been present. They must have been inclined, by personality, experience and outlook to the artistic rationale of Warhol, and yet they must have resisted to some extent the influence of the Warhol environment. Something meshed: events; personalities; ideas conscious and less so about the nature of music, film, light, and about the direction and mood of America and its cultural life—its disguised paranoia, its hysterical fear of being involved, its icy demand to be entertained and not provoked. The Velvets are, in some ways, a logical extension of whatever aesthetic can be derived from the artistic productions associated with Warhol's name. This is said in knowledge of the fact that Warhol resists the type of propaganda which relates in public a definition of beauty, etc. Yet, it is possible to see similarities in form and in content between Warhol's work and the creations of the Underground.

The Underground is a band of surface simplicities. They play rock and their figures are not obviously complex. (Reed's vocal predecessors are identifiable; some are still performing: Jagger, Jerry Lee Lewis, parts of Presley, Morrison and the vinyl Buddy Holly.) Their music begins in simplicity; they recall, at times, the chord patterns of early rock groups—up-front percussion, repeated guitar chords of recognizable fingering, a definite melodic line with keyed shifts—all well-rehearsed, all beautifully performed. The Channel's "The Closer You Are"; "Tonight I Fell in Love" by the Tokens; the Marvelettes' "Please Mr. Postman" and "Little Girl of Mine" by the Cleftones; "Rave On" by Buddy Holly— these are all rock and roll numbers which the Velvets would find familiar and noteworthy in attitude and execution. The best rock groups, most of whom preceded by several years the later Beatles-Stones-Kinks models, share an insight with these models and with the Velvets about the essential nature of rock; they recognize its basic rudimental simplicity of appeal and production, its reliance upon apparently rough-cut rhythmic diamonds for the purposes of decorating a sentiment, a belief, a discovery. They understood long ago how briefly rock would stand if it were based upon patterns too far-ranging and convoluted for a bass guitar and a drum to support. Early rock may not have approached the situational profundity of the present—but no one has gone very far beyond it in arrangement and instrumentative *conception*.

The Velvets are made whole by such a conception—one which doesn't ignore complexity, but chooses to avoid it. The most recent manifestations in rock of the principle of simplicity are found in the music of the most successful rock bands: *Something Else* by the Kinks, *Beggars Banquet* by the Rolling Stones, *The Velvet Underground No. 3* by the Velvets. Yet they are distinguished, all of them, by the material to which the musical conception has been ordered. The subject matter of "David Watts," "Salt of the Earth," "Pale Blue Eyes" is instantly recognizable as the area of concern of the Kinks, the Stones, the Underground. Here, too, is a key on the simplicity rationale: one never mistakes the work of such an artist—his product is his signature. And if the Velvets determine, for the most part, the musical processes in their work, the material and the processes must be seen in the context of the Warhol environment.

⌘

When the Velvets formed and played their first gig in a New Jersey gym, they were four musicians with differing abilities, styles and tastes. Cale could, and often did, out play most rock musicians on a variety of instruments; with the Velvets, he concentrated on bizarre and virtuoso electric viola and organ playing. Maureen Tucker, self-schooled in a percussion system of rudiments and endurance, brought the Bo Diddley and African styles to a unique and reliable compound. With her bass drum turned on its side, she did a number on rock drummers not by expanding the conventional rock fills, but by modifying them. Sterling Morrison added a line to the group traceable to the components of his own personality: direct, candid, impatient of cant, frequently reticent by choice, always ready to provide a comment necessary to the musical continuity. Lou Reed, in whose image the Velvets have discovered many of the enduring features of their work, played lead, wrote songs and sang them with a restrained flair and a conviction about their essential merit characteristic of the best rock vocalists. These four musicians played a music of repetition, commingled with harsh accents, control and New York City overdrive. Their moves led to descriptions legitimate and understandable but frequently off-center: menace, contempt, obsessive hostility, surliness. Their service as house-band for the Exploding Plastic Inevitable helped in the embellishment of their reputation. Nico sang trance like, fixated, aloof, her beauty as removed from conventional concepts of warmth as a polar cap; Warhol's shows filled the space around the music with images as disturbing and abrasive to the mind as the situations in several of Reed's songs. The situation of the Underground, as a component in Warhol's system, helped them to develop as a group fertilized by an original and uncompromising mind.

The peculiar nature of rock music makes strong demands upon the performer. It provides him with a release and a freedom not previously known to popular artists who wished to deal successfully with the dilemma of American life—its commerce and its culture. Rock performers stand as naked on a stage as any politician in the first chilly hours of defeat. A rock band which doesn't find a personal unity and cohesion on other than musical levels will find itself ultimately falling apart. Rock is best because it depends on a shared emotion, a collective response. It functions almost like a church providing shelter for those of uncommon background who share a common belief. Nonsectarian, it can still be dogmatic and slightly larcenous. But it's there that you find the intensity, the tainted madness of the convinced, the celebrated and the hopeful.

It is experience which brings to any rock group the proof of its value or the refutation of its plea to be heard. Rock, like life, has its cheap thrills, its staggering surprises, its small compensations and its large-scale squandering of resources. The Velvets hung together through moments of bleak economic outlook, personal confusion and professional neglect. With the demise of the Inevitable, the Velvets were thrown back upon themselves, forced to discover the kind of band they had been in the process of becoming. In a sense, they were as much victimized by their relationship with Warhol as they were helped by such a close contact with the bizarre consistency of his mind. They never insisted, except through their music and then only subtly, on their independence as a group. Their songs only helped to support the generally accepted notion that they explored those areas of society inhabited by pop figurines—as though the world had been made bad to be the decor for a sermon. The Velvets sang "Heroin"—don't all those underground creeps take it? They sang about lesbians, the frenetic trip for a connection, the cruel sham of New York City ("I'll Be Your Mirror," "Waitin' for My Man," "All Tomorrow's Parties"). The cultural attitudes and realities in their songs seemed to have originated in the social ambience whirling around Warhol like an industrial spoor. Yet they were more correctly associated with the visions inside and not hovering above that head. "Venus in Furs," "White Light/White Heat," "There She Goes Again" are certainly the products of a city governed by Lindsay and mired in decades of its own muck. But neither Warhol nor Lou Reed created New York—they only live there.

All those songs, however, are less remarkable for their subject matter than for the musical ordering to which they submit. Warhol explored the meaning of repetition—the Velvets do it, not with commonplace images, but with notes. "All Tomorrow's Parties" is a tableau, and the picture doesn't change, the scene is the same, the stanzas don't vary.

"Heroin" functions as a dynamic persona, a mask which moves from anticipation to ecstasy, from the strung-out decision to shoot-up to the slightly furious paradise of a run. Warhol was satisfied to repeat, with variations in color, location, and personnel, images of the ordinary. The Velvets took his lead. The disjunction and displacement of life in New York performs precisely the same kind of operation, from the ordinary to the bizarre, on its citizens—frequent, habitual confrontations with the sewer lead to a comfortable feeling, a sense of appropriateness which the less adventuresome or simply wealthier burghers find in a daily diet of TV and the *New York Times*. Anything, no matter how lurid, off-beat, far-out, or freaky, can be made to look ordinary if you see it enough. It can lead you to ask, with Dylan, what else have they got left.

⌘

Several clearly catalogued figures in art, music and urban development contribute to the material and performance technique of the Velvets. Major commercial enterprises and movements in the rock industry did not. The *Sgt. Pepper* era, San Francisco rock, the blues revival, the tainted and synthetic soul products of Motown—all were temporary and without influence in the minds and work of many rock purists, the Velvets among them. The latter, however, are drawn to the current rock creations, which recall in some way the sound and the attitude of the first rock era. Peripheral phenomena are just that: secondary and maybe inevitable, but not necessary to the music—self-inflating disc-jockeys, hyper-excited promotions, falsely enthusiastic and apprecia-tive record company execs, flock-like audiences. The bustle and frantic moves of a coming group are part of the commercial reality to the business—they must be dealt with and accepted as "real," not right.

For the Velvets to be associated on a personal and professional basis with Warhol was an experience of incalculable importance. Through him was transmitted, even if only by implication, unconscious support or opposition to a world of artistic endeavor and conception not usually given to the rock performer. Lennon, for example, is getting it second-hand through Yoko Ono; the Stones aren't getting it at all. The Velvets pass slightly beyond the rock groups for whom cross-fertilization means a careful attentiveness to what other successful bands are doing, in music and elsewhere. The Velvets were able to examine at second- and sometimes first-hand new processes and their effects upon clever and intelligent people involved in activities often quite removed from rock. For them cross-fertilization meant a drug-scene, certainly, but one quite different from the antiseptic and almost obscenely safe world of the Beatles or a Buffalo Springfield bust. It also meant contact on a performing level with novelty and originality, with the incipient moments of a new idea and its initial public expression. Light-shows, for example, in the Velvets' world were no discordant or irrelevant pastiche, no tiresome stylization, no synthetic prettiness or calculated and scoured freak-out.

The Velvet Underground, then, derives, in part, from a cultural scene peculiar to New York. The many faces in the scene are traceable, some with more difficulty than others. "Pop" is certainly a major and, for a while in their careers, a persistent influence. Yet, "pure" rock is as important to their musical production as Pop was to their artistic conceptions. For those who grew up in New York, who came to what insurance salesmen call maturity during the early and middle sixties, rock means certain specific songs and groups, and will continue to mean only those plus whatever new releases or bands resemble them, in performance and attitude, most closely. The Supremes aren't the greatest black girl-group in rock; they're only the richest. Purists remember the Chantels, who were there first with "Maybe" and their immediate successors, the Shirelles, who sang "Will You Still Love Me Tomorrow." Purists were in grammar school (or should have been) when the Penguins made "Earth Angel," but they loved it with the fervor and insight of a post-pubescent. Rock purists didn't need the Bee Gees or Joshua Rifkin to find out about fag-rock: Danny and the Juniors did it better. Social comment? The great Crystals songs: "He's a Rebel," "Uptown," etc.; the Drifters, early and late; the Corsairs' "Smoky Places." The Velvets are hip to this tradition, which is a factor in the development of their repertoire. Unlike many rock artists insecure in their self-conception and undermined by a lack of confidence in their pose, the Velvets say little about what it is they know or do. Yet, their performances reflect knowledge as well as a feeling about rock, and reveal them, from one point of view, as the most conceptually intellectualizing. The Velvets, by contrast, sing with no parenthetical explications, a song called "Rock and Roll," and it sounds less like "A Day in the Life" (which barely qualifies as rock) than "Tonight Tonight" by the Mellokings. Both songs are happy to be contained within limits.

Through two albums the Velvets persevered in their creations. The first album reflected many of the influences, the involvements and the concerns of the band and particularly of Reed. "Waiting for My Man," "European Son," "There She Goes Again"—the entire album is, as Reed once described the band's performance at the Cinematheque, "a dog-whistle for all the freaks in the city." Yet, in addition to that, it contained elements of musical achievement (rock and roll conception and memories) to which the group would cling during the months after their split from Warhol.

The second album must be rated on its technical deficiencies, not its aspirations. "Lady Godiva" and "I Heard Her Call My Name" are badly mixed; "Sister Ray" hasn't the magnificently precise and lucid breaks and changes of the in-person performances; "White Light/White Heat" is more frantic, less accurate than the live version. There are numerous reasons for the failure of the LP. The conflicts which divided the group were becoming more apparent and more certainly insoluble. The split between Cale and the others permitted Reed to present the group with a number of simple and beautiful songs, far removed, not from his prior excellence, but from the neurotic obsessions of the years with Cale.

Their latest album is technically perfect and substantially different from the music of the first two. Reed's songs are self-aware, not self-conscious; his singing is predictably superior to most rock vocalizing; the band plays with a care, a punctuality and a self-assurance too often undetermined by Cale's flamboyant figures. Their third LP, with "Candy Says" (the Velvets singing "doo-doo-wah! wah!"), "Pale Blue Eyes" (a successor to "If I Fell" and "Love Minus Zero: No Limit"), "I'm Beginning to See the Light" (rock and roll music in its pure state) is matter-of-factly stunning in the depth and normalcy of its emotion, in the care of its execution and in the perfectly realized self-conception it reveals. The Velvets are passing beyond the cities they live and play in and rising to the occasion of consistent and almost easy brilliance.

REVIEW OF *THE VELVET UNDERGROUND*

Lester Bangs

Rolling Stone, #33

THE VELVET UNDERGROUND ARE ALIVE AND WELL (WHICH IN ITSELF MAY surprise some people) and ever-changing. How do you define a group like this, who moved from "Heroin" to "Jesus" in two short years? It is not enough to say that they have one of the broadest ranges of any group extant; this should be apparent to anyone who has listened closely to their three albums. The real question is what this music is about—smack, math, deviate sex and drugdreams, or something deeper?

Their spiritual odyssey ranges from an early blast of sadomasochistic self-loathing called "I'm So Fucked Up," through the furious nihilism of "Heroin" and the metaphysical quest implied in the words "I'm searching for my mainline," to this album, which combines almost overpowering musical lyricism with deeply yearning, compassionate lyrics to let us all know that they are finally "Beginning to See the Light."

Can this be the same bunch of junkie-faggot-sadomasochist-speedfreaks who roared their anger and their pain in storms of screaming feedback and words spat out like strings of epithets? Yes. Yes, it can, and this is perhaps the most important lesson of the Velvet Underground: the power of the human soul to transcend its darker levels.

The songs on this album are about equally divided between the subjects of love and freedom. So many of them are about love, in fact, that one wonders if Lou Reed, the malevolent Burroughsian Death Dwarf who had previously never written a complimentary song about anybody, has not himself fallen in love. The opening song, "Candy Says," is about a young girl who would like to "know completely what the others so discreetly talk about." The fact that this and about half the other tracks on the albums are ballads marks another radical departure for the Velvets. The next track is a deep throbbing thing in which he chides perhaps the same girl for her confusion with a great chorus: "Lady be good / Do what you should / You know it'll be alright." John Cale's organ work on this track is stark and spare and, as usual, brilliant—this time as much for what he leaves out as what he puts in.

Then there is "Some Kinda Love," a grooving Latiny thing, somewhat like Donovan but much more earthy, and with words that will kill you: "Put the jelly on your shoulders / Let us do what you feel most / that from which you recoil / Uh still makes your eyes moist."

Perhaps the greatest surprise here is "Jesus," a prayer no less. The yearning for the state of grace reflected there culminates in "I'm Set Free," a joyous hymn of liberation. The Velvets never seemed so beautifully close to the Byrds before.

The album is unfortunately not without its weak tracks though. "The Murder Mystery" is an eight minute exercise in aural overload that annoys after a few listenings, and "Pale Blue Eyes" is a folky ballad that never really gets off the ground either musically or lyrically. On the whole I didn't feel that this album matched up to *White Light/White Heat*, but it will still go a long way toward convincing the unbelievers that the Velvet Underground can write and play any kind of music they want to with equal brilliance.

I'M BEGINNING TO SEE THE LIGHT
(In Which New Records by Bob Dylan and
the Velvet Underground Are Given Some
Attention, and Other Things Happen)

Paul Williams

Planet, May 15, 1969

b.

Everybody loves the Velvets' new LP! I am surprised, I am delighted! I
mean—my friends who hear the album ask to hear it again, they walk
around singing it, they talk about it during dinner. They buy copies
themselves if they have phonographs. They drop by to hear it otherwise. *The Velvet Underground*, their third album, on MGM, is currently
competing for attention with Dylan's spanking new love-gift—and
holding its own! It's my own favorite album since *Forever Changes*.
And I haven't had so much luck in turning people onto a record since
The Doors. That came out in winter 1967, concurrent with an album
called *The Velvet Underground & Nico*. I was an eager propagandist
for that first Doors LP in those days, and somehow never paid much attention to the one or two Velvet evangelists afoot. Almost two years
later, last fall, I began to open my ears. "Let me tell you people what
I've found."

"I met myself in a dream, and I just want to tell ya everything was all right." I think the Velvets are speaking to the insides of our minds today, as the Band did last summer, the Beatles the summer before that, the Stones even earlier on in our lives. "No kinds of love are better than others." *The Velvet Underground* is one of those few albums that allow us to suspect great music is being created in our time. On the inner sleeve of my copy of *Nashville Skyline*, I read some fascinating propaganda for the medium Dylan's message is impressed upon (the word "tape" was never once mentioned in the spiel, but I surmise some threat is felt) and came upon this shocking reminder: long-playing records are this year twenty-one years old, mere children by this world's standards. 1948, same year as Stevie Winwood, Israel, and me! Why is all this barely mature stuff taken so seriously? . . .

9.

We just listen to the Velvet album over and over. Sometimes "Some Kinda Love" is the track that most amazes me, the way it rolls and barks, so sweet, so sensitive. Reminding me always of a formal French lovesong & the blues of John Lee Hooker. Earlier I was amazed that one song could resemble such apparently diverse stuff; now I am so busy being amazed by Lou Reed's voice, the depth of humanity it encloses and breathes, and by his words, and by the guitar, bass, drums singing along, I am so thoroughly and immediately astonished by everything I hear in this song, now, every time I listen, that I no longer can focus on resemblances. I can only absorb, opening every receptor in my nervous system in my effort to feel this incredible moment more fully. One word for this music is "sensual."

Another word is "human." Not just the words, which really do speak directly to our human situation, but the music, especially the performances: there is something so real, so immediate and personal, in the movement of these songs, the touch of fingers to guitar strings, the extension of energy through a drumstick so that it is strike and touch both, an intimate, human action, you can feel this in the music as it touches you, strikes you, awakening in you a knowledge of the texture and movement of being alive. Bass notes like pulse beats, spoken words like the sensory explosion of opening my eyes.

"Got my eyes wide open"—the Velvets have always been in touch with the world. Now they are making that world, the real one, palatable, not by sugar-coating but by being gentle. The penetrating. Magic on the level of the Beatles, stark and subtle awareness on some higher level still, the Velvets have finally made an album we can all listen to; they have found a way to be even more honest. They have brought the whole world—not just the harmless parts—closer, and without scaring anyone. Now, *that's* revolution! We're set free.

h.

If you like Bob Dylan's new album, move to the country. If you're already in the country, I suppose the proper response to the record is to make love more, and better. Shine on brightly. Relax.

i.

It's frustrating. This essay feels like it's done, and yet there's so much more I want to say. About the Velvet album: how it moves, stopping and starting, the break in "Candy Says" ("if I could walk away from *me*") which is simply the best example I can think of of how beautiful motion can be, the breakthrough in "The Murder Mystery" (the listener is set up, the repetition of the word "structures" becomes increasingly ominous, both streams call for attention more and more in their quiet ways, until you're completely split and suddenly realize that the piano is a part of both streams and something else, at which point, with the aid of the word "perverse" and a sense of timing that is

evidence of genius, you break through, three streams become a thousand, the song wanders to an ending and you are left on a higher
plane—and ready to hear "Afterhours"), the way everyone identifies
with "Jesus," the way everyone walks around singing "Afterhours" and
plays it again when the album's over. I want to get into a rap on subject matter, how "Some Kinda Love" is about the worthiness of casual
affairs ("Situations arise / Because of the weather / And no kinds of
love / Are better than others") and "Pale Blue Eyes" is about more
than adultery, maybe the significance of adultery's *texture*. I want to
declare that "I'm beginning to see the light" is the best line I've heard
in months, and the song is better, and the "How does it feel to be
loved" ending is almost more than I can hold in . . . which is fine, because the next song is "I'm Set Free" ("I've been set free, and / I've
been bound"), in which the growth cycle of release leading to greater
need leading to grander release, etc., is not merely described but created, expressed, performed. And followed by "That's the Story of My
Life," another perfect transition: ". . . that's the difference between
wrong and right. But Billy said, both those words are dead. . . . " (It is
incredible how this album talks about almost everything that is worth
talking about these days, and has a revelation to offer in almost every
area! And the music, the music. . . . But I guess that's what it means to
be completely in harmony with the moment.) I want to discuss so
many things, all those wonderful lines in "The Murder Mystery" and
what they do to your head as they seep, one by one, into consciousness—I would like to analyze every line of "Afterhours" and of course
Maureen's magnificent vocal as a study of the nature of perfection in
this century—I would like to play this album with you about a hundred times and share more every time. Not to mention that I could
write volumes about *Nashville Skyline* or just "Lay Lady Lay" and my
own lovelife during the past week . . . and I've certainly much more to
say about birth, how people being born and words being born have so
much in common & how the "population explosion" as ungraspable

metaphor and fact rules not only our subconscious at this time but our literature. . . .

But shit, this essay is over, it was over before I set down the letter i. This is all afterthought, a sneaky effort at releasing pent-up tension of expression, giving birth. . . .

I'm beginning to see the light.

REVIEW OF *THE VELVET UNDERGROUND*

Adrian Ribola

O*z*, May 1969

THE VELVET UNDERGROUND HAVE ALWAYS BEEN A GROUP WHO TURNED AS
many stomachs as they blew minds: not everyone can groove on them.
Their attraction (or repulsion) lies in the extreme areas in which they
operate: insistent, relentless rhythms . . . hysterical organ and guitar
. . . wrecked vocals. A cut like "Sister Ray" on their last album makes a
direct bid on the metabolism, you either escape or surrender. Their music is always unsettling and disturbing: their heads adrift in Burroughs-
land, a sickly sweet, rotten smell in the air . . . songs of Strange
Pleasures, subversive and corrupt. Yet here we are with "Jesus," a long
way from "Heroin" in the space of one LP. Have they really hung up
their spurs and the whip of shiny, shiny leather with the sailor's suit
and cap? Have the Flowers of Evil started to bloom?

Perhaps they haven't gone through changes so much as modifica-
tion; the wolf and the lamb walk hand in hand. For the first time Velvet shares top billing with Underground. They've stopped rushing on
their run and slowed the pace to a processional dawdle. But though
everything has been toned in low key it's still unmistakably them. It's
got "feel" alright, but it's a kind of ghoulish corpse-like feel. Gone are
the walls of sound and vast textural contrasts, in comes a sad liturgical

droning, the wailing of the converted sinner (but with his tongue slyly
in his cheek). One doesn't really have faith in their faith, and it's
probably wisest to give up very early trying. Cop out of value judge-
ments, write it off as some variation on camp (which VU have always
been strong on anyway) and you can relax and enjoy it.

Songs on this album are divided between heaven and hell, and the
casual listener will be forgiven if he doesn't notice the difference. "Jesus" is pure, simple, moving and undeniably sincere. But then there's
"Some Kinda Love" which is another thing altogether . . . shall we say
"hard core necrophilia"? The lyrics are the filthiest. "Put jelly on your
shoulders and lie down upon the carpet . . . " or, "In some kinds of love
the possibilities are endless—and for me to miss one would be ground-
less. . . ." "Murder Mystery," in which chick drummer Maureen Tucker
takes to song, is a cross between the Mothers and the Billy Cotton
Band Show, and reminiscent of the saga of Walter Jeffries on *White
Light/White Heat*. Maureen also takes the honors on "Afterhours" and
gets into a nice Vera Lynn bag . . . in fact she warbles delightfully.

Velvet Underground don't really sound together on this album,
either as a group or individuals, which I have a sneaking suspicion was
what they might have been aiming at. Luckily too, for if they made it
they would lose their quality as a group . . . fragmentation is more
their scene. The style of this album is the antithesis of their style before. By replacing blatant freak value with subtler means they end up
sounding more bizarre than ever. Tired cliche, but this album really
does grow on you . . . like a malignant tumor.

INTERVIEW WITH LOU REED

Ramblin' Jim Martin

Open City, #78

IT'S 11 O'CLOCK AND THE CHICAGO TRANSIT AUTHORITY IS ON STAGE downstairs and I'm upstairs "interviewing" Lou Reed, lead guitarist with the Velvet Underground, doing a gig at the Whisk and here in L.A. to cut a third album with Verve. The group is composed of Reed; Sterling Morrison, rhythm; Maureen Tucker on drums; and a newcomer, Doug [Yule] on bass—replacing John Cale, who played bass, electric viola, piano and organ. Cale is now producing Nico.

Some small talk about rock criticism (Reed doesn't take reviews seriously: thinks rock critics have much more important things to write about, and, since most critics know nothing about the music, he thinks all reviews suck). Then he characterizes the Underground's music by calling it "simple rock and roll":

LOU: The music is very simple . . . simple rock and roll. It never was anything else; it's not advanced, doesn't have any messages, and it's very simple rock and roll. It's just songs. Anytime anybody says "interpreting," I immediately grow scales. . . .

JIM: Does the group still do "Sister Ray" (*White Light/White Heat*)?

LOU: We do "Sister Ray" every time we play.

JIM: In the second set?

LOU: Yeah, because you don't want to follow it with anything. Mainly, the instruments are wrecked by the time we finish. We close out with it. You see, "Sister Ray" depends on whether we're playing part two, part three. . . . "Sister Ray" in its entirety might run three days sometime, depending upon the energy level of the group, but, you know we have tapes of this, but we won't release them because it's more than an hour long already. . . .

JIM: Why not put it all on one album?

LOU: Uh, because it's not practical; there's no reason to. When it's justifiable to put something like that out, we'd do it, you under-stand? There's no point in putting that out now. One, no one would buy it, except a few local freaks, right? Two, the record company would lose money, so then, three, we'd get it in the end. In other words, why haven't the Beatles put out something four days long? Well, the Beatles are just getting around to putting out something they're allowed to now. If they'd done it in the first place they'd have bombed and it just wouldn't have made it. You know, you un-derstand? You have to deserve to be able to do it.

Reed now explains why he doesn't believe in evolution.

LOU: I don't believe people came from apes. . . . I mean, I won't use the old riff about why hasn't some chimp turned into a man? You know, at the local zoo or something. But evolution is just silly, it's just one way of trying to explain unexplainables to children. I mean people keep trying to say you're evolved, but it's just that there's one level showing through one week and another level the next, you know? . . .

JIM: Are you conscious of influences of any kind—musically, literar-ily, etc.?

LOU: Sure, everybody. I probably, you know, listen to everybody everyone else listens to. (*Laughs*) My influences wouldn't be any different from yours.

JIM: You like Clapton, Hendrix . . . ?

LOU: (*Laughs*) I just like everybody. . . . I don't like to say bad things about people. . . . I've seen Hendrix jam and when he's jamming, he's really lovely, a good guitar player, and I understand that Eric Clapton did the guitar thing on "Sour Milk Sea." . . . I'm not sure I enjoy the groups they're in. . . . I'm not sure I enjoy blues guitar playing. In fact, I'm sure I don't. . . . I think Jim McGuinn is a very good guitar player, really exciting, you know: to this day, no one has done a better solo than "Eight Miles High." I mean, people should really support the Byrds; the Byrds are divine.

JIM: But they keep changing all the time—

LOU: So WHAT? People are so fucked up, they say, "You changed, you didn't stay the same": so? Yeah, so WHAT? It's the Byrds.

JIM: But if you liked something they did at one point and then they changed, and—

LOU: Tough. That's ridiculous. I mean, people don't own people; YOU don't own people. On the one hand, you're saying you're in favor of evolution, and on the other hand, what if it evolves into something I don't like. Maybe YOU should evolve.

JIM: In the performances of "I'm Waiting for the Man" at the Whisky, the VU plays the song at a slower tempo than on their first album, *The Velvet Underground & Nico* (also Verve). Why?

LOU: Oh, yeah, we were tired of it fast. . . . The lyrics are made up on stage; they're not written. . . .

JIM: You improvise?

LOU: Right. I mean, like "I'm Waiting for the Man" was written, "Venus in Furs" was written, "Sister Ray" evolved. . . .

JIM: The group doesn't do "Venus in Furs" anymore.

LOU: Listen, if you were playing "Heroin" every night, you could understand what could happen to you, you know? See, we have to be careful that we enjoy doing it each time, and like we really do enjoy it each time, and when we don't enjoy them we don't do it.

JIM: You played at the Avalon in San Francisco recently?

LOU: Yeah, I didn't enjoy that one, because, uh, I'd never, we just got, we'd never been in a room that big in our lives, and uh, our amplification wasn't ready for it, and we couldn't really hear what was going on, so it was really very difficult for us. You should always try to show up wherever you're going to play two days ahead and get a chance to test out the sound system. With them, you couldn't, because you're interested in changing with the other people. And in a big place it really becomes hard, you have to go through the motions not because you want to, but because you can't hear. You have to hear, right? I mean, even if Beethoven was deaf, he wasn't gigging with Brahms or something in, uh, you know, the middle of the Avalon; you know, it would have been a totally different thing. . . . Can you imagine that? I mean, if all the dead people who played music were suddenly around gigging? You know, Beethoven meets Mozart, you know. They could bill it "Battle of the Keys," yeah, right in the middle of Shrine Pinnacle, you know, Ludwig. . . . You know, . . . that's what people are kind of doing now with Lesser Mortals; they're just gonna destroy them all, you know, because people they're doing that to are not at that level. It's just like saying, you know, "Battle of the Blues Guitarists: Betty Grable Versus Kate Smith." Yeah. Who cares, right? It's on that level. A toy level. That's the level everything's on these days, what's being done. . . . People who are, like really attempting to do something, like I think the Doors now and then . . . like Jim Morrison's trying to do something, which is a lot more than anyone else around here is doing . . . he's like, trying to do something for people, you understand? I mean, he's getting up there in front of all those kids, and he's not dumb, he knows exactly what he's doing; he's going through all this whole number—for them, and that's very nice, very religious: rock is getting very religious. I know they're doing it, and I think we're doing it and I can't think of anybody else who's doing it on that level.

JIM: But you don't have a religious feeling, except in the sense that there's almost a ritual-like quality to your sets—

LOU: I believe in rituals. I firmly believe in rituals and traditions. Like, I believe in dressing up before you go on, and wearing certain things you don't wear any other time. And, I believe you get up there and everything is set up a certain way, and everything's counted off a certain way, and it's very methodical, you know, because it's like a litany, you know what I mean? And it's your own, you know, which is much more groovy anyway and like if people are there something takes place that doesn't take place in any other situation, and like that's why, you know, I really enjoy playing; I mean, there's certain things you do up there you just can't do in any other place, and . . . continually working with people—that's fantastic, man.

JIM: But some audiences may be dull. What can you do with an audience which won't respond?

LOU: Make them respond. . . . I try to do whatever it is to get them going, so that I can get going. In other words, I see no point in haggling over details, you understand? The thing is, I'll select whatever it is within our realm. I mean, we're not going up there and doing "Louie, Louie." One of the reasons I won't do "Louie, Louie," by the way, is because of the guitar solo involved. It's one of the classic guitar solos of all time. I mean, the Kinks tried to do "Louie', Louie" and couldn't. No, you know I really believe like, people paid money, and I'm accepting it, you know? I'm not out there playing free, you know—that doesn't mean you bend over 100 percent—I mean, we're up there to play certain things and we're going to make it happen with them or without them, hopefully with them.

JIM: How did the group come to do the film *Exploding Plastic Inevitable*?

LOU: I wasn't even there. I was in the hospital. All they did was some character filmed the show, I mean, we did the first light shows; some people don't know that, but anyway, light shows have evolved into another thing, and we just don't have any control over light shows, except we keep telling them to please don't use strobes; you know we try to inject some of our own taste, somehow, but now light shows are all over the place. What happened then—this was in '66, you know?—a cat came down and he filmed them in Chicago. It was all just a lot of fun. It was misinterpreted up and down the line. You know, we were supposed to be some strange leather freaks, drug addicts, S&M, you know, on and on; I mean, until this day, you know—

JIM: Well, you were being produced by Warhol—

LOU: Yeah, but what does that mean? Some people think he's the greatest artist not only of our time but maybe of a lot of other times. I don't want to go into it. . . . He made a 25-hour movie that, probably, may not even in your lifetime get to be shown. It was shown just once, in New York. . . . It was called *Four Star*. He's so good; the Factory is so fine, and he's so great, I mean, that's why we've never been touched by him; I mean we can't take that, I mean we learned very early in the game, I mean, we knew how good we were and we knew how good he was, and yet we were hearing all these things; so he never touched us, but he is simply—and I don't want to get into a conversation about Andy Warhol—but he is simply the Best, that's all there is to it; he is the Finest. And should it come out, and it'll be coming out soon. . . . He said the Empire State Building's a star, which, I'm telling you, where his head is, he's you know, right there. You know, in New York, you look up in the sky and you say I can't see any stars. . . . There's no way of communicating with where he's at. . . . He's just been shot; he's lucky to be alive, and he's scared. . . . A 25-hour movie, man, is just fantastic. . . . Like he did silk screens of the Mona Lisa. Sixty Mona Lisas and when they all wind up you look at the hands, right? Who else but Andy could get you away from the smile? . . . He tape recorded all the conversations in Grand Central Station and published them. There's gonna be a book coming out, Ondine's book, Andy turned on his tape recorder and got Ondine for like 24 hours. Ondine is the most incredible rapper going, and it's published. . . . He transcribed it over a period of two or three years; like one chapter's missing because one of the high school girls who typed it up, her mother found a chapter and burned it. But anyway, Ondine is the Pope. This book, it was just like *Ulysses*; and you read it like it was James Joyce revisited. It's fantastic. You see, it's the most fantastic book you've ever seen. . . . It includes everything everyone said in 24 hours. And that includes the grocery man, the taxicab driver; if you couldn't understand what they said, it says "Inaudible." . . . All right, that's the end of the Andy rap. We're not connected with Andy anymore. . . .

JIM: What happened to Tom Wilson (*producer of the second VU LP*)?

LOU: Tom Wilson went independent. He was very good at discovering self-contained groups that can handle themselves. Like we're a self-contained unit that can handle ourselves. . . . I like Tom Wilson, personally. . . .

(*Inaudible*)

I dig L.A. by the way. I think the kids are just fabulous. You gotta understand what it's like being from New York. You can't put us down for being from New York just like we don't put you down for coming out here. Like, everytime people find out you're from another place, they go through a whole rap, you know, like "Oh, how do you like it . . . ?!" You know, that whole crock of shit, right? But I think the kids here are great. The Whisky is a great club. Like all the people put it down, but it's still a great club, like we do a show up here and play, and nobody bugs anybody else. You know the Strip and the cops it's really scarey, and I don't understand that, but I remember the last time we were here: those cops, I mean really, you know, I'd stay far away from them, but the kids, they'd walk right up to them. You know, last night when we walked out, they were beating somebody up. But the kids, it's . . . they're just great.

You see, in New York it's a totally different scene; it all happens faster and you become enamored to a lot of things and then, on the other hand, you're kind of callous to a lot of other things. Out here it's just more relaxed, you know, like what happens when you get involved with a person there and you become pushy and aggressive, and they're out here saying, "Hurry up, why?" You dig it? They say, like you know, the sun's out, here's some pot, and you know? You'd say, come on let's go, right? It's just a different way of going about it. You know one's not better than another: they're just different. But I'm tired of running into this, you know, the New York freak image. I mean I don't wear my motorcycle jacket anymore just so I don't get involved in that.

JIM: How did you happen to come to call yourselves the Velvet Underground?

LOU: It's a dirty book. (*Laughs*) There's a dirty book, you know, it's the funniest dirty book I've ever read. Not only that was super-funny, but like we played a Philadelphia club and we found out that, like the daughter of the guy who wrote the book was taking tickets at this club in Philadelphia and we said, "How fantastic!" and we sent down and said, "Would you autograph this book?" and she said, "How dare you?! He's dead of cancer. . . . " But it was such a great time with the book, you know? . . . "Into the murky depths of depravity and debauchery with the Velvet Underground" . . . this is TOO good, I mean just the name, I love the ring of it, Velvet Underground: it sounded so nice. . . .

JIM: What does it mean?

LOU: It couldn't mean anything, you know? I mean, if you just think of "velvet underground" that's kind of a nice, pleasing, womb-oriented thought, you know what I mean? Cabbages and kings? It doesn't mean anything.

JIM: About the titles of your songs—

LOU: They're supposed to be in order, like for instance, I had a dream, you know I had an eyeball store, you know, and you'd walk into the store and they'd have all these glass cases with all these different eyes there. I won't be able to unscrew my head and wash out the blue and everything, and I figured if I had new eyes, it would clean things up and make it easier. You could put in one green one and one yellow one.

JIM: Did you ever get them?

LOU: Yeah, I went into a taxidermist's in the garment district and they had eyeballs there, glass eyes, but they had bat wings and everything, you know, 'cause a friend of mine was turned away from customs for witchcraft because she was covered, you know, with rat's tails. . . . That's Oreon, she was the female Ondine . . . a witch.

JIM: Do you like electronic music?

LOU: Not at all. I think if electronic composers could play rock and roll then electronic music might get interesting.

JIM: I recently got hold of John Cale's "Loop," a seven minute piece for guitar distortion and feedback, published recently in *Aspen* Magazine. It is beyond what instruments can do, normally, and it—

LOU: I have to make myself perfectly clear on this: that was something John did, and I'm not interested in that kind of thing, per se, very much. . . .

JIM: But it's, I mean I can hear it in your music—

LOU: You're reading it into it: I don't know how to explain it to you. But, once you get up to a certain level, I mean, I don't play my guitar like a guitar, I think of it like a tuba, you understand? It's not a guitar, it's a tuba. . . . I usually think of myself as a renaissance chorus on the guitar. . . . I mean, I know a lot of guitar players do that. You go like this on the fuzz, daaaaaaaaaa—and what happens is that you don't get just one note like a guitar, you may get eight notes, like daaaaahhhhheeeee. . . . You start hearing some really strange things. . . . We used to call it the Cloud, and like, on certain songs, we used to consciously enter the Cloud and you just hear all these funny things. They're not you, but you know they're being caused by the guitar, right? . . . and it's not just me, I mean, I've had people come up to me and say, "Man! Who was singing those choir parts? Who was playing trumpet?" There's no trumpet. The thing is, if you know how to operate an amplifier and make all these things happen . . . and like, we do, but I don't want to spend all my life doin' it. Like, there's no candy stores. I'd like to go for a soda.

JIM: I noticed that Gary Kellgren of the Record Plant in New York engineered the second album (and, later, Jimi Hendrix's *Electric Ladyland*). Did he have much to do with it, really?

LOU: We haven't had much experience with Gary, because we weren't in the Record Plant, which is his studio, but at that time, his studio was about the size of this room (*about 18' × 25'*). Now, can you imagine us recording in a studio the size of this room? Listen, in three years of playing, we've had less than three days of recording time. . . . Our first album was released six months late, right? because the record company was afraid because of "Heroin" and, two, because the manager of the Mothers didn't want Frank's album to be like our first one—there were no psychedelic albums no hip albums, then, and theirs was coming out first. . . . I'm not saying anything evil towards anybody, but there was panic, and ours came out six months later. That's what goes on. Three days in three years in recording studios.

The telephone rings from downstairs. Someone answers.
"Is that it?" Reed asks. "We're on."

IT'S A SHAME THAT NOBODY LISTENS

Richard Williams

Melody Maker, October 25, 1969

THE VELVET UNDERGROUND HAVE MADE JUST THREE ALBUMS, NONE OF which have sold particularly well in Britain. But that trio of albums constitutes a body of work which is easily as impressive as any in rock.

If you doubt that statement, then it's unlikely that you've listened hard to the albums, because they yield up their treasure only to a listener who is prepared to treat them with respect and intelligence.

The group was spawned a couple of years ago, part of Andy Warhol's Exploding Plastic Inevitable multi-media troupe. It was immediately obvious that they were very different from the hundreds of other groups springing up during the American Rock Renaissance.

Their music was hard, ugly and based in a kind of sado-masochistic world which few dared enter. The first album, called *The Velvet Underground and Nico*, was produced by Warhol and released here on Verve, and a scary document it is.

Three tracks feature Nico, the beautiful blonde singer whose voice has a unique deathly pallor. "Femme Fatale" takes a standard pop-song form and turns it into something tantalizing and frightening, while "All Tomorrow's Parties" is a grim view of the life of a Lower East Side good-time girl.

"Parties" and another track, "Venus in Furs," share the group's best trademark: a kind of heavy, almost martial beat, very hypnotic and quite unrelated to any other music you can think of. They arrived at this, I think, because of the presence of a girl drummer, who is most definitely not a joke. She adds to the already somewhat surrealistic charisma of the group, and the fact that she isn't a "real" drummer means that the music isn't cluttered up with pat, meaningless cliches.

"Heroin" is another superlative cut, featuring leader Lou [Reed's] voice on top and sometimes inside of screeching feedback and electric viola, played by John Cale. It builds to a mind-shattering climax which is best not heard at all by those of a nervous disposition.

By the time their second album, White Light/White Heat (Verve) came round, Nico had left the band, and they had got further into some of the McLuhanistic tricks hinted at in the first album. "The Gift," for example, is a horror-story narrated by Cale over a hard-rock backing, and it's teasingly difficult to catch the lyric content.

On "Sister Ray," the album's long track, they explore sound, with howling feedback and screeching organ making some of the most modern music ever heard. Like many of their compositions, this track never resolves: one gets the feeling that it could go on and on.

The third album, on MGM, was almost totally ignored in this country, and [Melody Maker]'s reviewer dismissed it with a contemptuous: "Not sensational, but interesting with the group now into the gentleness and beauty bit."

Nothing could be further from the truth. The songs were, in the main, quieter and more restrained, but the old cruelty was still there, manifesting itself in the overall mood and many of the words—if anybody bothered to listen to them.

For a start, nobody realized that the whole album was a continuous suite, although not billed as such. It traced the progress of a girl, Candy, from permissiveness through a realization of evil, and back to decadence.

The tracks are linked so inextricably that it's difficult to talk about them separately, but "I'm Set Free" is probably the best tune they've written (with the terrifying beat again), and "What Goes On" contains brilliant organ and guitar.

Typically, the key track—"Murder Mystery"—has been distorted so that the words can't be heard, but it serves, as the group intended, to make the listener think hard. This suite is so subtle and sophisticated that it's on a par with *Tommy*, and so far ahead of *Sgt. Pepper* that it makes that album sound like a series of nursery rhymes.

It's beginning to look as if the Velvet Underground will never make it, commercially. Nevertheless, groups like them do the spadework which enables less-talented musicians to progress. It's just a shame that nobody listens.

1970-71

Held Over For The Entire Summer!

THE VELVET UNDERGROUND

ATANTIC RECORDING ARTISTS

Wednesday Thru Sunday

11 PM & 1 AM

•

UPSTAIRS AT

MAX'S KANSAS CITY

213 Park Ave. South (At 17th St.) 777-7870

FIRST NY APPEARANCE IN 3 YEARS
THE VELVET UNDERGROUND
MAX'S KANSAS CITY   JUNE 24-28   JULY 1-5

A ROCK BAND CAN BE A FORM OF YOGA

Lita Eliscu

Crawdaddy, January 1970

"I'M A CHANNEL. I BRING THINGS TO OTHER PEOPLE, THINGS PEOPLE HAVE given me. I brought the Alice A. Bailey books to him not as a *gift*, but so he could learn what the information was, understand it and tell me and then I could talk about it to others."

. . . Alice A. Bailey, her books of knowledge, all 24 volumes, for the recruits of the new civilization, "The teaching planned by the Hierarchy to precede and condition the New Age, the Aquarian Age . . ." and Lou Reed is a channel. And so am I. And everyone, and the more you open the output, the greater the input. . . .

The Velvet Underground is one of the few groups to afford imaginations the play of universes, of astrological heavens, of grounds and spaces as wide as time itself. Each album, and there are three, is a progression, the stuff and elements of how-to Yellow Brick Road, but the detours are your own business. The most popular method of nearly describing something which is nearly what the Underground might be about in a hip, capsulated form is "Heroin" to "Jesus"—both song titles and both brand names.

What I remember of a conversation with Lou Reed before listening to it played back on the tape:

Slang, what happens when life is taken over by slang so that the non-specific meaningless definitions become our lives;

and *Communication*, reaching out to people, to everyone as a minimum, and if you don't succeed in reaching us all, it is your fault;

and *A Life of Positive Actions*, trying not to commit negative actions is a lifetime occupation;

and *Wanting to Reach everybody*.

All the ways are the same.

There is a way to all-knowledge.

You just have to find one that is right for you.

To know when to touch something, to be in a condition which allows you to utilize the information at hand; to be pure and strong enough to use the power which is there. To know the right time and place to match energy with matter. In my time, yes.

"And what I'm tryin' to find out—a rock band can be a form of yoga and you can put a high percentage of the energy through there . . . the records are all letters to people I want to get in touch with . . . vibrators, vibrations . . .

"You just might get everyone going at the same time and BAM! I know just enough to get by doing rock and roll, which is a small part of the world—not as important as most people think it is—but it may be the most important social force going, is what I think rock and roll is. I think it's leading to something else which is the *real* potent quality. . . . When people are dancing mindlessly, and your mind's just not there, dancing to that rhythm—well, that's not the only rhythm going."

A conversation, a propos:

ME: You have to realize that theoretically you want to reach everyone but that really you can't.

REED: I can try.

M: Well, some people won't have the courage to meet you halfway.

R: I'll go more than halfway; I'll go all the way.

M: That won't help them; if someone doesn't go halfway, then he isn't part of the Creation of the Involvement, and the meeting will pass through him, by him.

R: Well, if I go all the way, then maybe they'll go all the way and we'll go through each other like this, Choom! and come out the other side. . . .

It's like a tree; you can't see it all at once, you have to stand up close sometimes, go back far other times, and it keeps changing meantimes.

I want to be a tree.

People never want to get past right and wrong, it is such a convenient stopping place, a well-accepted one, almost well-respected. It takes purity to see clearly that the Universe Energy never stops so that "stopping" is a onesided myth and it takes courage to keep on going because poppy fields seem the perfect place for a nap. That's a line from "Story of My Life." "It's the difference between wrong and right, but Billy said, both those words are dead, that's the story of my life."

. . . Keys to people; you would have sat here politely, blankly answering/asking questions until I came up with a key which turned into you, the person, not the personality. No, I was going to drop a few things here and there, and either you were here or you weren't.

Well then, are you a pogostick or running water; which way do you find to action: over or around, through at all costs including jumping over and on top of people or the way of gentle perseverance, chancing that you miss the right time and place?

"Tauruses are the only people who make me laugh—in all the nice ways, even over the phone."

A *guide*: all quoted phrases are direct quotes of someone during the interview; passages which are not quoted are responses to thoughts which passed either during the interview directly or in an inter/view afterwards while playing back the tapes. Some direct quotes are not in quotes. All thoughts in the piece have to do with the Velvet Underground and the energy they created, either directly or indirectly.

Every word is based on reality. Reality, after all, is all there is that we know because if someone thought it up, then it exists.

Only reality counts.

All real living is meeting, and you know, if we all split, who would be around here to make it go.

A dark door and who is behind it: each person, it is true, has a dark door to himself and you can knock and ask to be let in, but once you are there, let me tell you, there will be a moment of panic and the only thought—Don't show fear in front of wild animals; then, you'll remember he is a friend.

But the existence of that moment is all so real. R. D. Laing is a nice man on the path to somewhere, on one side of a two-way street, recognizing the need to go through the madness and come out on the other side—

"What's really funny is that after you do it, it's over and then you just go through the motions of . . . publishing, copyrighting or whatever." What is true humility and does it count when you admit to yourself that even though you are trying, you can't feel completely humble: that part of you is *proud* to be aware that you are trying to feel humble? Does trying . . . to say you are trying as hard as you can, and still realize that you are not using all of your self? Does trying count, does it really pay off to try your best? What happens when someone achieves personal grace with less personal effort, and achieves it completely? Did they try their best a long time ago . . . ?

The Velvet Underground is a rock and roll group who, like the Rolling Stones, saw the need early to push people out of their normally bound perceptions, and also came to the conclusion that paranoia, fear and shocking truth were convenient, dependable tools. Who knows how big the iceberg is, or the true color of a white bear . . . underlying the obvious stream of conscious thought supplying the Velvet's songs with their sophistication, complex people and gutter (or gut) stories has always been the undercurrent tug of the Universe Energy tides from moons and suns.

I threw the I Ching and got a strange set of hexagrams; first, Standstill, which explains that at the moment of standstill is born the end of standing still and the beginning of change . . . and it is true that the Velvets are at the center where perspectives of time and space would make it seem that they are unmoving, having no need to move. Nine in the 4th line says, "He who acts at the command of the highest remains without blame. Those of like mind partake of the blessings."

And the hexagram becomes Contemplation which says, "Contemplation of the divine meaning underlying the workings of the universe gives to the man who is called upon to influence others the means of producing like effects. . . . Thus a hidden spiritual power emanates from them, influencing and dominating others without their being aware of how it happens."

Sure.

The three albums form a textured progression into a land of pure question-asking, of "I'm Beginning to See the Light," "I've Been Set Free and I've Been Bound (to find a new illusion)," of "Jesus," and through to "Afterhours": "If you close the door, the night could last forever and I'd never have to see the day again."

Songs about eating, sleeping, love and the cliche which is life itself, each past action understood and therefore done with, done for. But living, becoming, are not cliches and it is on the tightrope separating and uniting the two that the Velvet Underground has so successfully been existing.

"She wanted to talk about divine grace and all that, which was fine, but I had to know—"

"Yeah, she should have thrown me out and of course I see now that she was testing me: I didn't see before because I was too insecure and unsure to recognize the spirit behind rampant smiling indifference. How many years of people has she seen wanting a crutch instead of life itself?"

He could be ruling the world—very subtly. But he could be controlling it.

At this point during the interview, we talked about slang and com-munication, one of us making the point that communication is always for the other—or another—person, and is done to get that person to understand you. The danger of slang, of pre-agreeing to nothing, is a meaningless generality, so that you become Everyman's mirror image and are therefore unable to blow your nose without stopping to think and compensate for right-becoming-left. So "the point is, why dontcha be specific?"

A *specific question*: If you want to use songs as letters to people and want to reach everyone, and assume you do meet these people some times, then also given that I have said that it is the yoga exercise as-pects of your songs which made me want to do this interview, which is an *inter*-view implying at least two sides . . . then why do you say we should do whatever *I* want to do because you don't want to do this? How can you be doing something you don't want to do? How can *you* be wanting to "do what I want to do"? Can you do something which someone else wants to do and not want to do it, too?

Then I would say let the public be the judge.

—No, you'd say, fuck you . . .

'cause you'd do it.

I would say in my own defense that you should like me because I'm not such a bad person.

A *question*: Do you remember going to Syracuse University, living with a girl, and a girl across the hall who played guitar . . . ?

"If I heard the records, I'd say, 'There's someone talking to me for *real* over there.'"

Doug Yule is really a 4th member, he's not sitting in for John Cale . . . everything is where it's supposed to be. We're really a young group, we really haven't started to do yet whatever it is we do. Which is to play rock and roll music. We were first with everything, we preceded it all: light shows, feedback, mixed media . . . back in the old Cinema-theque on Lafayette Street. There was no St. Mark's Place at that time.

Angus MacLise

Piero Heliczer

Barbara Rubin

Flesh and blood, not print in books or on tongues but people.

This is a view from one side, as it should be. It is possible to listen to the Velvets and remain unmoved; I know some people who have done so. Still, the world is changing. . . .

Still, for those who like interviews, here is some:

"And Ray Milland has all this money in his suitcase and Anthony Quinn knows, but pretends he doesn't, and asks him, 'What you got in the suitcase?' and Ray Milland says, 'Uh, underwear.' And Quinn says, 'Oh yeah?' and Milland says, 'You take care of your end and I'll take care of mine,' and Mo says to me, 'Do you think that was a purposeful pun?'"

Ensuing discussion of puns in personal life, and early Hollywood movies.

"Stars are fabulous."

"*Outcast* by Ernie and Eddie! It's what the Stones are just getting into today . . . you can hear the double basses . . . mmm."

In the same vein:

"You know 'Gloria'?"

—By Van Morrison?

"Hoooooh, no. By the Cadillacs. And the Four Jesters and I think the Diablos did a version, too."

Pet theories:

1. AM *radio* is the only thing telling reality, so I am more inter-ested in singles. If you want to know what they are thinking out there: well (plus: The average straphanger has a better idea of what's happening in New York City than anyone else).
2. Modern Romance, *Teeny bop magazines*—. I love them; I'd love to see a teeny bop magazine aimed at me.
3. I'm not especially intrigued by *my own point of view*.

—What do you think you're doing, then?

Making little plays.

 4. *Horror movies.*

"No, no, my horror movie is better than yours . . . 'The Undertaker and His Friends'—they murder somebody, carve him up and bring him back to the butcher shop in the back, put him in this vat of acid. His girlfriend comes by, says she has a stomach-ache and they say, 'Well, we'll operate; they chloroform her, cut out her stomach—on screen!— you see every wriggling, thumping . . . then they chop off her arm, put it through a meat grinder. And at this moment, the hero comes in and asks what's for lunch and they wink and say, 'Chopmeat. . . .'" People were walking out in droves . . . and then at the end all the characters come out and wink at the audience and do a little dance!!!"

C/O THE VELVET UNDERGROUND, NEW YORK

Robert Greenfield

Fusion, March 6, 1970

NONE OF THIS CONCERNS ANYTHING EXCEPT MAYBE THE BACK ROOM AT Max's Kansas City which is on Union Square in Manhattan but not worth finding any more. Lou Reed says Max's is over and like usual he is a-fucking right.

The Velvet Underground has:

A. Pioneered mixed-media on the East Coast at the Cinema-Tek on Great Jones Street by playing behind the screen as movies ran. Of course they were the band in Andy's Exploding Plastic Inevitable.

B. Opened up the East Village, changing it from a quiet, unreachable-by-subway neighborhood of Polish dance-halls and burlesque bars into the death-rap freak center of New York that it is today. All because the Dom was the place to go when they played there for six months in early '66.

C. Played the worst gig in the history of rock at Poor Richard's on Sedgewick Street in Chicago in July, 1967, with the temperature at a hundred and six degrees. The room wasn't ventilated, the amps too big. Things went bad right from the start. Andy had been promised to a slew of radio and TV stations. He couldn't make it and sent Brigid Polk instead, dressed in a white suit. No one bought that. Lou Reed wasn't there either so the Velvets went on without a lead singer. All the pop paper and *Playboy* people were there to dig New York's latest. The zooming films and the flashing strobes and the blaring rock . . . people threw up and left believing the Velvets to be the most insane people walking the earth. "Boldly shocking," they were, these four kids from Long Island.

But listen. Fuck that. Maureen really typed up *a*, Andy Warhol's attempt at a novel. Only she left out all the dirty words because . . . well that's the way she is. And Andy had to put them all back in.

Maureen beats the drums. Beats them. Her brother's been writing the GAN (Great American Novel) for six years in their mother's house in Levittown. He went to Spain for a year and sent Sterling Morrison a postcard from Germany that said, "Hey, I've learned to juggle," and "I said hello to Vincent Price (really)."

So travel back now through time. To the streets of New York before the revolution that never was. Sterl and Lou have retired from music. Both are through with Syracuse University in one way or another (as is Felix of "The Rascals" but side trips are only that). Somehow Al Aronowitz, who's hanging heavy with Brian Jones and the Rolling Stones and writing for the *Sat Eve Post* and getting into the scene, managing a group called the Myddle Class, offers Lou and Sterl and John Cale a gig. They pick up on Maureen cause she's got an amp and she replaces Angus, the original drummer, who's split to India. They play Summit High School. In Summit, New Jersey.

Pan those faces very fast. Mr. Director, this is Summit High. New Jersey is another country and this is high school gymnasium New Jersey sweat socks romance. Here is the Velvet Underground doing "Venus in Furs" and "Heroin" for seventy-five bucks and quickly in and out. But Sterl thinks he remembers two girls fainting. Leave it in if it plays. Ride them out of town on a proverbial rail with the gym in flames behind them as Summit's teenagers greedily tie off.

The Underground go into the Cafe Bizarre on Bleecker Street where a guy stands in front pulling kids in off the street. The kids are cookie cutter jobs all in pea coats with Thera-Blem on their faces, sniffling and saying "Meyann" talking about scoring nickel bags of grass while they worry about the last bus from Port Authority back to Graded and Saddle River and Summit, great mother womb New Jersey.

The Velvets do all right considering they're all pretty drugged. The manager then tells them they're drinking too much milk, cut it out. Little does he know. As they conspire to have themselves fired before New Year's Eve. However, before New Year's come Andy. . . .

No need to say Christ almighty here. They were the band he was looking for. This total environment trip was kicking around in the back of his head somewhere. So it began.

Brian Jones drops into the Factory one day. In tow there's this fantastic flying dutchman of a chick. Andy asks her what it is that she does. . . . In a Grimm's fairy tale Wagnerian gothic voice, she groans, "I zeeeung!" Nico joins the Velvet Underground.

Working at the Dom. Hanging at Max's.

They make it out to LA to play the Trip. The troupe consists of fourteen people and all are essential to the act. Gerard Malanga dances dream-like in front of the Velvets while they work. He wears a Marlon Brando T-shirt. Works out with toy barbells on-stage. When they get to "Heroin," he shoots up with an oversized horse needle. Then he lights a candle. Andy and Danny Williams and Paul Morrissey work the lights and the slides and the films.

Each night when the show ends, they repair to this castle up in the Hollywood Hills near Griffith Park. About thirty kids from New York are there with them. Severn Dardern lives downstairs and all the old heads wear nothing but monk's robes. The ceilings are high arched and vaulted, braziers burn through the night. Ghostlike figures glide, room to room, at three ay em. Pacific Coast Drug Time.

After a week and a half, Sterl moves to the Tropicana. "One day Andy cooked for everybody there," Sterl says.

What did he make?

"Eggs. What else?"

But the coast is bad vibes. The Mothers of Invention jump on the bill in LA and the hometown crowds cheer them and boo the Velvets. Everyone runs out of money. It costs thirty-eight hundred to get back to New York City. Bill Graham flies down to look at them. He books them into the Old Fillmore. Ralph Gleason calls them pure trash. Bill Graham echoes the sentiment and they've never worked either of the Fillmores since.

Back they come winging to New York, newyawk . . . sadomasochistic strungout manhole cover in a body shirt with a big collar. Ponder that image as we sacrifice art for the direct interview.

AN INTERVIEW WITH LOU REED—composed of direct quotes except that he didn't know he was being listened to so that it may not all be direct. (It may in fact be totally made up or said by someone else and attributed to Lou.)

"God, you get out on the road into these towns with one television station. Merv Griffin. You get so sick for New York. You have to grab a copy of *Vogue*."

"But the people are really nice. We met this kid in Seattle who had three to five years to live. Some kind of terminal illness. I said, 'Excuse me, but what does that do to your head.' I mean, I'd be off to Africa to get it all in. He said, No, he liked the people and the place."

Lou's left hand flickers to his face.

Some questions here. Andy?

"I don't see him much. I'm never in New York. Fifteen days out of the last four months. I know where he is. He's waiting. They're all bored."

Dallas?

"It's getting too hip. People there who've done the New York thing backwards and left to live on x acres with no smoke."

Billy Name?

"Billy Name's really brilliant. He's the one who painted the Factory silver. He's been in that closet for a year now. He's not coming out."

George Plimpton?

"Plimpton sucks. We played a party at his house. I asked him for this poster and he wouldn't give it to me because it was a work of art. Listen, I crumpled up my Marylin Monroe picture by Andy and left it in a friend's house. When I came back it was framed behind glass and HIS Marylin Monroe picture. Anyway, we started playing and all his guests said—How do you dance to it? Ginsberg and Orlovsky started writhing about in the corner and they all looked and said, 'Oh, is that what [to] do to it?'"

The chronology resumes.

The Velvets as society's darlings. Two benefits for Merce Cunningham, one at the Brooklyn Academy of Music, one run by Mrs. William Paley, known as "Babe" to her friends. A party for the fun couple Stavros Niarchos and Anne Ford. Gian-Carlo Menotti begins a collection to send them to the Spoleto Festival in Italy. Sterl says send us—screw the festival, we won't come back. Ten cents is collected.

They work at Philip Johnson's house in Stanhope, Connecticut. Johnson's an architect. His house is on a mountain. Braziers burn (again). It's the Garden of Eden. In Stanhope, Conn., Kort Von Meyer, a UCLA professor turned rock freak, wearing a white linen suit, puffing on a foot long cigar, with wraparound dark sunglasses speaking in an unintelligible Latin accent, tells people he is a Brazilian peasant lord. They believe him.

Old Sterl; out of Freeport, Long Island, wearing wicked green velvet cut into a suit by Betsy Johnson, making that Max's back room scene, knowing he is right in the middle of the hippest hurricane currently blowing in New York, has one complaint. "No rye at any of those parties. Never a drop. And no beer either."

In the Fall of '66, they work a Motown gig in Detroit along with the Yardbirds. Andy shows. Officiates at a mock wedding in an open field as the Velvets' road manager crushes a car with a sledgehammer. Fantastic.

John Cale leaves as a result of hassling and Doug replaces him. Nico splits. Andy loses interest. Stays on as manager then gives it up.

The banana album gets yanked off the market because Eric Emerson's picture is on it without a release. MGM goes through five presidents in eight months or something like that. Distribution reeks. The Velvets cut two more albums for them anyway. The banana album cannot be held down. Sells 215,000 copies with 700–1000 orders still coming in monthly.

Valerie Solanis ("a peripheral lunatic" one of the Velvets calls her) shoots Andy. The *New York Times* covers it. Viva, originally a household word in the kitchen, becomes one in the living room. Lou Reed stops singing "Heroin" because, well, when all these guys come up to you on the bandstand after the set and say, "Uh yeah, wow . . . I got into shooting cause of you man. The first time I ever did any. . . ." When that's not at all what the song is about. And who has the time to explain?

As Sterl says, "Everybody's beaten. We've all lost on every possible level. In sixty-five and sixty-six, even in sixty-eight, you could feel that something was about to happen. Now it's happened . . . and the merchandisers are rich. We are all shucked, hyped . . . screwed."

The Velvets keep on. Six hundred one week. Twenty-five hundred the next. Creedence Clearwater did it for ten years before they made it. A new contract with Atlantic is coming up.

Within the month, you can catch the Velvet Underground at Head Quarters in Reading, Pa., or at the Main Point in Bryn Mawr. It's just down the cross-country street from Max's in Andy Warhol America, hard by Union Square Park but the back room's empty . . . and not really worth finding any more.

AN INTERVIEW WITH STERLING MORRISON

Greg Barrios

Fusion, March 6, 1970

STERLING MORRISON WAS ONCE DESCRIBED AS THE MOST UNDER-RATED person living. He has been with the Velvet Underground since the dawn of history and hopefully will continue in that capacity forever. He was also called indomitable as well as an astute Italian duke. In any case, he is generally conceded to be a superior musician, as far above in talent as he is distant from the hype of current guitarists. In an interview while on tour in Texas, he spoke with Greg Barrios.

The group originally included Angus MacLise?
You know all kinds of secrets. . . . How did you find that out? Yes, originally we were just jamming around and lived in this unheated apartment and Angus lived in the unheated apartment next door. He had just come back from India. He didn't want to be in a group, though, he thought it was fun to play music now and then whenever he felt like it; so Angus couldn't be the drummer though we were good friends. At that time, we did some of the absolutely first mixed media things. . . .
. . . the Exploding Plastic Inevitable?
No, before that. The antecedent of that was done in the old Cinematheque—all done by film people—things which Angus called

ritual happenings. "Rites of the Dream Weapon"—did you ever see a poster for that? Yes, that was the first one. Before Ken Kesey or anybody. Angus had seen a lot of Dervish dancing while he was in India. He had been there for eight years and he came back with his raga scales and assortment of drums and so we used to put on these things and they had films. Piero Heliczer was involved in that.

I've seen his Dirt.

Yeah, and his New Jerusalem. Piero just had a showing about a month ago. He's back in the country. He's enigmatic.

I gather from some of his poetry . . .

What was that? Aquarium Productions?

No. Some items in the Film-makers coop catalog and newsletters.

There are really underground personages who have never been transformed by public acclaim. People like Piero, Angus, Tony Conrad, and Walter DeMaria, though Walter is doing some things in art at present. Underground movies didn't mean a thing in 1964 in New York. You were just sneaking around with no money.

There are many of them still like that, even those who have produced important works like Jack Smith.

Well, yes, and take someone ever more amazing like Harry Smith who should be restrained from destroying his films. He makes those incredible hand-drawn cartoon films. I don't know how long it takes him, they're amazing. Have you seen any of those?

I've seen the Mirror Animations which is quite short.

They're really marvelous. And every once in a while Harry flips out and destroys all he can get his hands on.

I met him once at the Chelsea Hotel with Barbara Rubin.

Yes. Barbara is one of the illuminaries.

Getting back to the group. Where did the name Velvet Underground come from? Did Andy—

No, this was before that.

Was the group composed of yourself, Maureen, and John Cale at the time?

Right and Lou Reed. And every group has to have a name so one
day we saw the name on a book.

That paperback S&M book?

Yes, and we said, that's nice. It's abstract and the word underground
meant something, and so we said sure why not—never figuring we
would rise above our particular little echelon at the time, so that
was fun. It was outrageous, the only people playing in New York
City at the time were ourselves and the Fugs. We were lurking
around the old Cinematheque and the Bridge and occasional gala
underground events at the Village Gate downstairs. It was us and
the Fugs—living in the Lower East Side with around $25 a month
combined (just about).

**The first introduction I had to the group was an NET film on tele-
vision in late 1965. The film was on Andy Warhol and it showed
him holding a tryout for a group to use in his EPI.**

It wasn't a tryout at all. They didn't know what was happening.
They came there to do a thing on Andy and found us. We were already working with him.

Part of that film used your music alone. It was very nice.

They (people from NET) didn't know what to make of it except
that it sounded very peaceful and what we were playing was actually an instrumental version of "Heroin." The final thing as they
were showing the credits and it went droning on, that's what that
was. They didn't know what was going on. The Factory (Warhol's
studio) in those days was so hectic and they had certain security
measures to enforce.

**The second time I heard the group was on the soundtrack of Andy's
film Hedy in 1966.**

Oh, *Hedy*. Mrs. Lamarr!

**Yes. I thought the music added to the pretentious mood of the film.
It was very funny.**

The movie was very funny. Almost everyone had a cameo part in
the film. I think Jack Smith played the judge.

It was Harvey Tavel. I think Ronnie Tavel wrote the script. How did the group actually become connected with Warhol for a period of time?

He heard us playing in the Village. Barbara Rubin brought Gerard Malanga to hear us and he brought Andy. He thought it would be real nice—he always had the idea to do a media type thing with all types of films, with all possible ways to involve people.

Did that begin at the Dom on St. Mark's Place?

Yes. And that wised us up in a hurry about where business begins and that sort of thing. We had the Dom and a three year lease believe it or not. It really sickens me still when I go to St. Mark's Place because more than anyone we invented that street. There was nothing going on there. Absolutely nothing. The Spa at one end and just Polish type stores, and Khadija Design, and the Bridge at the other end. No one had been there very long. Khadija had been there longer than anyone. It was an African clothing store. That was in 1964. Somehow we showed up at the Dom looking for a big room, and we said, ah, Dom (Polish for home), this is it. No one went down to St. Mark's Place. No people coming in off the street. There was no point in being there. It appeared to be a disaster.

No concerts in Tompkins Square Park going on at that time?

No. This was way before that. If it was used I don't know what for. So we got the building for three years and we opened it up and did extremely well. The people came down there and a person who worked in our box office said I've got an idea, why don't we go and play in California. We said sure, why not. So we all went out to California even though we had been at the Dom for about a month.

Was that the trip to California which they said they weren't ready for?

Yes, we played at the Fillmore and the Trip. We had a great time. I loved it, and when we came back we went back to our room since that was our thing. We owned it for three years, and when we came back we discovered it was now called the Balloon Farm. Actually our lease had been torn up and the director of the Polish home had been bribed and bought off and so our building had been taken away from us and later sold to the Electric Circus for around $300,000. We did have some valuable property—so I discovered early in life that when you have something valuable someone is going to try and take it away from you unless you go around knowing things. I couldn't believe something like that could happen and if you bother to sue or do anything like that—by the time it came up in the courts, you'd passed caring.

Were items like the Whip Dance with Gerard Malanga and Ingrid Superstar used all along?

Gerard and Mary (Waronov), though Ingrid did some. They could do anything they wanted. The actual number of people who would travel with us varied. The dances were Gerard's domain, and the lights Andy's. We only worried about the music. The way the Whip Dance came about was when someone gave Gerard a bullwhip and one particular night—the night he came down to hear us in the Village, he happened to be carrying it with him and later he started dancing with it. There was no deep dark S&M motivations. Someone gave him the whip just for laughs. He also used flashlights and lifted weights. Gerard is amazing. He was a regular on Allen Freed's old TV show.

The Big Beat? Wasn't Baby Jane Holzer also on there?

Jane used to be around there, too. When Allen Freed got kicked off the air, his final publicity picture was of him and two regulars. Gerard happened to be one of them.

When did Nico join the group?

Well, she appeared with us at the Dom, so it was right before that.

Was it Andy's idea that she join the group?

She was around because of Andy, but he couldn't talk us really into anything. We thought it would be a good idea. I mean that's how the whole thing was worked on the first album: *The Velvet Underground and Nico*. In other words, we were a unit with or without her. And she could do some things we really like, so we said do some songs. It was a complicated working arrangement because she said if I don't sing, I don't do anything. So it was always a question of how many songs Nico would do, should she do all of them, which we didn't want, and that was the only cumbersome aspect of it.

Last night as Doug was singing "I'll Be Your Mirror" I detected the Germanic accent. . . .

Oh yeah, we mimic the way she did it. She never said, "I'll be your mirror," it was "I be your mirrah." It's amazing how those songs are still so good.

What was the reaction to the first "banana" album? I know many people couldn't get into things like "European Son" and a couple of the other cuts.

"European Son" is very tame now. It happens to be melodic and if anyone actually listens to it, "European Son" turns out to be comprehensible in the light of all that has come since—not just our work but everyone's. It's that just for the time it was done it's amazing. We figured that on our first album it was a novel idea just to have long tracks. I'm not referring to any particular song, but any song running 8 or 9 minutes. People just weren't doing that—regardless of what the content of the track was—everyone's album cuts had to be 2:30 or 2:45 minutes.

The three minute song.

Then here's "European Son" which ran eight minutes or something. And basically all the songs on the first albums are longish though there are a few short ones. "All Tomorrow's Parties" is rather long.

I have your first single which has an abbreviated version of "All Tomorrow's Parties" on it.

Well don't lose it. I really liked that record. You can't get copies of it anymore. I have about two of those singles. There were never that many. "White Light/White Heat" was also a single. I don't have many of those either.

I heard many rumors as to why Nico left the group. Would you clarify that?

It was all very informal. We stopped working for a while. We used to do that periodically—just refused to do anything. Nico needed money so she went out on her own. She was working downstairs at the Dom (Stanley's) and we said sure, do anything you want, and so she was doing that. We'd take turns backing her up. I'd do it for one week, then John Cale, Lou, Ramblin' Jack Elliott, Jackson Browne—everyone was showing up as Nico's accompanist. When we decided to start work again we told her about it, and she said, oh, I have three more weeks here. So we told her to decide what she wanted to do and she decided that perhaps she could go on her own and be a big star, and we said okay. There never was any ill feelings. For in-stance, Lou played and composed some of the selections for her first album on Verve.

Didn't you help compose the song "Chelsea Girls" for her?

Yes, I did some meddling with chords.

I liked the first album she did. It was mostly Jackson Browne but it did have some Dylan on it.

Dylan was always giving her songs.

There have been rumors that he wrote several songs with her in mind?

I don't know, perhaps. It's very hard to avoid these people in New York. Dylan was always lurking around.

Didn't Andy use Dylan in a film?

There was one film with Paul Caruso called, *The Bob Dylan Story*. I don't think Andy has ever shown it. It was hysterical. They got Marlowe Dupont to play Al Grossman. Paul Caruso not only looks [like] Bob Dylan but as a super caricature he makes even Hendrix look pale by comparison. This was around 1966 when the film was made and his hair was way out here. When he was walking down the street you had to step out of his way. On the eve of the filming, Paul had a change of heart and got his hair cut off—closer to his head—and he must have removed about a foot so everyone was upset about that. Then Dylan had this accident and that was why the film was never shown.

What was the general reaction to the Velvet Underground's second album?

They were stunned.

[By] the fact that Nico wasn't on there?

Oh no. By what the album was—kind of raw electronics (most of it). We liked the album very much. Generally reaction to our albums is late in coming. They just lay around for a year and then people start to pick up on them. There isn't much you can say about your own albums.

Have you always had the liberty to put on your albums what you wanted?

Yes . . . it was kind of . . . we just did it. The company wasn't especially aware of what we were doing.

The production credit for the first album lists Andy Warhol as producer. I assume he doesn't operate like Phil Spector?

No. This was "producer" in the sense of producing a film. We used some of his money and our money. Whoever had any money that just went all into it. Andy was the producer but we were the "executive producers" too. We made the record ourselves and then brought it around and MGM said they liked it. We just never cared to do it the way most people do.

There have been some bad reactions in critical circles toward narrative things like "The Gift" and "The Murder Mystery." Last night, Lou said that he wasn't going to do any more of the narrative things because of the reaction to them. He felt "The Murder Mystery" succeeded. I do too.

I thought they liked "The Gift." I don't know. They might react against "The Murder Mystery" but "The Gift" is more coherent. I thought people liked it.

Do you perform either one on stage?

We used to play the music from "The Gift" occasionally. We never did perform "The Murder Mystery," it's too hard. Anything involving narration is really ridiculous to try and do before a live audience.

Now with the third album you have some people saying, "Now they're on to Jesus." Can you say that's a progression?

No. It's just something that you do.

In other words, they keep looking for another "Heroin," or "Sister Ray," and so forth.

I think the third album is a lot more subtle.

Exactly. There doesn't seem to be anything that really comes out and grabs you like "Sister Ray." (Excluding "The Murder Mystery" of course.)

That's okay by us. As an album, I think it holds up better than the other ones. The others, when you listen to them, something reaches out and hits you over the head, and something else drops back. The new album is a lot more cohesive. I mean why would we do another "Sister Ray"? For our purposes, we've already covered that ground.

Well, since you are now on the MGM label, some people thought you might have toned down because of some pressure.

That was only an administrative change so that we can use a different sales manager or something like that. Also, they have a prettier label, aqua and gold; those were my junior high school colors (*laughter*).

Which of the three albums do you like best?

I don't know. It changes. Whichever one I haven't heard lately. If I have been listening to one . . . for instance, I didn't listen to the first album for a year . . . then I went back and decided I really like it. I'm sure no one plays much of what they do every day. You just let it sit around for a long time, then you drag them out and listen to them.

It was nice last night when you played "Femme Fatale" and "I'll Be Your Mirror" and later some new songs like "I Can't Stand It Anymore."

Yes, there's all kind of things. We just shuffle them around.

Do you think the group misses John Cale and his presence or not?

Yes . . . no . . . it's hard to answer.

I miss the viola.

Yes, but it wasn't used that much, and it wasn't an essential ingredient as far as we were concerned. Everyone thought when we first showed up doing that, it was a gimmick. It wasn't that at all. You could get a sound out of it that we thought suited the song. It was used only for about three songs.

I think It's a Beautiful Day makes excellent use of the electric violin.

The electric viola works better than the electric violin. One might say it's an electric violin but it's not. The electric viola registers a little deeper, so it has a nicer sound.

Have you heard John Cale's _Stooges_ album?

No, I haven't listened to that yet.

Have you heard the Stooges at all?

No.

Have you heard John's album with Nico, _The Marble Index_?

Yes, I like some of the songs on there. I haven't heard _The Stooges_ album, I'll have to do that.

They have some of the early qualities of the Stones way back when Phil Spector would sit in and . . .

. . . play zoom bass . . .

(_laughter_) If they sound that good I'll have to listen to them.

Which of the current groups do you really like? (Doug Yule interrupting: Taj Mahal.)

I do? (_Doug Yule_: Sure you do. I thought you did.) I've always liked the Byrds. I've always liked the Kinks. I like Dr. John's first album.

Gris-Gris?

Yes. (*Doug Yule*: The Rolling Stones.) Everyone likes them. Let's see who's unusual? (*Doug Yule*: Creedence Clearwater.) They get sort of monotonous. (*Doug Yule*: But they have some good stuff.) Yes. (*Doug Yule*: Just like us. We all have our ups and downs . . .) . . . and all arounds. Indeed. And Quicksilver, I like them too.

Are there any groups you think have imitated the Velvet Underground's style? Or songs?

Yeah, everybody, kind of. It doesn't pay to get into it, however, cause people might say, well you're imitating Josh White, or someone else. If you release records you hope people will listen to them and whatever they do with it you should be happy about it. There isn't anything to complain about.

What about people like Van Dyke Parks?

I dismiss him summarily. I don't care what he does. I don't think he has the credentials. Whatever he's supposed to be doing—he isn't good enough.

In the sense of a commercial success?

In any kind of success. If he's such a great musician then let him go to Tanglewood. His work just sounds like some clever exercises.

He does a creditable job in co-producing Guthrie's new album.

Oh, as a producer he might be able to do something. It's that I don't think classical music—or formal composition, if you will—needs people to release it on the unsuspecting pop world. If you want them to listen to that then go listen to Vivaldi or something Baroque.

But I don't just sense the classical influence . . .

Okay, so he's the great synthesizing mind of the 20th century, well he's not that either.

Do you consider Zappa more appropriate to that title?

Zappa is incapable of writing lyrics. He is shielding his musical deficiencies by proselytizing all these sundry groups that he appeals to. He just throws enough dribble into those songs, I don't know, I don't like their music. I like some of the people in the group. Zappa figures how many opposites can I weld together. I'll take this phrase from god knows who (i.e. Stockhausen—the magic name!) never heard of him. What is Zappa? I say Frank can I hear a song leaving out the garbage cans? I think that album *Freak Out* was such a shuck.

For instance, the following is something that would haunt me to the grave. He had this utterance in one of his albums—god knows which one—"I'm not saying I want to be black but there are times I wish I weren't white." Now how can anyone come on like that? And he just keeps going on. Now as a satirist, or something, he might be okay. Satirists are capable of knocking things. It's a label you can hide behind. You might say that I myself am knocking him, well, not really. He's doing something nobody else is doing. So in that sense he has his little niche.

There have been some comparisons drawn, somewhat outrageously, between the Velvet Underground and the MC5.

That's a comparison that would drive me to an early retirement.

What do you think of the MC5?

I think seldom of the MC5.

Is there anything we've left out?

Well I don't want it to appear that I'm knocking Zappa because too much has already gone down between us.

I thought his *We're Only in It for the Money* was fun. It was a good satire on what they saw in the Beatles' album.

Yes. But let me see him come out with something as good as *Sgt. Pepper*. If he comes out with one song that is as good as any song on *Sgt. Pepper* I revise my opinion. I can make fun of *Sgt. Pepper*. Everyone can. If anyone thinks that cover was clever, I have no art ability at all, and I can come up with one as funny. I mean here is what the Beatles did and without any stretch of the imagination one can come up with a parody. What Zappa saw in *Sgt. Pepper* was something good which showed real perception and talent, and lacking these attributes himself, he decided to do something else, and make fun of it. Is there anything on *We're Only in It for the Money* that compares even remotely with anything on the original?

Well, the attitude of Zappa on some of the songs toward runaways seems more realistic that the maudlin content of "She's Leaving Home."

Yes. But *Sgt. Pepper* is still a great album. When I think of the Mothers I don't think of anything they did—I just think of who they're imitating. Who Zappa is deriving his horn lines from and so forth. The Mothers started out in the early days as essentially an old rock/boogie group. Zappa was doing what he knew best: old rock. There was a real good guitar player on the first album by the name of Elliot. He left because Zappa saw a chink in the social structure and he was going to fill the hole. For better or worse, he did it.

Well, he's finally disbanded the whole group.

At last. The person Zappa always admired the most was his manager. He wanted to be his manager. Zappa is the kind of person who should be a manager or a publishing representative. He wants to be one of the really sleazy industry types. And he has some need for this too.

What direction do you want the Velvet Underground to go? Are you happy the way it's going now?

I'd like to see us have a hit single. It's really important that you do that. Our singles so far are a joke.

I thought some of the new songs you played last night have the potential to be good hits.

Everything, if perhaps not a hit, could be distributed. Most of our singles were never distributed. However, where they appeared on jukeboxes, people have really liked them. "White Light/White Heat" as a single is nice. That single was banned every place. When it was banned in San Francisco, we said, the hell with it. That's as far as it ever got.

You have a single out at present from the third album, "What Goes On."

That was not a real single. It was just a cut put on a single. There's a subtle distinction between what is a real release and what is a real real release.

In other words, a single produced for a market different from the album market.

It's hard to say. It might, it might not. We have all sorts of strange things lying around in the can, as they say. We record them and get tired of them before they're released. It happens many times. We get demos and we play the demos and get tired of them.

I think there is much humor in your music.

Oh, there is.

Many people, however, tend to emphasize the darker S&M qualities.

Yes, but this is not reflected in fact. We've made no attempt to dispel them but if anyone asks us, we say, no, don't be ridiculous. We owe that legacy to Gerard who in his infinite wisdom did all kinds of outrageous things. Suppose that title which we took for our name had been on a detective novel or whatever. It just happened that the book was about that. It was a really dumb book.

Many people consider the light show as an essential part of your image. Now that you are no longer associated with the EPI you no longer have any special lighting effects with your show.

We got away from that. Actually we built the light show at Fillmore Auditorium. Bill Graham didn't nor did any San Francisco entrepreneur. When we showed up Graham had a slide projector with a picture of the moon. We said, that's not a light show, Bill, sorry. That's one of the reasons that Graham really hates us.

In his recent book on San Francisco rock, Gleason says it (light shows) officially started in SF.

Marshall McLuhan gave us credit for it in his book. He's the only one.

Right. I remember the photo he used of the EPI and Velvet Underground in *The Medium Is the Message*. That was quite nice of him.
It was nice. He showed the group that did at all. People like Gleason—he was one of our archenemies. They had the thing sewed up. The reviewer has a piece of the action. Bill Graham has the room, he has a piece of the action too. San Francisco was rigged. It was like shooting fish in a barrel. The fish being the innocent heads prowling around Haight-Ashbury. We came out there as an unshakable entity. I'd never heard of Bill Graham, in fact. I've never heard of him since. I don't know who he is, I just thought he was an insane SOB, totally beneath my abilities to observe. He just didn't exist as far as I was concerned. An absolute nonentity. He knew what we thought of him. The day I arrived at his club, I was thrown out. I just walked in with my guitar and he said, you, get out of here. They told him, you've lost your mind, he's playing here tonight. He said, get out, get out, you son of a bitch. I wish I had. If any man really needs a beating, it's Bill Graham.

He, of course, has his own defense mechanism. He's currently telling everyone how SF will be dead without his Fillmore West.
Well, it was always like that. When we arrived it was an attack against their way of life. Graham made so much money that weekend we played at the Fillmore that he didn't believe it. That's what blew his mind. We arrived at a time before Jefferson Airplane was known to anyone, they didn't even have Grace Slick yet. Everyone was nowhere at the time, the Mothers, and of course, ourselves. Warhol was the name at the time that made the impact with the public.

What groups shared the bill with you that night?
The Mothers of Invention, you see. The Mothers were following us around California. They also had an audition group perform. During the show, Zappa would keep putting us down, like on the mike he would say, these guys really suck. But Zappa is really a great guy, if he weighed fifteen more pounds he'd be in a hospital. No, he's just a

jerk. So the Mothers were chasing us around California so we arrived in Bill Graham country. He always had an audition group. The reason for this was he didn't get any money. He would say, if you're really good, I'll let you play. This guy's an operator. The audition group that night happened to be the Jefferson Airplane, whom he was managing. They wanted publicity and the Mothers wanted publicity because there were so many people capitalizing on our show that night. We were just a neutral party. We were going back to New York to greener pastures, supposedly, but when we got back our club was gone.

I understand you spent much time in Boston after that.

Yes, because we were so furious about New York and a lot of people who should have been behind us at the time but weren't.

Were you there during the infamous Boston Sound period?

Yeah, Alan Lorber was responsible for that. He just wound up ruining a lot of Boston groups. Boston, however, is a really nice city, we have lots of fun there. It seems to have much more potential than San Francisco. So we played in Boston as opposed to New York City. Last time we played in New York was at the Brooklyn Academy, private parties, that sort of thing, superbenefits like the big NET one.

Have you been back to the Scene?

It's closed. The Mafia was beating people up. They were having these incredible fights, thugs coming in. So Steve Paul just shut it down. That was going on at Arthur's too. The liquor laws work in such a way that if you have a trouble spot your liquor license can be revoked. So organized crime comes in and says, I want a piece of the action, and they say, no, you can't have it. So they just start these giant fights there. And the clubs lose their license. That's what happened at Arthur's. The Mafia people will even beat themselves up just so the police will come. That's what happened at the Scene.

THE VELVET UNDERGROUND

Lenny Kaye

New Times, April 20, 1970

DARK BLUE. SPATTERED FRAGMENTS. SPLINTERS. PINPOINTS. IF YOU MIX STEEL and concrete and people, what do you get? *Whip it on me, Jack, whip it on me.* And over it all, strangely enough, a little clear white light that tumbles and gleams its way to the east, rolling and flowing along.

They don't work New York anymore. If you ask, they'll tell you it's because there aren't any clubs left to play here, or that they can't stand Bill Graham, or any number of other Official Reasons. But it's more than that, you know, much more. There was a scene here once, a collection of people, places and things; a meeting in time and space that happened at a single point and will probably never occur in just that way again.

The Velvet Underground were a part of that scene, articulated it, musically defined and eventually pointed to where it would all lead. And as the process moved on, as it eventually had to, they went along with it, still a step or two ahead of the rest, watching, alert for the signs of Change.

When you sit back and look around now, you should always remember one thing. They were there first.

In the comics, superheroes always have to be given origin stories. Superman was deposited on Earth after home-planet Krypton blew itself to smithereens with him as the only survivor. Spiderman was just plain Peter Parker until he was bit by a you-know-what. The fantastic Four got caught in a cosmic ray storm. The (old) Human Torch was created by a benevolent scientist.

For the Velvets, you could write the story in many different places. You might begin when Brooklyn-born Lou Reed, working as a kind of song-writing machine for Pickwick Records, first met John Cale, a Welsh musical drop-out from a massive Leonard Bernstein Composition and Theory Scholarship to Tanglewood. Reed had written a thing called "The Ostrich" and needed a group to take it around the local high schools and record hops. With Cale, he formed the Primitives, which lasted together for something like a week before falling apart.

Or you might begin in the depths of the lower *lower* East Side, a cold water wood-burning flat on Ludlow Street where Reed, Cale, Sterling Morrison, a drummer named Angus MacLise and various others spent a long winter in late 1965. As usual, they had been puttering around with forming a band, calling themselves such things as the Falling Spikes and the Warlocks, ultimately lighting on the paperback title of *Velvet Underground*. Nothing was very organized at the time; there were few amplifiers, only a couple of songs Lou had written a while back ("Heroin," "I'm Waiting for My Man"). And of course, there were no jobs.

Origins, lots of places, here's Summit, New Jersey, for instance, where Al Aronowitz got the group its first honest-to-god gig in the high school gym. "The Black Angel's Death Song" for the princely sum of seventy five dollars. Fantastic. Or maybe when they opened at the Cafe Bizarre, no drummer (Angus had split for India), and they got friend Maureen to bring down her set and Reed was still trying to find a drummer 'til showtime but no luck so finally he turned to Mo and asked if she could play those things and she said yes and another piece dropped neatly into place.

But if you want to write the story of the Velvet Underground, you have to begin far beyond any of the physical things that actually happened. You first have to look at New York City, the mother which spawned them, which gave them its inner fire, creating an umbilical attachment of emotion to a monstrous hulk of urban sprawl. You have to walk its streets, ride its subways, see it bustling and alive in the day, cold and haunted at night. And you have to love it, embrace and recognize its strange power, for there, if anywhere, can you find the roots.

Even as late as 1966, the Velvet Underground at the Cafe Bizarre must have been quite a sight to behold. While other groups around the MacDougal St. area were dabbling in variations of Byrds folk-rock and thinking how nice it was that the Lovin' Spoonful had *really* made it, the Velvets set out to cover a whole new territory. The thing was to be real, not merely superficial, and so years before Altamont, before the love-peace-death trip, before dope had become acceptable on a mass scale, the Velvets had moved into violence, drugs, an entire area of human consciousness that few, if any, had ever put to the rock 'n' roll form before.

And believe it or not, that was what it was. Rock 'n' roll. Plain and simple. Oh, they worked on it, adding things on top and bottom, releasing it from certain standards that had previously been held inviolable. Cale, for instance, had just come from working with LaMonte Young and his "Dream Symphonies," where they would experiment with holding sets of chords and notes for long periods of time. Sterling had studied classical trumpet; Lou had been working at the piano since the age of five.

But in the end, it was all rock 'n' roll. Maureen sat heavily in the back, smashing out a set of Bo Diddley–derived rhythms that seldom if ever varied. Cale and Morrison fell easily into the form, viola and guitar nailed on top. And Reed: he never expected anything more than an old time rock 'n' roller, except that his lyrics slowly changed from little fantasies about the girl next door. If you lived in the right place, that is.

It was at the Bizarre that the Velvets as a group first came into contact with Andy Warhol, and by extension, the entire New York avant-garde scene. Film-maker Barbara Rubin had brought Warhol down there one night and he immediately latched on to the atmosphere of perverse urban sexuality that was the Velvets' stock in trade. The timing was incredible. Warhol had just been offered a large sum of money to put on a show at Murray the K's burgeoning World out on the Island, and had been looking for a rock band to help him do it. With the Velvets, it was a perfect match.

In retrospect, the group's relationship with Warhol has never been made clear, probably because the sheer strength of the Warhol name has always made the pairing seem greater than it actually was. Though listed as producer on their first album, he never actually took a hand in the making of their music. Most of the early material had been written long before his arrival, and the basic sound was formulated and set down by the time of the job at the Bizarre. Essentially, his role seemed to be as a semi-manager, who guided the group only in terms of giving them an environment in which to expand. "Andy had sort of a good way of picking out situations for us to appear in," remembers John Cale. "He would almost invent places for us to play." After the group was fired from the Bizarre, Warhol brought them to the early Film-makers Cinematheque, gave then rehearsal space in the magic world of the Factory, and helped them find jobs and equipment.

It was at the Cinematheque that much of what was later put into the Exploding Plastic Inevitable first began to form. Andy would take a series of movies, then project them for the Velvets to accompany in a kind of live soundtrack. In addition, Warhol would experiment with light projections, the group playing free-form in back of the movie screen, trying to combine visual and auditory images into a searing whole. It was Mixed-Media even before such a word existed, an attempt at something New which only a breed of highly-tuned figures like Marshall McLuhan had been able to pick up and recognize.

The Cinematheque also brought Nico to the Velvets. She had been in Europe, dabbling on the fringes of the jet set, making a spot appearance in *La Dolce Vita*, and was now in a New York hotel telling people that she was a singer. Somewhere along the line, she had made a little 45 record and was continually dragging people up to her room to listen to it. The story (and its truth, of course, is irrelevant) is that she came to the Cinematheque one night with Brian Jones, saying she wanted to sing. Her first performance was Dylan's "I'll Keep It with Mine" (which she did while the Velvets backed her up) and after that, more or less officially joined the group.

With the obvious success of the Cinematheque behind them, Warhol moved his show to still-dormant St. Mark's Place, where they set up shop in an old Polish community hall called the Dom. There, they constructed a massive multi-media show known as the Exploding Plastic Inevitable, featuring lights, music, even a kind of dance and theater. Warhol would run the projections—fine, geometrically perfect patterns encircling the walls—the Velvets would play, old records blared out during the breaks. Gerard Malanga, dressed in leather and brandishing a whip, would dance with Mary Mite in front of the group, each pretending to beat the other. Even the audience couldn't escape; they too were part of the inevitable.

Reviewers who came drew parallels to Berlin in the depths of the thirties, but they missed the mark. It was New York in the sixties, the essence distilled and brought out, a city splitting apart and loving every minute of it.

In its own way, the group's debut album captured the Exploding Plastic Inevitable scene perfectly. *The Velvet Underground and Nico* was the first of the concept albums, first with cuts to break the three-minute barrier, drawing a picture that was at once sinister and beautiful, ranging from delicately-crafted melodic pieces to piercing shrieks of electronic energy. In some sense, it was a schizophrenic album, moving from one side of the coin to the other, always juxtaposing, asking a question in one song and then answering it in a totally different way with the next. Nico was the one who sang its dominant theme:

I'll be your mirror
Reflect what you are
In case you don't know . . .

Lou Reed refers to each of the group's albums as "chapters," and looking at how they fall into a line, one neatly after another, you can easily see that he's right. As a group, the Velvets' progression has never been the common move of good to bad, or even simple to complex, but rather from one total level to the next, each one explored, set down, and left to be built upon by the next. The albums stack on top of each other, and to pull one out and take it from its neighbors is to risk toppling the entire construct.

Almost prophetically, the first album set out a lot of the ways the Velvets would deal with their music in the future. Lyrically, the group would create little characters, tell stories about them, interlock each so that what was being spoken of would not be so much a set individual as an entire group. And regardless of how they came off to those who listened, these were not idealized portraits. *The Velvet Underground and Nico* contains a lot of ugliness, a lot of the down side of life that is so much an inescapable part of city living. "The Real Thing," says Reed, "is not something you'd want to idolize": once again, this passion to create something real. Yet the group's very fascination with the dark sides of the human nature automatically removed anyone (or anything) they were talking about from moral grounds. It existed, was something they particularly knew about, and in the end, that was all that was necessary. There was no good or bad, only shades of each.

The key to that first album is not "Heroin," though it clearly was the most popular song, receiving a rather large amount of airplay for something so taboo-ridden and straight-forward. Rather, the key lies throughout the entire record, culminating in the broken glass and shattered images of "European Son." Where many of the earlier cuts relied on their lyrics to create a mood, the entire second half of "European Son" stood on its music, a coda to the framework the rest of the album had attempted to set up. Everything that was a part of the Velvets' world—pain, angular passions, an underlying flow of violence, existence on the very edge of reality—took shape in the short minutes of that cut.

At first glance, *White Light/White Heat* seems a logical successor to the first album, taking everything worked out there and moving it another step further, a bit more hellish, a lot less romantic. Even musically, it builds on the same components: using the rhythmically hypnotic as a creative force, taking repetition as a guiding energy, purposefully throwing away accepted musical guide-lines in order to achieve a grander vision than mere instrumental proficiency.

But over that there was more happening within the album than just a standard growth. In essence, a drastic restatement had taken place; events had thrown the Velvets into a whole new stage of development. In the intervening time, the group had gone to California (doing the Trip, the early Fillmore) and had come back to find they had lost the Dom, their lease torn up, a future Electric Circus on the way. For a while, they tried to recreate the Inevitable in a little place called the Gymnasium, but it never quite turned out the way everyone had wanted. The spontaneity that had spurred the Inevitable in its finest moment was gone now, and to force things seemed somehow not right.

And increasingly, there were tensions within the group itself. The nervous energy that had once brought three independent sources of power together had begun to dissipate, and the resultant tensions were beginning to rumble and twitch beneath the surface. The first to slip away was Nico, already downstairs at the Dom appearing as a solo act with Jackson Browne, while a rift had begun to open between Reed and Cale.

"We were very distraught at the time," says Cale. "There was pressure building up—God knows from where—and we were all getting very frustrated." It was also about this time that they made moves to establish their independence from Warhol, who was getting more and more involved with his film-making and less concerned with the group.

It was in this atmosphere of strain, with formerly known and relied-upon landmarks crumbling around them, that the Velvets put together *White Light/White Heat*. You can hear it all reflected in the music. There is a feeling of hurriedness, an urgency which moves each cut up to a slightly greater level of intensity. The production is muddy (the group insisted on playing at full volume in the studio), which only served to heighten the quickened pulse of the album.

When you put the first and second albums side by side, there is a literal difference that you can almost reach out and touch. *The Velvet Underground and Nico* seems brighter with more colors, pictures, an almost fun painting of a banana on the front cover. *White Light/White Heat* stands in stark black and white, graced with an invisible death's head on its cover.

More, there is a very real element of paranoia to the album. "I Heard Her Call My Name" begins abruptly, almost as if it was afraid that the side would start without it. "The Gift" is an almost classic study in paranoia, possibly taking place all in the mind of Waldo, recited in a cool, emotionless tone by Cale that serves to bring it home even further. And on "Lady Godiva's Operation," a subliminal voice hisses out, "You're a boy—you're a girl," tense, accusing.

The climax of the album, "Sister Ray," gathers together the five previous cuts much the same as "European Son" did on *The Velvet Underground and Nico*. It is a story, first of all, with narration switched from person to person: the sailor, someone named Rosie, Sister Ray herself, several others. And there are events that take place: a killing, people wanting jobs to "try and earn a dollar," a variety of comings and goings. A little world, in other words, covered over by that strange desire for salvation which continually creeps up in Velvet lyrics. "I'm searchin' for my mainline," sings Reed, over and over and over until the words separate into syllables and finally to individual letters. Almost, if you'll pardon the comparison, like John and Yoko repeating their names through a whole side of a record, watching them break slowly down from things with a symbolic meaning to mere sounds from a human throat.

Musically, the group behind Reed solidly backs up the effect of the lyrics. Everything is based around one chord, cemented by a stolid, endlessly patient beat by Maureen. Guitars mingle and clash over the bottom, pieces of viola, organ and vague electronics fly around, but nothing can really rise too far over the drone on the floor. It encompasses everything. After ten minutes or so, as if to drive the point home, the Velvets abruptly cut the flow for just the briefest of moments, like a sudden light after a dark tunnel. Just to let you know.

At least here, if in no other place, we can use a Velvets composition as a basis to compare their approach with that of another group. About a year before "Sister Ray," the Seeds put together a song on their second album (*Web of Sound*) called "Up in Her Room," where they repeated that phrase over the course of fifteen-plus minutes, building the music with it in a kind of logical intensity. At least on a physical level both songs work much the same way. After x amount of time, they tend to create an environment of their own: listening to them is like humming in a room where another dozen people are humming also, in a constant pitch, never varying, unchanging.

But the Seeds are a California group, and just in terms of the different life-style, they operate in an entirely opposing fashion to the Velvets. Where Lou Reed spits out his words, knows their power, chooses them and realizes what he is aiming for in the way of effect, the Seeds have come about their sound in a much more elementary way. Most likely, they thought of it once in a practice, liked it, and decided to build a song around it. And from the appearance, they never thought of basing their music around a dominant aesthetic, never dawdling with such matters as theme, never cared much about things like context and meaning.

The difference is important. In terms of Art (capital A), the Seeds' approach is hit or miss, a product of spontaneous thinking that can only go as far as the initial creative impulse will take it. But the Velvets, a product in many ways of the New York avant-garde—who read, go to movies, obviously do a lot of heavy thinking—are used to intellectualizing about what they do. They function in the realm of Art, first and foremost, not only intrigued with matters of Style (as are the Seeds—and please don't misunderstand, there is much to be said for that), but also with matters of Content. The Velvets have always moved in terms of carefully thought out theories, knowing what they want to accomplish and how best to go about it.

Art-rock has become a much scorned term of late. In large part, I'd tend to go along with that: most of the stuff that has passed under the title has been little more than a combination of pretentious garbage and two-bit eclecticism, part of a seeming campaign to make rock "acceptable" for people who never much cared for it in the first place. But then there comes a group like the Velvet Underground, who takes the hidden powers in art-rock and slowly brings them to the light, giving the phrase some much-needed relevance once again.

And so today.

They've been on the road since the beginning of October, are tired, a little sick, weary and hurting to get back to New York. John Cale is no longer there, off producing and building his solo album. Doug Yule has come in to replace him, playing bass and organ. Maureen still stands when she plays the drums batting away, never missing a beat, Reed and Morrison are working immeasurably closer on the guitars, seemingly more in control of their instruments than previously. They still do some of the old songs on stage, but the present material is about half new and unrecorded.

In many ways, the Velvet Underground are a changed band. The frantic pushing that was so much a part of *White Light/White Heat* is gone now, replaced by an ethereal calm that seems to signify that the mainline has indeed been found, the next level ascended to and attained. Their third album is simply called *The Velvet Underground*, attesting to the fact that the separate pieces are gone now, that the group is for once a tight, cohesive single unit.

The music has changed also: the melodic lyricism that only crept up in part on the first two albums has by the third become dominant. Reed still asks his questions, creates his characters, sets up each song by the one before ("Jesus" leading into "I'm Beginning to See the Light" which in turn becomes "I'm Set Free"), but the way he goes about it is more methodical and paced. The urgency has disappeared; "The Murder Mystery," the third album equivalent of "Sister Ray" and "European Son," is almost pleasant to hear, combining a happy recitation from one speaker with a sad [one] from the other, creating something which is not so much opposing forces as interlocking halves.

The Velvet Underground is probably the group's most commercial album, yet like the others, it'll probably leave them in as large an obscurity as they now find themselves. When people do know about them, they remember "Heroin," or they think it's all a put-on, or they somehow lump them in with other New York underground groups like the Fugs. It's sad, of course. The Velvets are probably the most creative band in America today, dealing in an area which most other groups studiously avoid whenever possible: Life.

To be *real*, you see. Because if you can't do that, say the Velvets, you may as well not be doing anything at all.

THE VELVET UNDERGROUND: MUSIQUE AND MYSTIQUE UNVEILED

Phil Morris

Circus, June 1970

THEY WORK AS MUCH AS THEY WANT TO AND GET TOP BILLING IN THE MAJOR cities across the country. They have a particularly strong following in Boston, Los Angeles, San Francisco and Chicago. Their three albums have all received praise in reviews and the first one, which hit the charts *twice*, has sold 220,000 copies and is still selling. They are Velvet Underground.

And Fillmore East audiences requested them in a poll—they turned the gig down. So why aren't they considered a major group? Why have so many people never heard of them? Why the Velvet Underground mystique? Well, there are all of the "too weird, too far ahead of their time" kind of explanations.

The Velvets really *were* too weird for everyone except the most avant of the avant-garde in 1966. And it's doubtful that even those who accepted the strangeness of the band really knew what their music was about.

The Velvets' vision went far beyond the surface implications of their lyrics. They weren't merely into drugs and deviant sex. They were and are concerned with *art*. They were literate and articulate and they enjoyed using their intellect to create music that explored new concepts of form, content and presentation. And they chose the most modern tools of technological America with which to construct their pieces. For example, Lou Reed had all sorts of pre-amps and speed and tremolo controls built into his guitar so that it would literally play itself. He could make it play sixteen notes for every one he played, or, he could tune all the strings to one note, set the guitar up to feed back and leave the stage and go into the audience to listen to an incredible, totally mechanical music. (He did exactly that at the old Fillmore in San Francisco and Bill Graham promptly freaked out and ran around the stage disconnecting the amplifiers.) The Velvets were the first group to use controlled feedback and distortion and they used it like another instrument altogether, not as simply a variation on a guitar sound.

Currently, the band is about to begin work on a new record for Atlantic. They recently switched to that label from MGM, which some members of the group felt didn't know what to do with them so they didn't do much of anything as far as promotion and publicity was concerned.

The group is happy with their new affiliation. They feel they are now dealing with a record company that believes in what they're doing. And Lou says the new record will be the first "real" album the band has done.

They have enough material for at least two records and they will be working with a producer (possibly Jerry Ragavoy) who knows studio techniques—an area the band admits they know nothing about and have little interest in.

The forthcoming album will be broader than any of the others and will include a song called "Here Come the Waves," apparently a major work, and "I'm Stickin' with You," a country show tune by Maureen Tucker, the group's drummer.

In the past the Velvets have been dismissed by some (mostly those who have never heard them) as a pop art put-on. That classification undoubtedly stems from their association with Andy Warhol—although Andy is a very serious artist who never put anyone on in his life. Andy and the Velvets and Nico, an underground goddess of sorts who wanted badly to be a singer, staged the first of the mixed media shows called the Exploding Plastic Inevitable with music, light projections, dancers, leather, whips—just a total theater experience. It took place at the Dom, a bar on the then silent St. Mark's Place underneath the immense Polish National Hall which was to become the Balloon Farm (where the Mothers of Invention first played in New York) and later the Electric Circus.

Prior to the Exploding Plastic Inevitable (and what a prophetic title that was) the band had been rehearsing and experimenting in the Filmmakers' Cinematheque where they held what one observer called "ritual dances devised by dope fiends with nothing better to do."

Before that, the Velvets had been working at the Cafe Bizarre on West Third Street in the Village and it was there that they met Andy.

After the Inevitable, everyone in the group pooled their shares of the proceeds and rented a recording studio for one day and recorded the first album. Andy did the cover which consisted of a big yellow banana on a white background with instructions to "peel slowly and see" in small black letters. When the yellow banana was removed it revealed a slightly smaller reddish-pink one underneath. Andy was also credited with producing the record for whatever publicity value his name might have, but in actuality he had nothing to do with the group musically. And aside from singing on a couple of songs, neither did Nico.

That album, entitled *The Velvet Underground and Nico*, was a departure in many ways. From the pop art cover, to the length of the selections, to the lyric content ("Heroin," a junkie monologue; "Venus in Furs," a song of sado-masochism and leather fetishes), to the very sound and structure of the music, the record was a first in the annals of pop.

Musically, *The Velvet Underground and Nico* was a balance of disparate elements. The songs ranged from airy, melodic pieces to elec-

tronic thunderstorms of sound. No one had heard anything like it before and about the only traceable influence was the modified Bo Diddley beat of Maureen's drums. The long instrumental called "European
Son to Delmore Schwartz" bore kinship to avant-garde classical music
because of the backgrounds of Lou, Sterling Morrison and John Cale in
the classics. Schwartz it should be noted was a poet and literary figure
whom Lou and Sterl studied and drank with at Syracuse University.
Try *Selected Poems*, published by New Directions.

The record was poorly recorded and did not accurately represent the
fullness of the group's sound. But despite the technical faults of the recording, the music was there and it was strangely hypnotic and addictive.
On the surface it seemed very simple, but in fact, the Velvet Underground had already absorbed and incorporated many different styles into
one unified whole. The guitars droned and sensuously dribbled out notes
in a very Eastern way; visions of sheiks and harem girls and plodding
camels in the desert. Maureen's drumming was a distillation of all the
rock and roll that had gone before and yet she played with mallets on
two kettle drums while standing up. She's methodical and steady like
some entranced Zulu witch doctor. The vocal harmonies were lovely and
almost tender like the early black groups (the Moonglows, the Five
Satins, the Flamingos) but Lou Reed's singing and phrasing had a Dylanesque quality without any Byrds type folk-rock connotations.

All of these factors plus the classical, jazz and electronic ingredients
were present, but at no time did one get the impression that any of the diverse elements were conscious imitations. Their music was so much their
own. Instead of taking influences and trying to combine them, and push
them further to make something new, the Velvets sort of took everything
that was out there in the cosmos and brought it down to earth to share
with people. Their sound was ethereal and funky at the same time.

The group has done two more albums since then. The second, called
White Light/White Heat, had the same kind of balance between soft,
pretty songs and frantic, driving urgent material. The real standouts are
"I Heard Her Call My Name," which features an absolutely astounding

lead guitar part with mathematically balanced phrases and piercing but perfectly controlled feedback shrieks, and "Sister Ray," a very long epic filled with images of a sailor who "just got in from Carolina" and "didn't like the weather"; also present are Rosie, Sister Ray, people wanting jobs, and someone who continually yells: "I'm searchin' for my mainline, she keeps suckin' on my ding dong." The droning guitars set up a dreamy presence that subsides abruptly near the end of the piece. If you think acid-rock takes you into other realms, listen to "Sister Ray." You'll never be the same.

The third album, *The Velvet Underground*, is their most lyrical and haunting. Gone is the "other side" of the Velvets. The record flows easily with a gentle, melodic feel throughout. Many titles could be singled out such as "Candy Says," "Pale Blue Eyes," "Jesus," "I'm Set Free" ("I'm set free to find a new illusion"). There's a joy about it all even in the solemn songs. And Maureen sings one of her own tunes, a charming innocent thing called "Afterhours." As a whole, this album is probably their most successful in an artistic sense, but it is subtle and hasn't sold as well as the first two.

The Velvet Underground is a unique phenomenon in the pop world. A group that has survived and grown. (Doug Yule, bass and organ, replaced John Cale almost two years ago and the band now functions as an organic unit rather than separate parts.) What they do is totally real and honest and that approach will undoubtedly pay off eventually.

In the meantime the cult grows larger with every public appearance. They're the kind of group that people turn their friends on to and those who dig the Velvets are almost religious about it.

Perhaps in view of all that's gone down in the past four years, the public is now ready for the first Velvets album. But they had gone beyond that stage a long time ago. So maybe when the new Atlantic album is released, the group will again be too far ahead of their time for most listeners. Oh well, the Velvet Underground freaks will understand and jump for joy.

NO PALE IMITATION

Richard Nusser

The Village Voice, July 2, 1970

THE VELVET UNDERGROUND AT MAX'S KANSAS CITY? AT FIRST, I THOUGHT IT was some kind of joke. As if someone was trying to rig a re-run of the Terrible Sixties by conjuring up old ghosts in old haunts. The Velvets, after all, had been the darlings of the Pop/amphetamine culture, whose spiritual center was often to be found at the round table in Max's back room, and it was not inconceivable to imagine some entrepreneur attempting to cash in on what would certainly be a premature revival of those jaded, faded years.

But no. The Velvets have changed considerably since they left Warhol's gang. No more demonic assaults on the audience. No more ear-wrenching shrieks of art. No more esoterica. "We once did an album with a pop painter," Lou Reed told the audience last Wednesday as the group began a two-week engagement upstairs at Max's, "because we wanted to help him out." "You're doing better without him," a fan yelled back.

And so they are. It seems the Velvets are now back to where they once belonged, functioning as a genuine rock & roll dance band, dedicated to laying down strong rhythms and a steady beat that gets the vital juices flowing. No fuzz tones, no academic exercises. They were always good musicians, sometimes precocious and lacking discipline, but admired by their peers nevertheless, for originality and innovation. Now they are all bloody virtuosos, with a mature sense of knowing when they are good and enjoying it. The result can be positively exhilarating.

The audience told me that. Opening night, of course, was something of an event, a kind of Old Home Week that brought together various elements of the rock/pop hierarchy; plus nostalgia seekers and true believers, most of whom had not seen the Velvets since they exercised at the Gymnasium three years ago. I don't know what they expected to hear, but they certainly weren't disappointed.

The Velvets served up scads of crisp, new material, along with what Lou calls "rock & roll versions" of the group's old standards, like "I'll Be Your Mirror" and "I'm Waiting for My Man." The first set was done "in concert," with the audience seated behind tables, but in no time at all everyone was fighting the urge to dance. People started smiling, sometimes in amazement, as the boys began pulling these incredible notes from their instruments, and then they started beating time on their knees and bobbing their heads.

By the time they were halfway through the first set people were yelling "Right on," and you know what that can do to a performer, especially if he's white and the guy yelling is black. The room is very small, and very conducive to that kind of rapport. After two nights of this the group was firmly convinced that they had done the right thing by coming into Max's to make their return appearance on a New York stage.

By Friday night they were at the peak of their power. The word must have gotten out that the Velvets were back and in rare form, because the audience was right there from the beginning. They applauded the first notes of each old number and when Doug Yule, playing lead guitar, went into a bluesy, heart-tugging solo on "Sweet Nothing," which is the Velvets' "Hey Jude," they went wild, interrupting it twice with applause.

I don't know what effect this will have on their careers, but judging from past audience reactions to the Velvets (and other groups), I would say things are at an all-time high. I, for one, have always believed that the Velvets have never received the attention they deserve, but I attributed this to the fact that they have never tried to be commercial. They seemed to enjoy being arty and esoteric. I also think that they were so indigenous to New York City that they were probably too sophisticated for the rest of the country. Oh they have always had a loyal following, even in the most obscure burgs, but it was all purists. No mass market. They're more eclectic now, so things may change.

They have made significant contributions to rock music, that's for sure. They have influenced many groups, including the Beatles, the Stones and the Airplane (who lifted one of Maureen Tucker's drum riffs line for line and used it on one of their biggest singles). The Velvets are also the foremost exponents of something I call white/urban East Coast rhythm and blues, a form that doesn't rely on a white singer doing black face. All rock has black roots, but the Velvets are one of the few groups around (along with the Stones) who have succeeded in developing their own style without coming off like a pale imitation. They have managed to evoke a culture born of the Long Island Expressway and what's wrong with that?

They'll be at Max's another week, at least. Two shows a night, Wednesday through Sunday, starting at 11:30. There's a $3 admission fee, but once inside you can relax and enjoy. "There's no hustle."

REVIEW OF THE VELVET UNDERGROUND AT MAX'S KANSAS CITY

Mike Jahn

The New York Times, July 4, 1970

Max's Kansas City, NYC, Summer 1970

THE VELVET UNDERGROUND WAS PLAYING EXPERIMENTAL ROCK IN 1965 when the Beatles just wanted to hold your hand and San Francisco was still the place where Tony Bennett left his heart.

The group came to prominence in 1965 and 1968 through an association with Andy Warhol and Nico, the singer and actress. The musicians played a long standing engagement at the Balloon Farm, now the Electric Circus, on St. Mark's Place, where they were a part of Warhol's mixed-media show, the Exploding Plastic Inevitable. They are appearing through tomorrow at Max's Kansas City, their first New York appearance in three years.

The music, which after all this time rates very high, is more rhythmic and forceful than ever before. The Velvet Underground plays a hard rock that is powerful and tight as a raised fist; so unified and together that it just rolls itself into a knot and throbs.

The group defies categorization as well as any other group currently making the rounds. Better to say that their music is loud, driving, with remarkable interchange of dynamics between guitars and bass, and that awesome sense of unity. The vocals tend to be second rate and subservient to the instrumental, which is a common condition.

The musicians should be seen more often than once every three years; they make 80 percent of today's popular rock groups seem pointless and amateurish.

The Velvet Underground consists of Lou Reed, vocals and guitar; Sterling Morrison, guitar; Doug Yule, bass and vocals; and Bill Yule, sitting in on drums.

PUTTING ON THE STYLE TO COVER UP THE AGONY

Dick Fountain

Friends, #18, November 13, 1970

WHILE SEARCHING FOR AN OPENING TO THIS PIECE, A DISTURBING CHUNK of rock history crept out of the garbage bin that I call my memory. Namely, "Putting on the Agony, Putting on the Style." As you might expect from such a song, the psychology is all wrong. So to introduce New York I'm going to modify it, so: "Putting on the Style to Cover Up the Agony." In Rock Music particularly Style is hard to define (if anyone wants to) and even harder to locate geographically. Partly because for a long time everybody has been listening to American records. So all these guys from all over make records but at our end they all come out of one record shop and come out kinda shuffled. Sure you can tie down musical styles pretty well. (In fact, *Rolling Stone* has raised this endeavor to the level of an art form, i.e., an industry). For example, the Chicago Blues Style, the earlier Memphis–New Orleans Blues Style, the Sun Sound, the Nashville Style, etc. But if you want to go further than just analyzing here are the symptoms of a disease (to wit; capitalism). Of course, some people swallow their distaste and make a living out of it. The point of all this is to show that the mass music termed "rock" consists of different styles; not

only musically different but reflecting different ways of living. In particular, to talk about New York and the Velvet Underground. I've
been digging the Velvets for quite a time and then I noticed that
their music on record was different from that of the Seekers, the Jefferson Airplane and, say, Blood, Sweat and Tears, to choose three at
random. So far, so good. Profound critical insights. Now having
served a stretch in New York I think I can place those differences a
bit more accurately, and present my findings for your education and
titillation.

So here I was in New York, and with no bread. So I have to get a
job. (A defeat in itself.) I get a job as a busboy in Max's Kansas City,
a restaurant of some repute in Union Square.

> Take a walk, down Union Square,
> You never know what you're gonna find there.
> You gotta run, run, run, run, etc.

Nature of clientele: rich hippies, rich artists, rich fags, fag hippies,
hippie artists, arty fags, underground film stars, underground artists,
underground rich hippie artists, rock stars and their dogs, rich underground arty dogs, etc.

Nature of busboy: one who cleans up tables, lays new tablecloths,
serves coffee, trips over rock stars' fucking Great Danes and spills coffee on rich arty underground floor. Wears long hair and Mickey Mouse
t-shirt.

To set the scene: 1 A.M., low ceiling, dark rooms faintly lit by red
lights on the tables. Crowded with long hair, patent leather, buck-
skin, lurex tights. Air filled with cries of "Too Much! Dynamite! Darling, you can't mean . . . ! Eat shit! Look it's Warren! Over here
Taylor! I said sour fucking cream and chives! Hey, that bastard hasn't
paid!" The vibes run somewhere between a mental institution and a
film set.

Jackie and Candy Darling sweep in fluttering false eyelashes and being *charming* all over the place.

In the back room ten or so of Wendy Ashol's "Factory" discuss heat-
edly a Shakespeare sonnet (!), of which none of them can recite a line.
Taylor Mode, of rich underground arty film fame, awakes suddenly as a
waitress treads on his drooping eyelid. Behind on the wall, a large pink
and purple photoscreen print of a girl getting fucked with her knees
up to her ears, smiling sweetly. (For years I thought Burroughs has a
lurid imagination. He cheated. He wrote it all down from life.)

The waitresses rush around in black, harassed. They come in two
sorts, hard and soft. The soft ones often crack up.

The busboys come in three sorts. Fast ones who come in on speed.
Slow ones who come in on smack. Spaced out ones who smoke grass
in the Gents. I went in straight once or twice.

To continue, impatient reader, after I've been working a week it's
announced that a group is going to play in the upstairs room four
nights a week for two months. The Velvet Underground playing their
first New York gig in three years.

To digress a little. Some people claim that in their third album
the Velvets went soft, after the hardness of "Sister Ray," "Heroin,"
"Waiting for the Man." Well I had my doubts, but now to find out.

First evening, a fair crowd, $2.50 to get in. The band comes on and
tunes up for about 30 minutes. It consists of Lou Reed on lead in skin
tight black trousers and t-shirt, very thin and pale with an amazingly
butch hair cut. Sterling Morrison looking hippy on second lead. Doug
who looks like Bob Dylan on *Blonde on Blonde* on bass, and Doug's
bruvver on drums (sitting in for Maureen Tucker who was out of action for the summer). Doug's bruvver has long, long blond hair.

The tuning up finished, Lou goes to the mike and starts the thing.
"Good evening, we're the Velvet Underground. We'd like to start with
a tune we recorded a few years back to get a hit for a poor pop artist."
Sniggers from the audience.

Blat! Straight into "I'm Waiting for the Man." Very, very heavy. Much more musicianly than the old records (tricky bass and drums, very tight, been together a while). So much for the soft theory.

They sound something like the old Velvets, the old Who and Creedence Clearwater stuck together. Hard rock with the trademark of Lou Reed's Bo Diddley strumming. Maureen Tucker's stethoscopic drumming isn't there, but Doug's bruvver swings a lot more.

The evening continues with "White Light/White Heat" at pain threshold volume and rocking like fuck. Lou Reed, hand on hip, hand waving, head nodding with a little sneer, makes Jagger look like Val Doonican.

Then Doug sings "I'm Set Free" from the third album, starting soft but building up to Hendrix proportions.

To cut it short, I was knocked out; I came half expecting to be disappointed and left shattered.

Their act was a mixture of oldies: "I'll Be Your Mirror" (Doug and Lou singing hoarse harmonies), "Some Kinds of Love," "Beginning to See the Light," "Candy Says," and a long Bo Diddley hypnotic version of "What Goes On" that ends up like a dirt track race; a sprinkling of new songs, the best being: "Sweet Jane," "A Story Song" and "Cool It Down," which is a somewhat ambiguous warning:

> *Cool it down, you going too fast*
> *Cool it down, don't you want it to last?*

And a sicky called "The Golden Age of Movies" about a decrepit film star. The chorus would be sentimental:

> *You're over the hill right now,*
> *and looking for love.*

If it were not for the broad grin with which it is delivered.

The rich arty underground hippie audience danced into a stupor throughout the second set until the last number, a slow country harmony heavy number called "Sweet Nothing":

> *Say a word for old Jimmy Brown*
> *he ain't got nothing at all,*
> *threw the poor boy right out on the street*
> *they even took the shoes right off his feet*
> *Oh sweet nothing he ain't got nothing at all . . .*

Repeat for several verses substituting different names. Build up to climax with Doug playing lead sounding like Delaney and Bonnie's old lead. Nice stuff.

Tumultuous applause and cries of More! Best fucking band in New York! Best fucking band in America ya fuck! (This from two kids with pupils like full stops.)

Then a chant of Heroin, Heroin, Heroin! Great reluctance and embarrassment on the stand. Final capitulation. "This is an old song." Subtly altered lyrics.

> *I know just where I'm going*
>   (What's this!)
> *I'm going to try for the kingdom if I can*
>   (Surely not a God freak!)
> *'Cos it makes me feel like I'm a man*
>   (Wait for it)
> *When I put a spike into my vein . . .*
>   (Absolute silence—heavy breathing)

A little smoother than the record, a little less menacing, but pretty fucking powerful. The show breaks up in silence, no more encores, snippets of hushed conversation. "Where can we cop at this time." I start to rearrange the tables.

The next month I got to know a lot more about New York, working four nights a week, getting robbed at knife point on my way home by Jimmy Brown and his friends who ain't got nothing at all.

And a visit to Co-op City in the Bronx, a stonehenge circle of 70 [story] tower blocks with shops, cinemas, a hospital, schools, everything necessary for a comfortable living death. Too far from anywhere to walk. So ten story car parks form the outer circle. Met a bunch of freaks in the middle sitting on the plastic grass. (It's washable and it lasts forever, they call it Astro Turf. There's one thing however, it does burn.) Playing guitars and singing "Down by the River" they greeted us like they'd been on a desert island, which they were. "Got any smack?" "Any downs?" "The cat who was pushin' here got busted with two ounces of smack. Watch the pig over there, he can spot new faces!" Went up on the roof for a smoke, left in a hurry, with a small shred of comfort. If freaks can emerge and survive in Co-op City they can do it anywhere. The end may be in sight.

Meeting 18 year old school-girls who do up two bags of Meth a day.

Seeing dead guys OD'd and pigs prodding them with their night sticks.

One night an ex-cook throws a wrought iron chair through the plate-glass window of Max's and tries to cut the owner's throat with a splinter of glass. I feel great sympathy for this bold act of insurrection. Turns out though, he's raving about how they stole his left ball and half an inch of his cock after putting drugs in his food. Not far off at that.

Chat to members of the band now and again but can't face an "interview." (That lump of *Rolling Stone* reportage above took a lot of living with.) Sterling Morrison said, "Yes and no" when asked if they still do dope. Cryptic. Yes, they were sorry they had never made it to England. Apparently years ago before Ashol discovered them, Miles of I.T. wanted to bring them over for a show. But hassles and being hassles it had to be done through the business and the business turned out to be Brian Epstein, who died inconveniently before the show could be arranged. And they never made it. And Jim Callaghan missed a chance to shine unequaled since the deportation of Lenny Bruce.

Their fourth album is due out soon, they seemed pleased with it a lot of their new old-time rock and roll stuff on it.

Altogether cooled down a lot from the early smack speed smashed scenes: ▪

Cool it down, don't you want to last.

But that doesn't make them a new Plastic Ono Band by any means, the edges are still very sharp. One night Lou Reed gets talkative (usually sits in a booth and drinks beer in between sets) and tells how he'd been in the business for x years when they met Warhol, and talks of clubs in the old days where he had to bus tables between sets to make his bread. Tells us how during tonight's set two sailors in uniform came in and met two girls and danced and left and he thought that was nice. So did I.

Going from this land and to that, wearing a sailor's suit and cap.

❧

Fight Love Pollution (venereal disease)—inscription on a New York match box

So back to the beginning, to the question of style. The Velvet Underground have got a reputation as a hard band, a sick band, a bad-vibes band (leaving aside the question of the third album for rock musicologist historian academic wankers to pick over). What is unsaid but implied is that this is an image they put on, a hype, a good gimmick, etc., like Dr. John and his phony voodoo or Black Sabbath or . . . need I name more. In fact it's merely an honest description of the experience of most people living in the sickest city capitalism has so far spewed up. But more important it's not far removed from the experience of lots of other people in London, Manchester, Paris, Rome, Detroit and even, dare I say it, San Francisco.

What makes the Velvets almost unique is that the scene they sprang from, i.e., an unashamedly decadent New York avant-garde art scene, has at least produced sufficient lucidity to describe this experience in some of the best (and most beautiful) songs in rock. (I say almost unique because Bob Dylan managed it before he became just another country station with nothing to turn off.)

Not that describing it changes anything. Not that the Velvets are revolutionaries (even now it's fashionable to be a Volunteer).

They just want to be a rock band. And just write serious songs about things that happen. And sell records. And they just happen to be a little too intelligent to fall for all the cock about flowers in your hair and golden acid cities in the sky.

They are the only white blues band around. Not a white band that can play black blues. (There are two or three of those who are pretty fuckin' good.) But a band that has invented a white blues.

> 'Cause when the smack begins to flow
> then I really don't care anymore about
> all the tensions in this town and
> all the politicians making crazy sounds and
> everybody putting everybody down and
> all the dead bodies piling up all around
> and thank God that I'm not aware
> and thank God that I just don't care.

Just don't care. Decadent detached and a bit cruel. But it is a solution of sorts to the problem of how not to die of boredom. It makes more sense than to pretend that there is no problem and that it's all sweetness and "are you a Scorpio, man." And it's less treacherous than singing about revolution whilst raking in millions from your pacified audience.

One day when the Rock Machine has been smashed along with the rest of our chains, I'm going to remember a few of Lou Reed's songs.

Tom Mancuso

Kansas City in the Summertime: The Velvet Underground at Max's

Another in our relentless campaign to shed some light on just where the best rock and roll music is played.
We've said it before, of course.
And we'll probably have to say it again.

A black woman teases the music she is dancing to: her hips touch it only every other beat. The song says

she ain't got nothing at all
every day she falls in love
and every night she falls

but she has the music and it is making her smile. The band is The Velvet Underground, and they don't mind sharing the magic and the stage. There is no more light on Lou Reed [vocals, guitar], Sterling Morrison [rhythm guitar], Doug [bass, vocals] or Billy Yule [temporary substitute for drummer Maureen Tucker] than there is on the black woman, and twenty-five other people, dancing in front of them, upstairs, at Max's Kansas City in New York. The music's in everyone, Wednesday through Sunday, all summer long.

Before the first set begins, around eleven thirty, Lou Reed carries in his guitar, checks its tuning, takes off his nylon windbreaker, and then talks to people. He wears tennis shoes and the way he walks, even the way he talks, has an athletic composure, a reserved confidence. Lou Reed has "always wanted to play in a rock 'n' roll band." He does, and he describes what he does as "like meeting people." If someone sings one of his songs, "it's like humming your name." Another way in which he describes what he enjoys about music compares it to sports: "It's the *playing* that's nice." Modest ambitions, pleasures, and metaphors are unexpected from a rock 'n' roll star. "I'm not a star" he says, but access to either the first or third of the Velvets' albums would prove him wrong. It is more likely that he is a star whose style requests different responses than Dylan's prankishness did, or Jagger's indifference and Lennon's proselytizing do.

Lou Reed "says it"—a phrase he uses for the lyrics he prefers, direct, aphoristic, and "unafraid of being corny." (He mentioned "Fallin' Off the Edge of the World," "Whispering," and "I Can't Tell the Bottom from the Top," as examples.) "I know how it is now. I don't know how it was" leaves the past, and past associations, where they are. "You know, whatever works out" explains the selection of songs for the new album, due out from Atlantic in a month, but also the steadied un-milking attitude that The Velvets have toward music and performing.

The first set starts with "I'm Waiting for My Man," sometimes in the original version, sometimes in an awful, rollicking version. Other songs that show up from the old albums are "White Light/White Heat," "Sister Ray," "I'm Set Free," "Some Kinda Love" (a tampered-with version), "I'll Be Your Mirror" (Doug sings), and "Heroin." Some of the new songs are: 1) "Sweet Jane"—a Dylan-like combination of hard

Holwell Anger

yearning and careful statement that upends, with a simple refrain, the idea "that life is just dirt/that women never really faint/and only children blush"; 2) "Who Loves the Sun...(since you broke my heart)"—a says-it song about an (un)erringly sympathetic man who feels sorry for the sun in place of himself. The implication is that the size and importance of his need is also the size and importance of his gift: even when he's turning off he can't help but turn on; 3) "A New Age"—a strong song that doesn't resort to a prophet's ego for its power, and includes some nimble lyrics: "And when you kissed Robert Mitchum/Gee but I thought you'd never catch 'im"; 4) "Head Held High"—a likely single (after reluctant dismissal, one by one, of four or five others) that will feel as satisfying, perhaps, as The Byrds' "My Back Pages"; 5) "Sweet Nothing," "Rock 'n' Roll," "Here Come[s] the Waves," and "Lonesome Cowboy Bil " are just as good as any of the others.

The characters of these new songs (e.g., Jane, a clerk; Jack, a banker; the fat, blond actress; and Lonesome Cowboy Bill who "rides the rodeo/buckin' broncs and sippin' wine...) seem to be hurt, anonymous people "looking for love" and treated to The Velvets' sympathy and care. They are isolated in direct line, but different fashion, with the outcast Severin, or even the self-castrating Candy, of the earlier albums. The things they say, and the things said to them, keep the religious poignance of the third album. The music, however, resembles the harder sounds of the first and second albums, but without their rage for order.

The Velvet Underground's performance has, historically, fed on a resourceful handling of continuity and change. Nico and John Cale left at different times, each taking away something special, but somehow the group has not diminished. Even the summer absence of Maureen Tucker, whose head-on drumming is, for some, the best in rock, has not prevented The Velvets from making Billy's rolling style seem an asset. Sterling Morrison avoids, as the rest of the group does, virtuoso powerplays, but, unlike the others, he must have to remind his hands not to do it. Doug's guitar work is good and his vocals have a lean innocence that's exciting—provided the song hasn't been sung before by Reed or Nico. Reed's vocals and lyrics vary from slurring indifference and literary refinement to prayerful earnestness and bubblegum simplicity. Yet without its range of personalities and its skilled inflections, Reed's voice could still contest Jagger's in originality. Dylan's lyrics shriveled to inanity without their amphetamine mannerism. Lou Reed's lyrics have faced down equally steep, stylistic changes and found new edges to cut their excellence.

KANSAS CITY IN THE SUMMERTIME: THE VELVET UNDERGROUND AT MAX'S

Tom Mancuso

Fusion, September 8, 1970

A BLACK WOMAN TEASES THE MUSIC SHE IS DANCING TO: HER HIPS TOUCH IT only every other beat. The song says:

> *she ain't got nothing at all*
> *every day she falls in love*
> *and every night she falls*

but she has the music and it is making her smile. The band is the Velvet Underground and they don't mind sharing the magic and the stage. There is no more light on Lou Reed (vocals, guitar), Sterling Morrison (rhythm guitar), Doug (bass, vocals), or Billy Yule (temporary substitute for drummer Maureen Tucker) than there is on the black woman, and twenty-five other people, dancing in front of them, upstairs, at Max's Kansas City in New York. The music's in everyone, Wednesday through Sunday, all summer long.

Before the first set begins, around eleven thirty, Lou Reed carries in his guitar, checks its tuning, takes off his nylon wind-breaker, and then talks to people. He wears tennis shoes and the way he walks, even the way he talks, has an athletic composure, a reserved confidence. Lou Reed has "always wanted to play in a rock 'n' roll band." He does, and he describes what he does as "like meeting people." If someone sings one of his songs, "it's like humming your name." Another way in which he describes what he enjoys about music compares it to sports: "It's the playing that's nice." Modest ambitions, pleasures, and metaphors are unexpected from a rock 'n' roll star. "I'm not a star," he says, but access to either the first or third of the Velvets' albums would prove him wrong. It is more likely that he is a star whose style requests different responses than Dylan's prankishness did, or Jagger's indifference and Lennon's proselytizing do.

Lou Reed "says it"—a phrase he uses for the lyrics he prefers, direct, aphoristic, and "unafraid of being corny." (He mentioned "Fallin' Off the Edge of the World," "Whispering," and "I Can't Tell the Bottom from the Top" as examples.) "I know how it is now. I don't know how it was" leaves the past, and past associations, where they are. "You know, whatever works out" explains the selection of songs for the new album, due out from Atlantic in a month, but also the steadied unmilking attitude that the Velvets have toward music and performing.

The first set starts with "I'm Waiting for My Man," sometimes in the original version, sometimes in an awful, rollicking version. Other songs that show up from the old albums are "White Light/White Heat," "Sister Ray," "I'm Set Free," "Some Kinda Love" (a tampered-with version), "I'll Be Your Mirror" (Doug sings), and "Heroin." Some of the new songs are: (1) "Sweet Jane"—a Dylan-like combination of hard yearning and careful statement that upends, with a simple refrain, the idea "that life is just dirt / that women never really faint / and only children blush"; (2) "Who Loves the Sun . . . (since you broke my heart)"—a says-it song about an (un)erringly sympathetic man who feels sorry for the sun in place of himself. The implication is that the size and importance of his need is also the size and importance of his gift: even when he's turning off he can't help but turn on; (3) "A New Age"—a strong song that doesn't resort to a prophet's ego for its power, and includes some nimble lyrics: "And when you kissed Robert Mitchum / Gee but I thought you'd never catch 'im"; (4) "Head Held High"—a likely single (after reluctant dismissal, one by one, of four or five others) that will feel as satisfying, perhaps, as the Byrds' "My Back Pages"; (5) "Sweet Nothing," "Rock & Roll," "Here Come the Waves," and "Lonesome Cowboy Bill" are just as good as any of the others.

The characters of these new songs (e.g., Jane, a clerk; Jack, a banker; the fat, blond actress; and Lonesome Cowboy Bill who "rides the rodeo / buckin' broncs and sippin' wine . . . ") seem to be hurt, anonymous people "looking for love" and treated to the Velvets' sympathy and care. They are isolated in direct line, but different fashion, with the outcast Severin, or even the self-castrating Candy, of the earlier albums. The things they say, and the things said to them, keep the religious poignance of the third album. The music, however, resembles the harder sounds of the first and second albums, but without their rage for order.

The Velvet Underground's performance has, historically, fed on a resourceful handling of continuity and change. Nico and John Cale left at different times, each taking away something special, but somehow the group has not diminished. Even the summer absence of Maureen Tucker, whose head-on drumming is, for some, the best in rock, has not prevented the Velvets from making Billy's rolling style seem an asset. Sterling Morrison avoids, as the rest of the group does, virtuoso powerplays, but, unlike the others, he must have to remind his hands not to do it. Doug's guitar work is good and his vocals have a lean innocence that's exciting—provided the song hasn't been sung before by Reed or Nico. Reed's vocals and lyrics vary from slurring indifference and literary refinement to prayerful earnestness and bubblegum simplicity. Yet without its range of personalities and its skilled inflections, Reed's voice could still contest Jagger's in originality. Dylan's lyrics shriveled to inanity without their amphetamine mannerism. Lou Reed's lyrics have faced down equally steep, stylistic changes and found new edges to cut their excellence.

In addition to the difficulty of personal and personnel changes, the Velvet Underground, now over five years old, has seemed to thrive in the midst of the culture's fumbling imagery. They used up the styles of the sixties, the hard drugs, the flamboyant distaste for society, the paranoia, and the withdrawal for identity, ahead of the decade. From mid-'68 to late '69 the "counter-culture," disillusioned with itself, searched for a non-paranoic life-style. It tried a dishonest rock 'n' roll revival (motivated by a sense of loss, not affection), a half-hearted recitation of contrived religious songs, and a split to the country that ignored, as a kind of preliminary proof, the consequent schizophrenia (present at both Woodstock and Altamont). Meanwhile the Velvet Underground had already released their third album, containing the most genuine roots-continuity in rock 'n' roll, and the only authentically religious songs. 1970: Dylan declared himself permanently impaired; the Beatles likewise; the Who still lie exhausted from their opera; and the Stones have yet to stand up to their vulgarized image and two below-standard albums. 1970: the Velvet Underground is playing in New York City—not the festival countryside—and planning to tour the country, a roomful at a time, beginning with the Whiskey in L.A. or the Matrix in San Francisco.

Out of the roomful at Max's, during the second set, a tall man leaned over to say, matter of factly, almost incidentally, that "the Velvet Underground is probably the best rock 'n' roll band in the world." The Velvets say that they try not to draw that kind of line, and the people dancing to their music could afford, naturally, only the time to be pleased with themselves.

REVIEW OF *LOADED*

Lenny Kaye

Rolling Stone, December 24, 1970

San Francisco, USA

LOU REED HAS ALWAYS STEADFASTLY MAINTAINED THAT THE VELVET Underground were just another Long Island rock 'n' roll band, but in the past, he really couldn't be blamed much if people didn't care to take him seriously. With a reputation based around such non–American Bandstand masterpieces as "Heroin" and "Sister Ray," not to mention a large avant-garde following which tended to downplay the Velvets' more Top–40 roots, the group certainly didn't come off as your usual rock'em-sock'em Action House combination.

Well, it now turns out that Reed was right all along, and the most surprising thing about the change in the group is that there has been no real change at all. *Loaded* is merely a refinement of the Velvet Underground's music as it has grown through the course of their past three albums, and if by this time around they seem like a tight version of your local neighborhood rockers, you only have to go back to their first release and listen to things like "I'm Waiting for the Man" and the "Hitch-Hike"–influenced "There She Goes Again" for any answers.

And yet, though the Velvet Underground on *Loaded* are more loose and straightforward than we've yet seen them, there is an under-current to the album that makes it more than any mere collection of goodtime cuts. Lou Reed's music has always concerned itself with the problem of salvation, whether it be through drugs and decadence (*The Velvet Underground and Nico*), or pseudo-religious symbolism ("Jesus," "I'm Beginning to See the Light"). Now, however, it's as if he's de-cided to come back where he most belongs: "Standing on the corner / Suitcase in my hand / Jack is in a corset, Jane is in her vest / And me, I'm in a rock 'n' roll band. . . ."

And once stated, the Velvets return to their theme again and again, clearly delighted with the freedom such a declaration gives them. Each cut on the album, regardless of its other merits, is first and fore-most a celebration of the spirit of rock 'n' roll, all pounded home as straight and true as an arrow. "Head Held High" is the kind of joyous shouter that just begs to be played at top volume, "Train Around the Bend" should satisfy all you hard blues fanatics out there, while "Lonesome Cowboy Bill" deserves a hallowed place on your favorite AM station. If Atlantic fails to get a Top–40 hit out of any of these, especially the last, they might think well of overhauling their entire corporate set-up.

Commercial potential not-withstanding. *Loaded* also shows off some of the incredible finesse that Lou Reed has developed over the years as a songwriter, especially in terms of lyrics. It's always struck me as strange that no one has ever attempted to record any of the Velvets' material, though it must be admitted that its previously bizarre nature probably tended to frighten many people off, but there should be no excuse with the present album. Building from chord progressions that are simple innovations on old familiars, Reed constructs a series of lit-tle stories, filling them with a cast of characters that came from some-where down everybody's block, each put together with a kind of inexorable logic that takes you from beginning to end with an ease that almost speaks of no movement at all.

In "New Age," for instance, he opens with what must be one of the strangest lines that have ever graced a rock 'n' roll song: "'Can I have your autograph?' / He said to the fat blond actress"—and from there, mingles cliche ("Something's got a hold on me / And I don't know what") with poignant little details about marble showers and Robert Mitchum, all combined into one of the most beautiful "love" songs to be heard in a while. Instead of taking the song through the standard verse-chorus-verse that might have been expected, the arrangement builds through three separate sections, each following perfectly on the heels of the last, culminating in a rush that takes you out beyond the boundaries of the song into the very grooves of the record itself.

And then there's "Rock and Roll," which tells the story of Ginny who was "just five years old," playing with the dials of her radio until she turned "on a New York station and she couldn't be-lieve what she heard at all." Or "Sweet Jane," possibly the Velvets' finest song since the cataclysmic "Sister Ray": "Ridin' in Stutz-Bearcat, Jim," says Reed in the midst of a vocal performance which would put Mick Jagger to shame, "You know those were different times / The poets they studied rules of verse / And the ladies, they rolled their eyes." You can talk all you want about your rock poets, but I can't think of many who could come close to matching that.

In fact, there's so much variety on the album that you could go through any number of the cuts and pick out much the same things, those extra little touches that make each one special and able to stand up in its own right. "Who Loves the Sun," a bouncy little number which opens up the record, closes with a few "Bah-bah-bah-bah's" that are reminiscent of the "doo-doo-wah's" which graced "Candy Says" on *The Velvet Underground*. "Cool It Down" quotes admirably from Lee Dorsey's "Workin' in a Coal Mine," while "I Found a Reason" contains a recitation straight out of any classic Fifties slow song. There's even a Velvets' hymn to close things out in the properly devotional way: "When you ain't got nothing," they sing in letter-perfect four part harmony, "You ain't got nuthin' at all . . . "

Yet as good as *Loaded* is (and as far as I'm concerned, it's easily one of the best albums to show up this or any year), there are some minor problems which tend to take away from its overall achievement. Namely, and whether it's the fault of the mix or the production is hard to say, it feels as if many of the harder songs on the album lack punch. The group as a whole performs well—Sterling Morrison's lead guitar is unerringly good (especially on the rave-up within "Oh, Sweet Nuthin'"), while Doug Yule's bass work frames each of the songs nicely—but it seems that something has been lost in the transfer of their material to tape.

Perhaps the explanation lies in the fact that *Loaded* was recorded before the Velvets undertook a summer-long engagement in the upstairs room at Max's Kansas City. There, playing five nights a week on what can only be called their home field, it was inevitable that their approach to the tunes on the album would change, become more refined and pointed as the group settled into what they were doing, giving them time to stretch out and expand upon each of the separate pieces.

Brigid Polk, a New York artist whose mediums are the Polaroid camera and the Sony cassette machine, has a series of tapes from those performances, and I would say without exaggeration that the music contained on them is some of the finest rock 'n' roll that has been played in many a year. On a small stage, surrounded by a mass of dancing bodies (and when was the last time you saw *that*), the Velvets fulfilled all of their early promise, taking even those classics which they had put aside for so long (such as "Heroin" and "Sunday Morning") and turning them out in newer, somehow brighter clothes. It was home-coming, in more ways than one, and there are few who were there that will soon forget it.

At this point, unfortunately, it remains to be seen whether such a thing will ever happen again. Due to a near-textbook case of management hassles, Lou Reed left the group toward the end of the Max's engagement, and though there is a possibility of reconciliation at some future date, the present situation doesn't look promising. In the meantime, the Velvets have added ex-Lost bass player Walter Powers to their number and are currently rehearsing for a tour. Reed, however, has always been the focal point of the group, the one who wrote their songs and provided their magic, and it is doubtful whether they can overcome his loss.

None of which can detract from any of the power and beauty contained in *Loaded*. In the midst of Reed's tale of five-year-old Ginny, he notes that, "Despite all the amputations, you know you could just go out and dance to a rock and roll station." And that, I guess, is what it's always been about.

LOU REED: GOT MY EYES WIDE OPEN

Walter Hitesman

Vibrations, #5

Now that the Velvet Underground has all but dissolved or at least down to one original member and Leader Lou
Reed is off to England to record a solo album – now <u>what</u> . . . Their first album the "banana" album was
electric 1966. The second <u>White Light/White Heat</u> was electric/"hard" 1968. Third a turnaround – acoustic/
"soft" 1969/and the fourth and last <u>Loaded</u> was neoclassic rock and roll 1970. Bananaalbum is shared by three
sensibilities – Reed's, Cale's and Nico's. (Nico by the way left after this one and Cale after two and have since
worked together.) The obvious differences are Cale the drone effect Nico reserve (both are European if that...)
while Reed himself covers it all and then some having written or co written all the stuff. There are three
separate types of material soft ballades ("Sunday Morning") a New York city rock and roll out of <u>Bringing It All
Back Home</u> ("There She Goes Again") and the outright drone ("All Tomorrow's Parties"). Of course "Heroin"'s
the all time Velvet hit/set-piece and part of its success lies in the fact that it can be taken literally(Cale's viola ill
the rush itself). Not so "Sister Ray" 17 min. in length featured on their second album and one of the all time as
they say long tracks . . . It is the fusion of Cale and the New York Rock side of Reed. The music has a fundamental ground the drone in which surface-variations swim – the whole primal energy flow chart. This ability of
the Velvets to remain constant sans any system (the Byrds from that other flatout town LA had one, LA a space
metaphor anyway while NY's rocket is the subway) this ability of the Velvets to remain constant sans any system
required as Wayne McGuire observed "spirit, energy and nervous system." The band's ultimate transcendence if
you will is in the exact opposite direction of a group like the Byrds – the Underground exerts a concentration/
pressure like a drill which to go anywhere has to remain in one spot. (To keep it up explains "Sister Ray" and
even getting it on in the first place their limited output perhaps.) Of course the triumph of the band is that it
was never merely repetitious altho that helped – Morrison and Tucker contributing classical concepts of their
roles, Tucker on drums for instance committing not a noticeable roll if any over the face of the first three
albums – a timekeeper period who during "Sister Ray" makes her transitions by simply bringing it up or letting
it down – while Morrison, who used to do laps around Central Park, is a rhythm guitar-middleman of strength
whose playing is straight up and down either for emphasis or to divide the rhythm or even carry the thrust. On
"Sis" he runs the gamut and endures with Maureen. The essential physicality of the song and the Velvets resting
on their back, the almost psychic sustainment Reed's with Cale's pure drone a formalized expression of it.

The title tune "White Light/White Heat" is an updated "Let's Go to the Hop" a wildcatting number in which Reed talks New York City jive in the intervals and "I Heard Her Call My Name" is "Waiting for the Man" from the first album all hopped up featuring a noletup guitar solo from Reed the implications of which according to Modern Lover Jonathan Richman have never been explored since but by Stooge Ron Asheton. The second album was made around the summer of love 1967 but it would be a disservice to Lou Reed to say that he was simply "right." The band has always rather embodied reality rather than taking a stand on it and some things are real. Which is to say that in this context the Velvets whose first three album covers were in black and white (second one black and black) were not merely non pyskilldellic or however you spell it and it is to Reed's credit too that he avoided on the other hand self-rightiousness or somekind of perverse Calvinistic thing. A word about production values. On the surface this album has a cruddy mix but the fact is it is a part of the sound of the record and inseperable from it original then and intrinsic. It's great when you realize that White Light/White Heat is recorded worse than the 45 version of "Let's Go to the Hop" and that is no mean feat. It is fitting too that a prime electric album like about close to 2/3's of the way through "Sister Ray" the thing which sounds as if you were tuned to a radio station loudly but a bit off the beam and the whole thing anyway was awash in an all-pervasive wetblanket of distortion — suddenly stops as Reed's guitar regurgitates out into a few growls before honing in on a razor thin beam which stops just short of Cale's entrance on the viola. But that sound had seemed a "given" of "Sister Ray" and to suddenly be without it is not unlike say a racecar driver at the Indy 500 starting to slow down and suddenly having his car disappear from under him (why the band gives you those transition splinters to grasp). Or "Candy Says" which begins the next album and is quiet and drawn out and deliberate and the tone . . . has changed. What an amazing period in between — Candy, Ray. The mix is now rock clear and stark purposely lacking resonance like a Bresson film I've been told. Exemplified perhaps by Tucker's lone cymbal smash in "I'm Set Free" which having no reverberation is all the more emphatic, tied to the action itself. "Candy" is the girl who hates her body and having to make the big decisions and the do-do-wahs at the end of the song are almost to sooth her. It is almost as if the remainder of the album were meant to help. The next song "What Goes On" upbeat and "Lady be good ... you know it'll be all right." Next "Some Kinda Love": "The possibilities endless" and/but "Some kinds of love are mistaken for vision." Followed by "Pale Blue Eyes," an incredibly beautiful, obscure delienation of an affair. The side closes with "Jesus": "Help me in my weakness . . . Help me find my proper place . . . " Turn it over for Reed's triptych of personal salvation (ya listin Candy?) in which his subtle command of tempo becomes obvious — (I'm) "Beginning to See the Light" which is not so much chugging as constantly revolving (and also happens to include the classic skitzo situation: "Here comes two of you/Which one will you choose?/One is black and one is blue/Don't know just what to do") proff of the pudding being the line "There are problems in these times but whooo — none of them are mine." Followed by "I'm Set Free" . . . "and I.ve been bound . . . I've been blinded by pain/Now I can see/What in the world has happened to me." The song peaks and subsides, builds and drops back with a gorgeous level guitar break midway through. Also a word about Velvet chorus work usually minimized but most effective when used like the chorus on "I Heard Her Call My Name" or here where Maureen says the word "pain" and Lou is joined on "I'm Set Free" — refrain by male stark open-throated singing. The Velvets never threw their rescources around. And thirdly the cryptic "That's the Story of My Live" the entire lyric of which is "That's the story of my life/That's the difference between wrong and right/But Billy said both those words are dead" — this one done to a bouncy, plucky beat . . . Maureen sings the last song (as Candy?) "Afterhours": "If you close the door the night could last forever/Leave the sunshine out and say hellow to never." This record No. 3 is Reed's word move. (Prior to that of "Heroin" was the soliloquy "Sister Ray" was the situation. The sailor from the former ("I wish that I'd sailed the darken seas on a great clipper ship") materializes in the latter ("he aims it at the sailor — and shoots him down dead on the floor") to perish. Where Dylan, the other NY poet, went to Greenwich Village for words Reed stuck to the street ("Sad Eyed Lady of the Lowlands/"Sister Ray"), and held adjectives in healthy contempt. Adjectives can be a dime a dozen. Dylan left the city with JW Harding and turned to myth while on the corresponding Velvet album No. 3 Reed keeps his city roots and writes in nonmythic terms — Candy being the only "made up" character on the album. Reed seems to be complex where Dylan is ambiguous — and sticks to New York playing music indigenous to the city rather than scenes there (like early folk). No. 3 turns out to be an incredibly sophisticated inner city folk/blues album. With Cale gone by No. 3 (replaced by Dougie Yule) the obvious drone is gone but not the Velvet ability to sustain. Even Loaded has a deliberateness to it and the obvious (highly colored) surface variety can not obscure. And while Loaded has its share of problems, not the least of which is that Reed was in the process of leaving the band at the time, it is still a lot of fun, parodying incidently the Beatles, Fleetwoods, CCR and even Dylan (vocal to "Sweet Jane"). And "Rock & Roll"'s five year old heroine Jenny is perhaps but a budding Candy. On "Jane" Reed in one fell swoop deals with a theme Dylan has been fencesitting for years — that of identity and adjustment. Right off Reed establishes who he is ("I'm in a rock and roll band"), and is an outsider to the conventional young couple he subsequently describes. He feels no compulsion to either join them or put them down. Reed had opened the song "Standing on the corner, suitcase in my hand," and one can only assume he himself was finally shoving off to another city — London — to make his solo album. Watch for it.

THE INSECTS OF
SOMEONE ELSE'S THOUGHTS

Geoffrey Cannon

Zigzag, #18, March 1971

EYES, IN NEW YORK, BETRAY, OR REVEAL, MORE OF A PERSON THAN ANYWHERE I've been in Europe. In the subways, most people avert any gaze, or else their eyes flicker and judder, subjects of pain and pressure. It's commonplace to meet professionally successful people who, as they talk, seem to focus on a point six feet beyond your head. And then there are the people whose spirit seems to have gone to lunch. They have the eyes of fish. They have abandoned the pretense of contact.

I had this in mind at the Electric Circus, December 30, watching Little Richard after 15 years of listening to his records, wondering how he came across. He wears black make-up on his lips and around his eyes, to intensify his stare. He flashed a glance, as he sang, at pretty much everyone in the audience. And his eyes said: Am I not a star? The star? And the audience, partly phased out by sleeplessness, partly by his gall, nevertheless said: Amen. He'd found his way of staying alive.

Lou Reed, too. You've only to listen to Velvet Underground albums to know what's been in his mind, these last years. I met him in Danny Fields' office, at Atlantic Records, on Broadway at 60th. And as he spoke, I was continually drawn to his eyes. They've as steady a gaze as those of anyone I've met. And they reveal the intensity, and the courtesy, that the eyes of the very best journalists have; the journalists who have the ability to see and hear anything, however painful, and yet make sense of it.

I'd written an article which proposed that the extreme terror and violence of Velvet Underground songs derived, not from imagination, but from his journalist's ability to mirror what there was—and is—to see in New York. I showed it to him tentatively. He read it and put it down, and looked at me, and said, "How did you know?" Most rock music writers go into their heads to create songs. In the old days, Lou carried a notebook everywhere. Years ago, he rented a $29 a month room on Ludlow Street. He and John Cale listened to the Who, and said to each other: that's it. And decided to put content into their songs, so that people listening would start up (and Lou mimed the reaction, hand to ear) and say, "What's that? Did you hear that?" That was what was on Lou's mind when he wrote "Heroin" and "The Black Angel's Death Song" and "I'll Be Your Mirror" for the first Velvets album. The last song, he said, is the key to the album.

And he sang the words that Nico sings, on that album:

> *I'll be your mirror*
> *Reflect what you are*
> *In case you don't know.*

He wanted to make a connection on that album, he said, so that kids with blasted minds could lift their confusion into the music. So that the music could feel their pain.

Did it work like that, with songs like "Heroin," I asked? Isn't it true that kids came up to you after Velvet's performances, and asked you where they could get heroin? More than that, Lou said, kids would say: hey, I shot up to your song. Hey, I nearly OD'd on that song. (Kids of 13 or 14.) "Heroin" was never a song I cared to sing too often, Lou said. Audiences would always ask for it; even this summer, when the Velvets played each night at Max's Kansas City, in Chelsea (NY). Maybe the kids did feel a connection with the song, which lifted off their sense of isolation. Maybe. There's a repeated line in "Heroin":

> *I guess*
> *I just don't know*
> *And I guess*
> *I just don't know.*

Who knows? There are now reckoned to be 50,000 people in New York with a dependence on heroin. Mayn't they have a song of their own?

Listen, Lou said: I was never a heroin addict. He paused. I had a toe in that situation, he said. Enough to see the tunnel. The tunnel downwards? I asked. The vortex, yes, he answered. "Heroin" isn't an up song, he said. But I think he knew that that statement wasn't true. "Heroin" is neither, of itself, up nor down. It's descriptive. A mirror. People will make of it what they will. At least it's illumination.

Lou's notebook. In those days, he said, people he hung around with, had a thing about magic markers. They'd sit about, looking to make pictures of their dreams with magic markers. And Lou would sit outside them with his notebook. They assumed he was making magic markings. In fact, he said, I was writing down all these weird things that people were saying. Being a journalist of the everyday situation of people in extreme circumstances. Or, rather, of people in an extreme city, who were, in their vulnerability, experiencing its extremity. Because they had no means to make a connection with its luxuries. Who were (and are) threatened with the dissolution of their minds, by what Lou called "the jim-jams of this town." People who were open wounds.

To be a writer, and to be a censor: those are two different occupations. A writer should reveal what he sees, hears, feels. Sometimes a writer has an obligation to be reckless. Unchronicled, misfortunes fester. But at the same time, Lou had no reckoning of himself as a doctor, lancing moral boils.

He spoke, at some length, of Ray Davies as a writer he felt some affinity with. In obvious respects, the Velvets and the Kinks are not alike. The music of the Kinks is a spare, unadventurous vehicle for Ray. The Velvet's music, on the other hand, is crucial to Lou, and John Cale, musically, [and] at least matched Lou's writing ability. All the same, there are connections. Lou said his idea was always to make each Velvets album a book; each song a little play. Books, films, records: he happened to choose records as a vehicle. So that kids could, listening, get that shock of recognition. "Wow, did you hear what that man is singing?" To steal their unaware consciousness.

Lou told a story about a girl called Alaska. (Alaska? That's right.) There was this story from England, Lou said, about a girl whose brain exploded from amphetamine. When the surgeon opened her head, for the autopsy, the brain was all—all scribed, as if by those rows of needles that record your physical functions in laboratories. Lou said that Alaska was like that. He wrote a song about her, which he never recorded, called "Stephanie Says," which revealed the secret of Alaska's name. She was cold through and through. The material for the song is in Lou's notebook. He thought of publishing it once, he said, but those crazy days are passed now.

Compare Lou's songs with Ray Davies songs like "Do You Remember Walter" and "People Take Pictures of Each Other." Same style, same type of mind, putting down detail, keeping off generalities. Writing about people in two very different cities; London and New York. One big difference: Lou brings the experience of his songs closer to himself, by singing in the first or second person, narrating events as if they are happening at the time he sings them, rather than in terms of their being past. This technique, with the Velvet's music, which on the first album sustains a tingling drone, obliges the listener to find sensations in himself which correspond to the state of mind of Lou Reed's singing alter ego. It forces the listener into the events of the song, as if they are happening to him. How's this, for example, for the paranoia of the mainliner, standing at Lexington and 125 Street:

> Hey white boy, what you doin' up town
> Hey white boy, you chasin' our women around . . .
> Oh, pardon me, sir, it's furthest from my mind;
> I'm just looking for a dear, dear friend of mine. . . .

The dear, dear friend is, of course, his connection.

The Velvets' first three albums all contained one track much longer than the rest, and therefore which set itself aside from them, and which infected the whole album with its complexity and ambiguity. The kind of track that encourages people to say (as Lou put it): "Wow, Lou, I really liked your last album, except for (. . .)." On the first album, this track is "European Son (to Delmore Schwartz)"; on the second "Sister Ray"; on the third "Murder Mystery." On the fourth album (*Loaded*) "New Age" might have developed into such a track, but it was edited by the rest of the band after Lou had left.

At one time, I wanted to be a novelist, Lou said. But I could never sustain that number of words. We were talking about Borges: Lou was intrigued that Borges had the ability to put the thought that most novels require, into 12 pages. What I was after with tracks like these, Lou said, was to attempt my own "Waste Land." The way I'd put it, Lou was attempting such a work that Susan Sontag most admires: whose surface is its structure, and which resists being pulled apart and reduced to anything other than what it itself is. That sounds both vague and pretentious. How else to put it? Sontag's idea is that creative work, to succeed, should be seen in terms of having its own life. If a piece of creative work can be assimilated (by its audience or by a critic) then it is merely commentary on an existing state of seeing reality, which depends on previous perceptions, cannot be altered. But as far as he himself was concerned, Lou was having brand new perceptions.

"Murder Mystery," for example. Did you know (I said to Lou) that, for sure, people in London, Paris, Hamburg, and Munich, and places north, east, west, and south, were crouching over their amps, switching from channel to channel, trying to make those words out? Oh, wow, really? said Lou. (And looked pleased.) Stereo! It suddenly came on him, like magic. "European Son" and "Sister Ray" had developed techniques of word—and instrument—overlay. And, on "The Gift," John Cale recites the story of Waldo's sad end on one channel (or, I should say, more clearly on one channel) while the music is on the other channel. Lou's idea, with "Murder Mystery," was to use words one way on one channel, another way on the other, synch them, so that listeners would find their way to listening first on one channel, then on the other, and afterwards on both. The first dialectical rock 'n' roll track. Left hand speaker equals thesis, right hand speaker equals antithesis. And the synthesis is in the listener's own head. So that there is no such thing as the meaning, objectively, of "Murder Mystery." Its meaning, for any listener, depends where his head is at.

Not, Lou said, that it exactly worked out like that. After recording the voice tracks, he found that one spoke at twice the speed of the other, as if one were recorded at 15, one at 7½. He decided that he should proceed assuming that this difference was meaningful. More than once, as he spoke, Lou mentioned his forgetfulness and impatience. Neither of us could tell whether this was a virtue or a fault. The right line between instinct and mathematics has to be drawn arbitrarily. On the other hand, it's too easy to make a mystique of mistakes. (Bird's squeaks, and Lady Day's cracked voice, add to our sense of their tragedy, not to the quality of their music.) I think Lou should have recorded both voice tracks of "Murder Mystery" at the same speed.

Lou Reed's ambitious tracks succeed, not because they are an extended, or elegant, illustration of any listener's existing perceptual framework, but because they themselves indicate a previously undelineated perceptual framework. The songs are part of an attitude of mind, part of an idea of reality, previously unexpressed, certainly in rock 'n' roll. They are not bendable towards existing ideals. They infect the mind of the listener with their immaculate structure, and work in terms of bending the listener's mind towards them. That's what's meant by their having a life of their own.

And Lou acknowledged that such a life exists independently of his own intentions. For example, we were talking about a line in "Heroin." Some months ago, I had spent a couple of evenings talking to John Cale. Filled with enthusiasm to be meeting a founder-member of the Velvets, I recited some of "Heroin," saying how amazing the imagery was, corresponding as it does to a sense of impossible alienated hope:

> *I wish that I was born a thousand years ago*
> *I wish that I'd sailed the Tonkin seas*
> *On a great big clipper ship*
> *Going from this land into that.*

No, said John. Not "Tonkin." "Darkened." No, no, I said. It was definitely "Tonkin." Listen, said John, gently nettled. I stood behind Lou singing that song, hundreds of times. It's "darkened." Well, I thought to myself, I hear "Tonkin," I prefer "Tonkin," and so, as far as I'm concerned, it is "Tonkin." That quick reference to a kind of Oriental Atlantis, flavored with a sense of Tongs, all those exotic evils kids read about in trash magazines: that's right for the song.

Meeting Lou, I mentioned all this to him. Yes, it is "darkened," he said. And, at the same time, warmed to the idea of "Tonkin." I needn't be the best poet of my own ideas, he said. And he said that listeners often improved his songs.

And also detected things in his songs, or in him, which he wasn't aware of. Another example. The first line of "Heroin" is "I don't know just where I'm going." After a Velvets concert one time, a kid rushed up to Lou, flashing excitement, and said: you changed the song. Why did you change the song? And Lou said: What're you talking about? And the kid said: you sang, "I know just where I'm going." And Lou said: nonsense, you are mistaken. Then, later, he sang the song to himself, and discovered that the kid was right. The change in the song corresponded, Lou decided, to a change in himself which he had not up to that time acknowledged. He was beginning to see the light, rather than the tunnel. The song was singing him. That is (to say it again), the song has a life of its own.

There again, take the made-up "Chinese" phrases in "The Black Angel's Death Song." They belong in the song. In a context saturated with imagery, they cool out the song, make its texture more open; allow the listener to find his own level and his own thoughts. As with "Sister Ray" and "Murder Mystery," the song is a mine in which ore of a particular nature can be quarried. To go back to the beginning of this article: Lou's style strikes me as courteous. In the midst of a music which has an incandescent and relentless beat, Lou creates space. Every time Lou's long songs are played, they sound different, and can never be pinned down, because they contain a factor which varies each time they are played: the listener's mind.

Is this writing trying to be an intellectual bathyscape dive into the Velvets' music, or a fave rave? A reasonable question. I can only answer it by mentioning Constantine Radoulovitch. Aside from Lou and Danny and me, in Danny's office, and Karin Berg from WBAI, there was also Constantine. He sat on the floor of the small room, by the door, knees hunched into his chin, holding a big book. As the conversations went on, plus telephone calls in and out, he'd take surreptitious photographs. Or glance up at the poster on the wall, advertising the Velvets' summer gig at Max's. Constantine lives in Arlington, Virginia. He was very tired, having taken a day off from the record store where he works; and traveled up starting in the early morning. He was also very hungry. If only I wasn't so tired and hungry, he said, I'd be enjoying this so much more. But I am enjoying it. Constantino's book contained all the Velvets' lyrics, plus commentary; two years ago, he heard *White Light/White Heat*, and he's been listening to the Velvets ever since. He is 17 years old. So is Constantine's interest intellectual, or fanatical? The answer is: both. That's the way the Velvets get you. Why don't you write a thesis on the Velvets at school? I asked him. Oh, I have, he said. Thirty pages. The teacher had little enthusiasm for it, he said.

As he spoke, Lou was saying that, this last summer, he'd found less and less enthusiasm, too; in his case, for continuing with the Velvets. His decision to split was influenced by Brian Jones' death, and I'd guess confirmed by the deaths of Jimi Hendrix and Janis Joplin. Many rock musicians have been hurt, or paralyzed, by having their persons sucked up and consumed by the vortex of their personae. *Loaded* was Lou's good-bye to the Velvets; he'd decided, in time, to become himself again. To proceed from beginning to see the light, to the beginning of a new age. He played some tapes of his new songs, and showed me a poem he'd written after seeing the film *Little Big Man*, in which he'd put himself in the head of an Indian chief feeling his people die. The poem contains the line "we are the insects of someone else's thoughts." The line works for a rock 'n' roll star, too.

Do you know, Lou said, that I've only ever received three, or four, letters from Europe, about my music? We were discussing why people were scared to approach him, and why no other band ever recorded his songs. The reason is to do with the completeness of his songs. People listen to the Velvets as individuals. It's always a surprise (a pleasant surprise) to find that a friend is also a Velvets devotee, because their music never addresses people collectively. That's right, said Lou. My songs are little letters. But, alas, he said, "I never got to people playing the records, so I could cheer if they got them right."

I'd like to put on top hat and tails, Lou said, like Marlene Dietrich in *The Blue Angel*, and do a number with a high soul chorus. And he mimed out the number, "Lonely Saturday Night," putting in the instruments with hums, and the "aahs" and "oohs" of the chorus. "The Velvet Underground wouldn't do that," he said. We laughed. And we talked a bit about John Cale's solo album *Vintage Violence*, and about Nico.

Lou had been reading Wilde's *De Profundis*, in an edition with an introduction by W. H. Auden, and had been annoyed by Auden's assertion that Wilde's reaching for Jesus was pathetic. That's the best part, Lou said. The book bit me. And, after a long search, he was reading Dante, in the translation used by Wilde.

Danny had to go. He took Constantine to the Village for a feed. Lou walked off in the other direction, in a leather jacket, no richer than when he'd started. Off 8th Avenue, copies of the Velvets' third album were selling at $1.50 each.

BEYOND WARHOL

Danny Goldberg

Circus, February 1971

THE VELVET UNDERGROUND ARE FAMOUS FOR THEIR ASSOCIATION WITH Andy Warhol, for singing songs about heroin and sex, for having rock's first female drummer, for being mysterious and remote, for being perverse and esoteric, for having a banana on their first album cover and for being written about with love by Lenny Kaye.

Like the Grateful Dead they remained the darlings of a relatively small set, either unwilling or unable to pierce the needle hole of hit record radio, and like the Dead, in spite of their long tenure as everybody's favorite starving superstars, their basic inborn instinct for rock and roll has driven them, albeit gradually, to the ranks of the finest and most popular American rock bands. The reasons have to do with their talent and perseverance (the band has been together more or less for five years!), with their vision and their integrated style, but mainly with the Mick Jagger of the group, its song-writer, lead singer, guitarist, pianist, and sex symbol, Lou Reed.

The Velvets' history is well known. They got together in Syracuse, surfaced in New York in 1966 playing the Cafe Bizarre where they met and fell in love with Andy Warhol, who was then at the peak of his pop art success. They teamed up with Nico, a Warhol superstar beauty, sang songs with lyrics that made the Rolling Stones look like prudes, and made history as part of a multi media event (the first and best . . .) called the Plastic Exploding Inevitable [sic] where they turned their back to the audience, and played very very loud. A legend of decadence evolved about the group as well as one of mind expanding music. They were the first and only east coast acid rock band of the period. They released three excellent albums on Verve and now MGM has released a "Best of" collection.

But the point of this article is not to further rehash what New York City acid was like in 1967 (an adorable but rather over reported square inch in the many acred farm of contemporary American consciousness). The point is to tell you about a new Atlantic album by the very same Velvets. It is an LP which neither imitates nor forgets the past. It's called *The Velvet Underground Loaded*, has a nondescript cover, and conveys the wonderful feeling that the Stones have in the past exclusively reserved: unforeseeable growth, immediate excitement and memorable new material.

Typically, *Loaded* is the completion not the beginning of another Velvet chapter; the album changed producers in midstream, resulted in some group dissension and ended an all summer engagement at Max's Kansas City where Lou Reed had returned rock joy to the sweaty cynical summer empire city. It's hard to tell what caused what—who left whom if at all, or what will happen in the months to come. Suffice it to say that the summer of 1970 has become instant Velvet Underground history as sure as 1967 was—and luckily for the present and future, *Loaded* exists as a lasting relic of the recent time.

Rock and roll, as we all know, went through somewhat of a plateau most of this summer. Festivals were plagued by government fear and quick buck promoters, and no revolutionary supergroup seemed on the horizon. New York, more than any other part of the country, craves freshness from its entertainers. Charles Manson could have been talking about New York when he wrote "Restless people from the sick city—but they're home now to make the sky look pretty. What can I do—I'm just a person?—this is the line we always seem to hear—you just sit—things get worse—watch TV and drink your beer." And if things are difficult for the average person, the imagined woes of the large core of avant garde are even worse. The Velvets were one of the first genuine rock groups to win the affection of the New York City art crowd. In June, Danny Fields, the young Atlantic Records savant who brought the group to the label, arranged for them to play the upstairs room at Max's Kansas City, the sprawling "in crowd" center of Gotham. Within the red lit walls of Max's, stars from Brian Jones to Bob Dylan, from Janis Joplin to Penny Arcade, have whiled away their late night hours.

The upstairs room is usually a "discotheque" but for the Velvets it became a concert hall. And for their opening night of a one week engagement—their first in native New York for close to two years— uncountable hundreds squeezed together at midnight hoping for a glimpse into the recent past that more had read about (or written about) than lived through.

But Lou Reed was too soulful to be an ivory tower golden oldie. There were changes from the old days. John Cale, producer of the first few albums, had left the group and was replaced on bass and organ by Doug Yule. Maureen Tucker was back with the group and played on the album.

The old Velvet sound combined a Dylanesque vocal with an eastern rock freak backing. In the old days Reed had concocted complex feedback systems where he would get dozens of notes for every string he touched. The new Velvets were unpretentious, tight, throbbing hard hard rock and roll, blistering with Reed's super voice of pleasure/ pain which sang songs no one had ever heard before. "Dance," he demanded raising his left hand with an intensity and grace which made him appear some beautiful combination of Frank Sinatra and Mick Jagger. And dance they did, even the most hardcore wallflowers. The diehard spectators and the impassioned table sitters could not help but move to the driving beat that the new Velvet Underground produced, driven by Sterling Morrison's lead guitar. It was Reed's show and no one would dispute it. In black tee shirt, his veins bulging from his muscular neck he played two sets a night—and not for the one week that had been originally scheduled but for the entire summer.

The Velvets' old professor Delmore Schwartz once wrote, "a cup of coffee can destroy your sadness," and the Velvet Underground were New York's cup of coffee throughout the summer smog. It must be observed that New York is one of the most performed-in cities in the nation—in addition to the always busy Fillmore East there is Unganos, the Bitter End, the Village Gaslight, and a dozen lesser known stages where pop music is offered. Yet it was Max's that led the most sophisticated rock audience in the world to dance as if they were in high school. And to return night after night because they actually enjoyed the music, not merely the social mannerism of a single viewing. Not since the early Lovin' Spoonful days had a rock band in New York continued to draw crowds for such a long period of time. Quite literally everyone of musical importance came to hear Lou belt out with exquisite contempt: "Oh sweet nothing / you ain't got nothing at all."

Naturally a scene sprang up. The group performed a couple of their old classics like "Heroin" or "I'm Waiting for My Man" each night, but they played them the new rock way—commanding respect and a love for their new style. Meanwhile rumors developed. Reed would appear to hate the gig on some nights, or to be at his happiest another. He gave interviews saying things like, "A rock band can be a form of yoga." And he exuded genuine rock—not an imitation of the fifties, or of the sixties—it was a timeless dynamite feeling that made people dance—and smile.

Meanwhile the Velvets were cutting the record *Loaded* in an involved and confusing manner. At first Adrian Barber, producer of the Iron Butterfly, was to be their producer—then Atlantic staffer Shel Kagen. Also involved was Geoffry Halsam, who did the final mix, and the group itself. The album is overall softer than their Max's sets; but the songs are the same and the album is a monument in rock history. Like Dylan, Lou Reed is an artist who changes faster than machines can record him.

At this writing there were rumors that the group had broken up and that Reed was in seclusion writing new songs. But with this group there is no telling what, if anything, the future will bring. The Velvets, thank God, are still unpredictable in an age of rock which revolves around record buying seasons and press releases more often than it does around the artist. Let us be thankful for *Loaded*, an inadequate but potent expression of that summer of 1970.

If nothing else, the album is concrete evidence of what the Velvet fans have always maintained: the group's early decadence and its continuing hassles do not change the fact that they are among the most complex, inventive and musical musicians in the world. They express the scathing, often nightmarish reality of the physical world, yet sing of inner love with a sensitivity that beckons angels. And in their most recent stage they combined their lyricism with their most centered rock music to date, maintaining their position in the dwindling handful of groups who perform rock as the divine momentary celebration it can be.

As Lou Reed passionately sings in "Rock and Roll," "Despite all that amputation you could just go out and listen to a rock and roll station." Or better still, get *Loaded*.

THE VELVET UNDERGROUND

Ben Edmonds

Fusion, February 5, 1971

THE DELIVERY OF A NEW MANUSCRIPT FROM THE VELVET UNDERGROUND commands attention and response in a manner which immediately and forever separates the Velvets from the commonplace. They travel in circles seldom glimpsed by even your heaviest of rock and roll bands, possessed of a continuity in conception and narrative unique to rock. Each of their albums is conceptually linked to those which proceeded it in the finest tradition of serial radio, an incisive statement both on its own and within the context of the past. But apart from being merely another chapter in the continuing story of the Velvet Underground, *Loaded* (Cotillion SD9034), the band's latest, is of even further concern in that it may very well prove to be the last Velvet Underground recording.

To begin somewhere, the air of controversy which currently clouds the Velvets' picture could stand to be cleared. Lou Reed, creative guiding light and image-filter since the band's inception in 1965, left the fold under strange and not totally amicable circumstances shortly after the completion of *Loaded*. Since the time of his departure, stories, some markedly bizarre, concerning the nature of his exit have been circulating. Unfounded though most of those stories obviously were from the very beginning, their very presence is nevertheless open evidence that something is amiss in the back room at Max's.

Loaded's cover credits are elementary fuel for the confusion, and would seem to lend credence to the belief that there was, and is still, a movement afoot to purge the band of Lou's influence. To begin with, Lou's name is listed third in the personnel account, when a band's leading figure is traditionally entitled to the first slot (as has been the case with the Velvets, too). Heading the pack this time is Doug Yule, and the catalogue of his contribution projects the image of a McCartney and, somebody obviously hopes, artistic successor to Lou. The most pungently offensive error, however, is the according of songwriting credits to Yule and Sterling Morrison. All of the songs on the album were written by Lou (as holds true for the third album as well, except that it was decided that Lou's prominence should be sublimated under a group logo), and with only one possible exception are almost instantly recognizable as such. Indeed, the songs of *Loaded* are as much an extension of Lou's creative psyche as ever; and are in some respects its finest flowering.

Though it be sheer ignorance to assume that one man makes a band, the Velvets, in essence, have always been Lou Reed. Even in the early stages; when the violent presence of John Cale confined two of rock's most prolific talents to the same band, the tap roots of the music could be traced to the reflective consciousness of Lou. To be sure, the Velvets' distinctive sound was based on a system of individual elements. Maureen Tucker (whom Lou describes as "the most adorable person on the face of the earth") held the key to the Velvets' cyclic repetition principle with her progressively simplistic drumming, and Cale's classically-oriented chaos was constantly challenging Reed for the floor. Sterling Morrison was the George Harrison of the group: the almost intimidatingly cool one who managed to tie it all together. And while you always knew that the music resulted from the collective attitudes and experiences of the band, ultimate realization was shaped by the brilliance of Lou.

The departure of John Cale is generally accepted as the dawning point of the band's second era, and generally for the wrong reasons. Many assumed that the chaos that left at approximately the same time as Cale was his personal domain, but this is not exactly so. The harshness mirrored in the Velvets' music during those days, though admittedly intensified by the demanding presence of Cale, found an easy outlet in Lou as well as John. When John left it merely allowed Lou the unchallenged freedom to confront another distinct side of his musical personality.

The addition of Doug Yule was, at the time, a crucially functional move. Like Cale, Yule is a very talented multi-instrumentalist, but the directional difference between them was essential to the success of Velvet music in the post-Cale period. Yule's orientation is along more traditional lines, and this outlook helps account for the relaxed brilliance with which the transition from the second to the third album was made. His was a complimentary magnificence. He had the artistic capacity to support the expansion of harmony and melody which Lou had envisioned ("After all," as Lou has said, "where can you go from 'Sister Ray' but to 'I'm Beginning to See the Light.'" No further explanation needed), but without the sometimes disruptive challenge of Cale.

Now that Lou has left, however, it would appear as though Doug is being promoted as his creative successor. This must be seen, at best, as a rather clumsy move. For, as with the others, Doug's contribution became distinctively Velvet only when filtered through the framework of Lou's conception. (The songs, after all, were always Lou's.) And neither Sterling nor Maureen is cut in the Roger McGuinn mold, so where does this leave us? With an album that looks suspiciously like the Velvets' last.

The Velvet Underground has always relied on implied knowledge for the base of their impact, and some people found the transition from the second to the third album perplexing. Because one gets the feeling that the Velvets always know more than they're willing to let on, people were nagged by the thought that the band just might be riffing them, a dilemma which should be firmly resolved for them through *Loaded*. The Velvets, even through the transition, have always maintained a straightforward and honest outlook on their situation.

The thematic transition was not nearly as hard to fathom as some would make it. There was always an underlying urgency manifested in Lou's outlook; not only did his songs reflect where he stood at the time, but the often tense need to experience the next step as well; the transition was logical, a necessary next step and, as usual, one giant step ahead of everybody else. He correctly anticipated and offered those qualities which would soon become of paramount Importance for continued survival: warmth, companionship and hope. It was a little like going from Andy's *a* to the Bible.

It's really a shame that one has to view *Loaded* from the perspective of demise, for the band as captured here is at their peak tightness. It is obviously their most studio-oriented album to date and, despite some minor problems still unresolved, a contrast in its sharp clarity with the shoddy production accorded their second album. In some instances, Lou's conception still outdistances the band's execution, but the gap was decidedly closing at the time this recording was made.

The irony of the fact that the Velvets' last gig together was upstairs at Max's notwithstanding, the possibilities involved in their summer-long city engagement appear to have had an effect on the direction of this album. Their ever-evolving simplistic conception has been channeled into its most relatable form yet, possibly inspired by the dance atmosphere of the Max's gig (an exposure they most certainly wouldn't have received in the cerebral ballroom situation). They're on highly personal terms. Some of the songs are extremely deserving of singles consideration, something the Velvets always have had the potential for but never before connected on.

Perhaps the most impressive musical facet of this album is the distinctive fusion of their two previously defined styles. The earlier Velvets approach concentrated on the low-register repetition and response, but the material on *Loaded* blends low-register overtones with an upper-register outlook which results in a simple rock and roll which is at once both gut-level and spiritually attractive.

Thematically, this new album must be seen as the logical extension of the lyrical and musical demeanor they introduced with their third album. The hard edge which they re-introduce here is a natural progression from the softly sedate disposition of that album—the combination of poetry and motion.

The Velvets, true to form, remain content to set situations and then let the audience play itself into them. They never pointed an accusing finger or drew your conclusions for you. The new situations, still being of a reflective nature, concern themselves with a world where shadows outweigh sunshine: the difference, however, is in perspective. While much of their earlier work employed larger-than-life distortion for effect, their new material is treated with compassion and genuine concern. Many contended that the negativity of their early period was strictly dead-end, but their present attitude leaves the door of salvation at least slightly ajar. Solutions must remain ours to find, for the Velvets deal in immediate reality and nothing more.

Despite the cries of outrage that the song will undoubtedly elicit from Velvet purists, "Who Loves the Sun" is perhaps the key to the album. It's outrageously simple and maybe even cute (it would most certainly have done the early Beatles justice), featuring some pleasantly nondescript singing by Doug and a childishly effective "ba ba ba ba" vocal background by Lou. Some might be tempted to dismiss the song as harmless or inconsequential, but the simple fact that Lou was capable of producing a song like this (keeping in mind that this is the same intellect that could produce a "Sister Ray") speaks volumes of the dimension of his compositional abilities. And that the band is able to execute it as perfectly point-blank as they do says as much for their discipline and development.

Check "Sweet Jane" to find some of the finest rock vocalizing ever captured on wax, courtesy of Lou Reed. Few could probably ever accuse him of having the prettiest voice in rock, but fewer still can dispute the contention that he possesses one of the most expressive. His range, considering the character assumption of his songs, is an almost necessary prerequisite for their successful execution. His "just watch me now" in the third verse is classic rock phrase-making, an area where Lou is unequaled. The only weak point is a badly slurred harmony lead-in to the final chorus, a momentary blemish on an otherwise magnificent song. The lyrics must rank among the finest Lou (or anybody else, for that matter) has conceived; his cultured eye is observantly fixed on the poetics of the street.

Loaded is an album of crucial touches. On virtually every song the Velvets incorporate subtle deviation, the sometimes unnoticed "little things" which distinguish their music from the superficially ordinary complexion of the riffs they lay down. On the negative side are the minor errors (mostly, on this album, in terms of production) which distract often as effectively. The flaws, however, serve to remind us that the Velvets, as with the music they choose to play, are essentially a diamond in the rough (though the sentiments they project are polished and razor sharp).

"Rock and Roll" is exactly as it appears: a brass tacks exposition of Velvet Underground rock perception. The historical continuity made obvious. They have always maintained that rock derives its basic impact and appeal from simplicity (even through the time when most of us had forgotten); this has been the conceptual foundation of their music. The comparatively up-to-snuff production affords us close range investigation of their method. The basic pattern of the essential rhythm guitar, the keep-the-beat stance of both the bass and drums, a lead guitar which is supplementary rather than focal, the building of impact through repetition: these characterizations mark not only the music of the Velvet Underground in particular, but the best rock and roll in general. (And the song itself, by the way, is excellent.)

The first three cuts on Loaded makes Lou's musical, as well as lyrical, domination of the album unavoidable. Gone, with only a couple of minor exceptions, is his dissonantly futuristic electric guitar. He concentrates on rhythm these days, and a majority of the time acoustically so. Both Doug and Sterling's lead runs are consistently nice, but the rhythm emerges here as the key, and it is Lou who makes it go.

"Cool It Down" is one of those songs where the conception outdistances the execution. The verses move in an uneasy, almost halting manner, a problem compounded by a horrendously uneven job of double-tracking the lead vocal. The tune would have moved infinitely smoother had the vocal been left singular. The chorus line very nearly pulls it out, but the song as a whole is never quite able to shake its skeletal feel.

Though "New Age" may not be the most immediately captivating cut, it must certainly be contended with as one of the album's most significant songs. A powerfully wistful glance at the fast-decayed glory of the Sixties, it presents the Velvets at the height of their scene-setting brilliance. They possess a fabulous sense of implied detail (both in terms of Lou's lyric and the band's performance); they say everything by saying very little. Doug's vocal is more plain than plaintive, for the Velvets find a more exacting perspective in seeming distance. (Velvet Underground songs are, almost paradoxically, both an expression of highly personal experience and a completely objective picture of that experience.) The sound of the ghostly distant piano creates the perfect mood. This song represents no instant revelation on the part of the Velvets—they have been aware of the dawning of a new age for quite some time now. That, you see, is what their third album was all about.

In "New Age" the Velvets reflect upon the fate of our self-indulgence in the Sixties. Our stars, like the emotionally destitute "fat blond actress" of that song, are clearly over the hill and gone. The Velvets could never be stars in the traditional sense, for they have always resided in a different galaxy. Yet they were perhaps the truest of luminaries: stars simply because they were stars, not because somebody chose to make them so.

I didn't particularly care for "Lonesome Cowboy Bill" the first few times I listened to it; it seemed a hurriedly clumsy mime of the now standard C&W riff. Like a number of songs on the album, however, it needs a little time to grow. It's an entertaining, almost comical, Walt Disney look at the Old West filtered through a Warhol fish-eye lens.

"I Found a Reason" introduces itself as a benign parody of Fifties rock syrup, but is stunned into simple beauty [by] Lou's last line in the spoken bridge ("I realize how many paths have crossed between us"), and subsequently fortified by the chorus which follows. Beauty literally pulled out of the air. It almost could have been on the third album, but is an integral part of the Velvets' expanded, scope picture here.

It used to be fashionable to define the difference between the West and East Coasts through the Grateful Dead and the Velvet Underground. Times have since changed, though, and that difference must now be seen as that between Creedence Clearwater Revival and the Velvets. (The Dead are rumored to be hiding out in Ohio somewhere.) One need only look at the formula for manufacture to see whose perspective is the more authentic. Creedence is rural assembly–line ready made, while the Velvets remain hand-crafted.

"Head Held High" and "Train Round the Bend" make it the least, although lyrical consideration for the latter may rescue it. "Head" comes off as a little too rushed for my taste (it, like several others, achieved a much greater degree of development during the Max's gig), while the musical components of "Train" (despite a nice feedback figure by Lou) just don't mesh as they should. They both suffer at the comparative absence of Lou's commanding rhythm guitar.

Although *Loaded* may frequently suggest mutated Creedence-like country overtones, you'll never catch the Velvets cavorting in a bucolic meadow for an album cover shot. The closest to the country the Velvets have yet come is still Central Park. They remain immediately discernible residents of New York City (their survival there must be considered something of a triumph in itself), but they're perhaps finding different ways of coping with its darkly attractive and distinctive form of death.

"Oh! Sweet Nuthin" is in many respects a lesser "New Age." Possessed of that same eloquent simplicity, it reverentially re-introduces the theme of loss and gentle desolation. The vocal work, with special regard to their harmony, is of high caliber. The instrumental track is solid and moves very well considering the song's length (7:23), but falls short of the fundamental hypnotism so familiar to them. Its effectiveness seems to be growing with repeated play, however, and it could be my favorite song next week.

It is in some ways fitting that this should be the final Velvet Underground album (reconciliation is possible, but not very), for they conducted us through the Sixties, sacrificing themselves for the experiences most of us never had to live through to dramatize the consequences of our life-style of that period. But the Sixties are gone, and we now find ourselves faced with the possibilities of a new age. The last decade left us with very few heroes deserving of our respect and fewer still we could (or even want to) carry with us into the Seventies. Fat blond actresses are excess baggage, they squandered the love we lavished on them and they now must find the roles reversed. The stage is ours this time around, we are the stars, and the ultimate fate of the play finally rides with the right actors. *Loaded* wipes the nostalgia from our eyes, and even goes so far as to discreetly imply some possible directions to seek. But win or lose, it's our ball game. And sitting over there in the corner is a restless Lou Reed, forcing back a knowing smile as he attentively awaits the outcome.

In the wake of Lou's exodus, the band leadership has been usurped by Doug Yule, while Walter Powers has been brought in to hold down the bass. Now of course Walter (formerly of the Lost and Listening) is a very magical person in his own right, but it is a distinctively Boston magic and hardly capable of filling the void left by Lou's departure. They still call themselves the Velvet Underground, but it all seems more than a little futile at this point.

The Velvet Underground were Athenians in the hungry arena of Rome. But now Lou has gone, and the Velvets have moved to Rome to contend for the crown. The battle, however, is already lost.

DEAD LIE THE VELVETS, UNDERGROUND

Lester Bangs

Creem, May 1971

THE VELVET UNDERGROUND HAVE BEEN ONE OF THE MOST CONSISTENTLY advanced musical organizations of our time, paid the price and endured on the strength of their commitment. The mass audience which they've deserved for so long may finally be coming around to them after exhausting all that "safer," flashier music which eventually proved so stereotyped. Not that there is anything intrinsically difficult about the Velvets' music, then or now, but a combination of bad press, guilt-by-association and public defensiveness have dogged them, absurdly, ever since they agreed to donate their manifold talents to dramatize the milieu of a Pop artist/filmmaker who had reached the stage where he needed a rock 'n' roll band to deliver both his vision and his image to every still-safe living room in Middle America.

So the Velvets hit the pop music scene with a grinding fanfare, and brought countless quivers to the flesh of harried parents gaping at their children huddled in quietly intense circles around speakers oozing the ultimate nightmare—a resinous hymn building into a roar of agonized hostility as inescapable as one honed fingernail shrieking across a blackboard: "Heroin / Be the death of me. . . . And thank your god that I'm *not* aware!"

If the kids embraced it with all the grim receptivity of a new age of ruthlessly self-consuming hedonism, the more respectable listeners set on high as arbiters of the kid culture—rock critics, writers of teen-mag album surveys, industry voices—flinched back with dual reflexes of shocked disapproval and glum silence: maybe this cancer (and isn't it aimed at our very vitals?) will just go away if we ignore it long enough.

Some of the more adventurous approached it with gimmicks: well, it has to do with Warhol, so it must be a put-on, right? Call it camp. Call it New York sickness and write it off musically—doesn't the chick drummer (and whoever heard of *that*, either?) lose the beat in "Heroin," isn't much of it grinding feedback noise? Who can take an album like this in the spring of '67, when the prospects for a Love Utopia shine so and *Sgt. Pepper* is just around the corner?

The early Velvet Underground certainly had a capacity to threaten people, whether they intended to or not, but what both their detractors and many of their most fanatical fans failed to grasp was the distance between the Velvets and their subject matter, a distance as implicit in "Venus in Furs" as in an America slice-of-life portrait like "Lonesome Cowboy Bill." The band has evolved through several fruitful stages of musical experimentation and thematic content in the last five years, some of the best of it unrecorded, but to many they are still a needle-driven instrument of Andy Warhol's supposed S&M conspiracy against the mass libido, and their first album remains their best seller while typing them yet as evil incarnate, spokesmen for the self-destructive fringe and parent of more precisely-aimed assaults like Alice Cooper and the Stooges.

Perhaps it's just that the Woodstock Nation has been brainwashed by the narcissistic, vibe-y albums of groups content to serve as PR squads for the youth culture's "beautiful young people" hype, and fails to see that art doesn't necessarily support darkness by treating it. In any case, the first Velvet Underground album is as solid a documentation of the last decade's malaise as we're going to see. "Heroin" is a classic treatment that stares death in the face and comes back poetic if unresolved. But all the Velvets' songs mark the progress toward that resolution, toward life and joy achieved honestly, outside all the counterfeit wisdom and popular shortcuts to salvation which have failed so miserably. The drug song that corrupts most is the one that advertises any chemical as the mechanism of ultimate self-realization. If heroin is the absolute alternative to enlightenment, it at least makes no false claims, and those who would use this music to score their own self-destructive programs will find no support from the Velvets.

I talked to Lou Reed last month and he spoke long and eloquently on this. He was especially surprised when I mentioned an anecdote of the *Rolling Stone* writer who has asked me if the Velvets were still doing "fag stuff": "We were never doing 'fag stuff,' although some people associated us with that. Just like some people that don't know her think that Maureen has some sort of really hard, dyke-ish image, and when they meet her they're surprised to find out what a beautiful, sensitive girl she really is. So I know that those first two albums and that image hurt us a lot. Those songs that everybody typed us with were reflections of certain scenes around us, and some of it manifested where we were at the time. But later we changed and our music changed but nobody else could seem to shake their pre-conceived notions. Like at the time I wrote 'Heroin' and 'Sister Ray,' I felt like a very rather negative, strung-out, violent, aggressive person. I meant those songs to sort of exorcise the darkness, or the self-destructive element in me, and hoped that other people would take them the same way. But when I began to see how people were responding to them it was disturbing. Because like people would come up and say, 'I shot up to "Heroin,"' things like that. For a while, I was even thinking that some of my songs might have contributed formatively to the consciousness of all these addictions and things going down with the kids today. But I don't think that anymore; it's really too awful a thing to consider.

"But I do know that that was only one aspect of our music, and we've gone through lots of changes since then, and I wish more people would recognize that fact. All of a sudden we started looking out when we went onstage and seeing audiences full of stoned-out, violent people asking for those songs. We didn't want to appear to be supporting that, which is why we won't play most of those songs anymore."

If the Velvets' first album was thematically grim, it was musically as bold as any statement from any band of the last five years. It rendered the dark street life of New York City in a vision as fully realized as anything in Burroughs or Alexander Trocchi's *Cain's Book*; songs like "Heroin" and "Waiting for the Man" were obvious, but "Sunday Morning" was so lush and lyrical that you might not at first notice that the words described urban paranoia with a terse chill: "Look out / The world's behind you / There's always someone around you / Who will call / It's nothing at all. . . ."

The humor in songs like "Femme Fatale" and "There She Goes Again" was missed by a lot of people, as was the wit of "The Black Angel's Death Song"'s authentically absorbed Oriental influence in the viola track (just compare its originality with the obvious "rag rock" scales indulged in by so many other groups at the time, and recall that the Velvets were doing it long before the rest, in 1965), and its lyrics with their strange smears of imagery ("So you fly / Through the cozy brown snow of the east . . . "). Which was also where Lou Reed began to branch out vocally into the distended chants that eventually became a whole system of delivery in "Sister Ray." Here it just found the syllables shifting from the word "choose" to briefly take wing in nonsense syllables, a kind of expletive shorthand: "I chi chi / Chi chi I / Chi chi chi / Ta ta kooah / If you choose / Choose to choose / Choose to go."

White Light/White Heat was the album, though, that firmly proved the Velvets to be much more than a Warhol phase, and established them for any one with ears to listen as one of the most dynamically experimental groups in or out of rock. This great album, which was all but ignored when it appeared, will probably stand to future listeners looking back as one of the milestones on the road to tonal and rhythmic liberation which is giving rock all the range and freedom of the new jazz. "Sister Ray" represented the ultimate extension of the pioneer work of the Yardbirds, marked the first truly successful attempt at applying the lessons of free jazz to rock, and threw a fierce light towards the future and further definitions in the new vocabulary by people like Beefheart and Tony Williams' Lifetime (dig especially the similarity between "Ray," a jam, and "Right On" on the Lifetime's second album). It also led Velvet fans to expect a consistent pattern of fiendishly intricate experiments, even though the band didn't want to limit and type themselves as part of the avant-garde any more than they expected to fixate themselves lyrically in the worlds of darkness conjured up by [the] first album and much of the second. Partly because they knew that they had many more stories to tell, and partly in response to an audience as unprepared for futuristic music as for nightworld lyrics, the Velvets left *White Light/White Heat* to stand, for the time being, as their ultimate statement in the new musical vocabulary of electronic abstraction.

Lou reminisces and shrugs: "Sister Ray's jam came about right there in the studio—we didn't use any splices or anything. I had been listening to a lot of Cecil Taylor and Ornette Coleman, and wanted to get something like that with a rock 'n' roll feeling. And I think we were successful, but I also think that we carried that about as far as we could, for our abilities as a band that was basically rock 'n' roll. Later, we continued to play that kind of music and I was really experimenting a lot with guitar, but most of the audiences in the clubs just weren't receptive to it at all."

But it wasn't only the outer-edge forays on Side Two which made *White Light/White Heat* a classic—each of the other songs was a solidly individualistic entity of its own, as distinct from the songs around it as from the dim gropings so many other groups were into at the time. The title track had steaming piano riffs and marvelous little rhymes that clicked through the funk with a perfect loose precision ("Watch that side, watch that side / Doncha know gon' be dead on arrival" or "Ohh, sputter butter, ev'body gone / Gon' see the mother") and "Lady

Godiva's Operation" injected a coarse urbane humor into the grandeur of a Byrds-like guitar riff, "turning on the machines that . . . " (enter Lou's streetkid cackle to finish the line begun in rather effete tones by John Cale's cultured voice) ". . . *sweetly pump air!*"

Perhaps the most interesting piece was "The Gift." Lots of oppressively banal "stories" and spoken passages have clogged LP grooves in the last few years, but only "The Gift" remains to stand as a successful fusion of literature and programmed rhythm—despite the contrived black humor of the denouement, the total work is witty, well-written and just realistic enough to be right on target. As Lou says today: "I wrote 'The Gift' while I was in college. I used to write lots of short stories, especially humorous pieces like that. So one night Cale and I were sitting around and he said, 'Let's put one of those stories to music.' So we did and I still wasn't sure about it—I'm never sure about things I write for about two weeks—but I guess it turned out really good." If the rest of them are as good as he guessed this one to be, we can only hope he finds some publishers.

Just how many leagues ahead of predictability the Velvets are was brought home stunningly in their third album, as the simplicity and eloquence of such little masterpieces as "Candy Says," "Some Kinda Love" and "I'm Set Free" permeated our consciousness as surely as the vast baroque architecture and deliberately placed sonic smog of "Sister Ray." But the sense of universality was new. Anybody should be able to see both themselves and others they've known in songs like "Candy Says"; as Lou Reed points out: "I've gotten to where I like 'pretty' stuff better (than drive and distortion) because you can be more subtle, really say something and sort of soothe, which is what a lot of people seem to need right now. Like I think if you came in after a really hard day at work and played that third album, it might really do you good. A calmative, some people might even call it muzak, but I think it can function on both that and the intellectual or artistic levels at the same time. Like when I wrote 'Jesus.' I said, 'My god, a hymn! and 'Candy Says,' which is probably the best song I've written, which describes a sort of person who's special, except that I think *all* of us have been through that in a way—young confused with the feeling that other people, or older people, know something you don't. And those and things like 'Sunday Morning' have always been my favorite Velvet Underground songs; I wish somebody else somewhere would record them."

"That's the Story of My Life" is really the story of the paradoxical mood of our times boiled into a couple of short sentences. What other band would answer "the difference between wrong and right" with "both those words are dead" and finish without drawing a moral conclusion? The Velvets' music, far from the pretentious dogma so rampant since 1967, solicits both intellectual involvement and an independent judgement.

The only song on the third album which has been called a failure, "The Murder Mystery," was conceived as a very ambitious experiment. Though it finally doesn't work, the song is still interesting, as is Lou's explanation: "'The Murder Mystery' was intended as a kind of application of modern literary techniques to rock 'n' roll. Like Burroughs and his fold-ins—I figured it'd have to work better here than on the printed page because here you've got a whole different dimension to work with in stereo sound, so the two verbal tracks overlap yet remain separate. Only the reproduction got kind of messed up so you can't even really understand the words if you separate the channels."

But the song I remember most particularly was one they did at a strange San Diego concert in 1968. They were on with Quicksilver Messenger Service, and much of the audience was apathetic or put off; they wanted those California acid-vibes instead of what they took for cold New York negativism. Lou Reed, himself, came out from the dressing room and walked around in the audience with his hands in his pockets, a slight, calm figure with a noncommittal expression on his face. Seemingly, nobody noticed him, because nobody said anything to him—although almost everybody in that place was so busy

being cool they could barely get up the gumption to dance, so it probably doesn't matter. My girl and I wanted to go up and say something
to Lou, shake his hand and tell him how much we dug his music, but I
was afraid. I thought he would be some maniac with rusty eyeballs or
something, the image made me nervous so we didn't approach him,
even though she said: "It seems to me like that was all they really
wanted, for someone to just come up and tell them they appreciate
what they're doing." And as usual she was right, as Lou confirmed
when I talked to him.

That was quite a night, though. In a way it was the ultimate Velvet
Underground concert. The audience was terrible; those that weren't
downright hostile kept interrupting the announcements between songs
to yell out what they wanted to hear, like "How about 'Heroin'!" and
even "Play 'Searchin' for My Mainline'!" But right in the middle of all
these bad vibes, the Velvets launched into a new song that was one of
the most incredible musical experiences of my concert career. Lou announced it as "Sister Ray, Part Two," but it sounded nothing like the
previous song. It was built on the most dolorous riff imaginable, just a
few scales rising and falling mournfully, somewhat like "Venus in Furs"
but less creaky, more deliberate and eloquent. The lyrics, many of which
Lou made up as he went along, seemed like some fantasy from an urban
inferno: "Sweet Sister Ray went to a movie / The floor was painted red
and the walls were green / 'Ooohh,' she cried / 'This is the strangest
movie I've ever seen.' . . . " But it was the chorus that was the most
moving: "Ohhhh, sweet rock and roll—it'll cleanse your soul. . . ."

That's classic, and no other group in America could have (or would
have) written and sung those words. In a way, there are some very old-
fashioned emotions in the Velvets' music. There is a strain of reverence that recurs, from "Heroin" to the song just described to "Jesus" to
"Ohh! Sweet Nuthin's." The yearning, hymnlike quality is the same—
it's just that the focus has shifted over the years. As Lou said recently:
"I think a lot of our music is about growing up, in a way. It's nice to be

mature, to be able to meet things rationally sometimes instead of with all this nervous sort of emotionalism."

ᔑᐯᔑ

Between *The Velvet Underground* and the long awaited *Loaded* lay a year and a half of hassles, conflicts, splits and realignments, sick rumors and ultimate triumphs. First on the slate was a parting of the ways with MGM; at the time each faction claimed the other was fired, but recent developments would seem to support the Velvets both in their claim and their actions. Christ, who else did the company *have?* I talked on the phone for upwards of an hour one day with a girl representing MGM in Los Angeles, and she was not at all sanguine about the part-ing. "What do you want to know about them for? They're *terrible!*"

"Well, I thought 'Heroin' was something of a sixties classic."

"Yeah, that was all right but the group itself . . . ugh! In the first place, no chick should ever play the drums. That is just not a woman's instrument. And the chick that plays 'em looks even more like a man than the lead singer looks like a woman."

Which reminded me of the time I met the Velvets in person. It's funny, but somehow you never expect people to be what they most simply are. You expect something larger than life, one way or the other; genius bemused on its lofty perch or *betes noires*, drugs and ruth-less cynicism and destruction barely tangible, like silt in the air. But when you shake hands and sit down to chat—son of a gun! They're average people! Just like everybody used to think that all jazz musi-cians were junkies, and never got up to change the baby's diapers in the middle of the night or anything. The Velvet Underground were outgoing individuals who claimed to use no drugs now, and were far more literate and intellectually inclined than your average run of pop groups. Lou Reed sat and talked with a relaxed intensity, clarifying where they'd been and what they still hoped to accomplish, together with their constant plans for achieving large-scale success without pandering in any direction; Sterling Morrison laid back with a lovely lady wrapped around him and a tolerant smile on his face, benignly consigning all the competition to oblivion; "Well, the Band is fine if you wanna go back to some rural agrarian society and sit on the front porch every night. . . . I mean, you know. I just can't understand this whole 'back to nature' thing—shit, I go lay on the beach at Coney Island and I get some nature, . . . " and Maureen chuckles, Maureen who has a certain emotional vulnerability about her that is most feminine and rarer than ever today, hurt in a way but also like somebody's kid sister, in fact like Lou Reed's kid sister.

When I met them, I thought to come on cool, so when the subject of drugs came up, I smiled very knowingly, "Well, I think you can take *any* drug, just so long as you don't take it too much or too often." And Lou Reed blandly replied, "Well, yeah, if you wanna be a smorgasbord schmuck." And people kept coming around, heads, groupies, a thirty-ish couple who reminded me of the kind of pre-hippie heads who used to make a big deal out of turning on and going to see 8½, smiling, "Well, we saw Julian Burroughs when we were in Paris and he said to send you all his regards. . . ." The Velvets in the middle of all this mildly amused, Lou setting Maureen on his knee, "Well, whaddaya think, kid, you wanna go get a pizza??"

The MGM girl went on, "The lead singer is the most absolutely spaced person I have ever met in my entire life. I think he was on speed all the time they were here. And on top of all that, he had the nerve to tell me what a fucked-up company MGM is, how much he hates the way we're handling 'em, and why don't we give 'em any promotion—he's sitting there running down the people who are giving me a paycheck every week! What am I supposed to do, agree with him? . . . They got a manager in New York that thinks they're the greatest thing in history. I'll give you his number, call him up, he'll talk your ear off about 'em for five hours. . . ."

So I called up personable Steve Sesnick, who came on just a tad like the classical stereotype of the fast-talking high-powered promoter, but was informative; yes, they had left MGM and were in the process of signing with Atlantic. MGM was fucked; he repeated what the band had told me, that they were given exactly one day to record each of their first three albums. Now that they'd gotten out of the Mike Curb-murk into better business arrangements, things were really going to soar. He had a vision for the band, "We're, what we're doing, is we're so far ahead of everybody else, and have been for five years—that we're just way out there where . . . way out in infinity. . . ."

That was a year ago, when all us fans in the hinterlands were gettin' anxious, going to the record store every day and expecting to see that Atlantic album, a great class label which help some fools take the Velvets seriously at last, old Ertegun/Wexler benchmark production and snazz packaging, the whole works. It was finally gonna happen. A lot of us thought it was about to happen when the local AM station bought a format called Funderground and "Heroin" made number one (why, it even beat out "Alice's Restaurant"!!) and a lot of other people got set (when the third album was released) for New York's contribution to the rock of ages to assume their deserved place in the public pantheon. But now it had to happen; the Velvets were playing live again, at Max's Kansas City in their old hometown, a celebrated summer long gig that knocked New York flat on its ass and spread the word cross-country. Legendary sets, some say the best live dance music by a white rock 'n' roll band ever caught and caught it is because there are tapes circulating in the East that would make a fantastic next Cotillion album (especially with conditions what they now be), or the bootleg of all time, if some enterprising madman were willing to invest a few vats of vinyl. All summer long the Velvets kicked out the jams, and more, because for every wailing, wiry firestorm there were some "Sweet Nuthin's" just down the track. It was a triumph. They went in to make their fourth album in New York's Atlantic studios. Now the time was finally on for the Velvets, rock 'n' roll princes right out of history if ever once seen clearly, and Lou Reed, non-*poseur* poet-craftsman that could become a Dylan for the 70's without even becoming self-conscious about it. The public was tired of its arch-superstars with their identical, impersonal funk-laden albums, their arrogant concert boredom and charisma of distance.

The Velvets went in and recorded. Slowly and at ease for the first time, learning. Holdups. Rumors that the producer (Adrian Barbour, maybe) wasn't showing up for sessions all that regularly. Some vague conflict. Other rumors had the album finished, the Velvets dissatisfied, back for more work. Perfectionist. Meanwhile there's some several thousand crazy kids (Velvet fans ain't no Mongol horde, but they'd rip the locks from doors and doors from jams to hear that music) out there across Southern California and the Corn Belt and up haulin' hod in North Dakota all jumpin' in ecstasy waitin' on the next big blast of Long Island sireen thunder. Rise and shine to "Heroin" in '67, "Sister Ray" pacing the long nights and lunging nerves of '68, "Set Free" in '69—these kids gotta have that music, man, they grew up with it whether you believe it or not, went on and through and off the chemical nightmare with that music scoring the process all the way, livid one year and lucid the next. Nobody who remembers all those songs and then waited all that time for Number Four could stand to wait much longer; just like they're not gonna stand for the prospect of no ascension from "Sweet Jane" and "Rock and Roll." Something had to give.

Something did. The strangest rumors started floating around. The first one was that Lou Reed was *dead*, that his manager had murdered him for reasons unknown and neither of them had been seen for several days. Nobody quite believed it but speculation was rife. On and off and on again as one shadowy tale tumbled into another; Lou Reed freaked out, flipped out, was incommunicado, and cracked under pressure and split for parts unknown, had freaked out and gone home to Long Island to live with his parents. "Oh well," said one cheerful cynic, "he writes all his best songs on Long Island anyway."

Which shows you just what kind of fine friends you get among your brethren and sistren along the showbiz mainline if you ever really *do* freak out. Jimi's dead, another star done gone. Janis kicks it and it

hurts even if you didn't like her music, Lou Reed flips out and skips
back to filial security, oh well, at least he's alive. I was having fantasies
about him staying on speed for the entire duration of the Max's engagement and falling in frothing fits and seared nerves to heal for another onslaught. Never mind what they tell you with their own
mouths—"White Light/White Heat" plays on, so's not quite dead on
arrival. Who shrinks from believing the worst? Who's ingenuous
enough to risk getting caught believing any better?

The bald facts of the matter are that Lou Reed did not in any way
flip or freak out, with or without drugs, even though it was such a hot
rumor that *Circus* Magazine (among others) picked it up, and *Rock*
Magazine, writing months after the fog of misunderstanding and misin-
formation had cleared, had him "disconnected from objective reality."

What happened, according to New York publicist Danny Fields,
writers like Lenny Kaye and Lisa Robinson and anyone else close
enough to the actual situation not to be taken in by the smokescreen,
was that a conflict developed, or had been developing for a long time,
between Lou and manager Sesnick. Apparently, Sesnick wanted the
group to move in certain directions (perhaps way out into . . . *infinity*):
Lou had other ideas and no compromise was possible. So Lou left and
did indeed go to Long Island, while the other members of the band,
for reasons unknown, stuck with Sesnick. Even though every song
they have ever written was, in significant part, Lou Reed work and
most of them flat Lou Reed originals; even though Lou was the leader
and guiding spirit of the band and always had been, much like Jagger
with the Stones, not only singing lead on the vast majority of songs
but developing most of the band's sonic innovations including that
wiry, unprecedented style of solo guitar attack used in "Ray" and
"Heard Her Call My Name," which he taught the other members of
the band and in which he, himself, played the best recorded solos. In
other words, Lou Reed is the total spirit and driving force behind the
Velvet Underground, as has been perfectly obvious for years to seemingly everyone but their "visionary" manager. When Cale was there,

they might have gotten along without Lou, because they were twin titans, the crowding of whose talents split the original Velvets much the same way that (to indulge a little sacrilege) Steve Stills and Neil Young burst the Buffalo Springfield. But now, without Lou, without Cale, relative newcomer Doug Yule seemingly at the helm, they could be little more than Danny Fields' nickname for the new group, "The Velveteen Underground" (or "Crushed Velvet"—ed.).

But it doesn't end there. As soon as Lou left, Sesnick started going around making statements to the effect that, yeah, they were gonna have a great band now that The Problem (which was his interpretation of Lou) was out of the way. Coincidentally, he also started dropping a story around town that the real reason for Lou's departure was that he had freaked out and had to get out of the main jetstream of the New York pop scene until he could handle things a little better.

With the unerring instincts that mark him a true standard-bearer in the Mathew Katz tradition, he went on to claim not only that Lou did not write most of the songs or shape the group's sound crucially, not only was the anti-egocentric practice of the Velvet Underground of marking their songs as collectively authored used to fuck Lou over and downgrade his reputation as a composer, but, according to Danny Fields, Sesnick even had the balls to start claiming that he wrote some of the songs himself!

Meanwhile, Lou Reed, sitting at home in Long Island, probably watching Hollywood Squares, neither shows his face nor says a word.

Look closely at the back of your Loaded album; an almost-empty recording studio, but who is that lone cat sitting over there at the piano? Some tireless genius so dedicated he stays on to work it on out even after everybody else has packed up and gone home? Is it Leon Russell? Elton John? No, no—it's—why it's jolly old Doug Yule, I do believe! Gee, Doug, I sure never knew you were bustin' your ass like that! And what else do we see here? The line-up . . . "dashing Doug Yule, stalwart Sterling Morrison, lazy Lou Reed, looks like he fell into the minor leagues, followed of course by milky-cheeked Moe Tucker.

And look at all those instruments after Doug's name . . . my, my, and playing lead guitar too, when all the time, I thought . . . one never knows do one? . . . "

Doug Yule is probably a very nice guy, and undoubtedly he's an extraordinary musician or Lou would never have hired him in the first place. But honest to God, this is the most outrageous misrepresentation and spit in the face of a great artist that I've ever seen on an album jacket. They don't come right out and *say* that this is a Doug Yule Production, they know they can't get away with that, but the implication is clear. It seemed like a nice gesture when the third album credited all songs to the band by group name—no ego problems or prima donnas *here*. It's fine for a group to think of itself as a thoroughly integrated, undifferentiated sound unit; God knows we've enough Jeff Becks. But when that spirit of cooperation is used to pull a fast one with every bit of artistic integrity the group stands for, you've got to indict not only the megalomaniac who conceived this tangle of idiotic, hopeless schemes but the musicians who let themselves be carried along with it as well.

I couldn't believe this story when I first heard it, and if it's as authentic as it seems, a lot of people are being used.

But in all those polemics, rumors, charges and chicaneries, real or imagined, there is one almost forgotten man: Lou Reed, himself, whom I spoke with long distance in the study of his father's law office in Long Island. And while everybody else on the line is fuming that either Sesnick is insane, or just, well, slightly unhinged by years of buzzsaw salesmanship, Lou refuses to fuel the fray, sling indictments or invective, but instead lays out the story as he sees it very calmly and carefully:

"I'm not going to make any accusations or blame anybody for what's happened to the Velvets because it's nobody's fault. It's just the way the business is. So some of the stories that've been circulating, I can see how people would've gotten these ideas because of the circumstances under which I left. I just walked out, because we didn't have any money, I didn't want to tour again—I can't get any writing done on tour, and the grind is terrible—and like some other members of the band, I've wondered for a long time if we were *ever* going to be accepted on a scale large enough to make us a 'Success.' . . .

"I can see why some of those rumors, like the one about me supposedly freaking out, might have gotten started, because I've been in kind of semi-hiding here. But they're directly the opposite from the truth. In fact, I'm probably one of the most anti-drug people around. . . . I don't mean that I wanna tell anybody else what to do, though, you know, because I think people resent that and it's none of my business anyway. I'm anti-drug in the sense that I think drugs are bad for Lou Reed. And I know a lot of people, like a lot of people I've known, experiment with a lot of these things as methods to solve problems or find outlets or whatever, but, when you find that they don't really work very good, you move on to something else. Like I haven't got any answers but the same ones everybody else has: yoga, health foods, all of that. . . . Lester, don't you think there might be some truth in the idea that marijuana leads to harder drugs?"

I hedged, venturing that I didn't know about that, but I did think that staying loaded on grass all the time tended to make you a perhaps innocuous, but nevertheless unproductive semi-vegetable. Still, I said, it's nice to jag off once in a while.

"Well, yeah," said Lou Reed, "it's great to have an outlet . . . kind of like going on vacation. But when you're on vacation all the time . . . you're never home, I guess."

᠅

All of this constitutes the atmosphere, then, of the season of *Loaded*, the fourth and arguably finest Velvet Underground album (though I'll still take *White Light/White Heat* on pure saber-toothed Energy Beyond the Highest Energies ever dreamed or garnered by any o' them Detroit killerboys or anybody else for that matter . . . personal 17-minute exorcism preference). Also, the absolutely final and unapproachable Rock and Roll Album of 1970. Which needed it and unputtered over Life Music like it as much as nay year since Gene Vincent kited off down the gulfstream. Also, and nobody believes it, except the band and Quickie Sesnick, the apparent final Velvet Underground album, *period.*

Be that as it may, though, thank god for trusty *Loaded*, which is not only a better album than *Revolver* but beats the last four Dylan albums all to hell and gone for my mind, in terms of what a Dylan album should be about and sound like if he would only do like I keep telling him. So I'll just hafta listen to Lou Reed, who is doing (just as ever since the Spring of *Pepper*) exactly what I wanta hear so I'll never have to tell him what to do and would feel cowed at the very thought of presuming so. Because Lou Reed, of all "poets," "songwriters," "balladeers" and energy jammers on the scene today, has a curious, unimpeachable dignity all his own, a dignity which simultaneously posits that he will hand you no bullshit and asks in turn only (I think) that this (call it person rather than "privacy") be respected. You'll never catch Lou pulling Tim Buckley's Little Boy Lost into Byronic Agony act, if he becomes a solo artist, or cynically manipulating an audience to volunteer hysteria like certain honk blues and black soul artists, when he is playing with a band and driving down the notes on that souped up axe he flays. Lou Reed (nor the Velvets when they were unified) would never exploit his audience, to put it in simpler syllables. And the deal, see, is that you accept what's given without qualification. As long as it's good. Because the Velvets gave and gave for years on years and people sat in clubs pursing their lips in cued contempt; or used the music like meth to promulgate their own hysterias, which amounts to the same thing—inattention.

Loaded is one of the most lazily listenable albums since *Moondance*. By which I mean that you can kick yourself back into your nook and relax, 'cause the Velvets do all the work for you. I suppose it's a necessary fashion in LPs today, times being what they are, that so many albums should be (either ineptly or quite intentionally) contrived in such a way that YOU, the poor weary listener, must stop acting the passive consumer and *invest* yourself in the album before you can get anything much out. 'Cause what you take from these cryptical constructions depends most weightily upon what you've bought. Kinda like a packrat, if you get my psychedelic meaning. Or a novel by one of them shifty-eyed Thomas Pynchon characters—it's not just a problem in music. I mean, it's gettin' to be fuckin' work to listen to music today, what with all those symmetrical dozens of couplets pregnant with convolutions of meaning, or all that magic-fingered musicianship you've gotta listen to close 'cause Don't You Know Who That Is Playing That Solo? But the Velvets, running gleefully upstream, as always, to counter each trend in popular contrivance with their sane, healthy instincts, just keep getting easier to listen to *and* hear all the time. No sweat, dad. And even if they never musicate together again, it's still nice to know, just like ole Van Morrison and some several other nice but volative folks, they've plowed their Walpurgisnachts and all such classy European Art terms just to mellow down easy like a natural man wants to in his day.

Loaded is simultaneously a high-sighted art-statement and the best affirmation yet that, just like Lou said in, why I believe it was the *Rolling Stone* review of this same album, they are really still just a rock 'n' roll band from Long Island. But whether you must descry the Artistes or the gullyjumpers just depends which of their manifold backyards yer playin' in. And sometimes they cross breed for a chunky solo right biff in the bazoois just delicated the slight degree by one frankly booshwah mauve boxing glove.

And what *that* syncromesh of half-struck metaphors means is that even though some of their more, shall we say, Elevated statements can be approached with all the attentive decorum proper to music of Significance (and they are that, too), they reflect Real Life rather then half-digested Soph Camp profundities, and more importantly, will also get your ya-yas out when you get tired of any and all meanings.

Furthermore, they never let their little Humor Senses toddle off out of the range of a fast resort when the going threatens to get a little bit lugubrious. In fact, according to Lou, the two most bittersweet songs which strike the most "serious" notes on the album were originally conceived in somewhat lighter tones: "I originally intended to do almost all of the vocals on this album, but I blew my voice out at Max's, so Doug took over on several of them, and the sense that the songs were handled and interpreted in got changed around a little—like 'New Age' was supposed to be funny, a girl thinking she was like a movie queen and the guy down the block was Robert Mitchum. And 'Sweet Nuthin' was even more different—it was intended as a rather sly song making fun of some people that it describes and not at all as the sort of very serious statement it ultimately became."

The nicest touch on the *Loaded* album, or at least the one that endears it most to me, is the fact that it contains not one but four Instant Rock 'n' Roll Classics. Their names, surprise, are "Sweet Jane," "Rock & Roll," "Head Held High" and "Train Round the Bend." "Sweet Jane" and "Train Round the Bend" have a suggestion about them of the kind of thing Dylan might be doing today if he'd gone on as a rock 'n' roll prince after *Blonde on Blonde* and elaborated that basic sheetmetal trainwhistle holler of his, instead of riverbeddin' down with a sheet of Corrs-cool Nashville steels and dandyfyin' himself up as the very scarecrow ghost of Preacher Gary Cooper come a-callin'. And now he's a very sedate man love with his house in hills w/kids and chickens and ducks so what's out here in Mudville for him? The challenge in songs like "Train Round the Bend," that's what.

This one song is one of the most definitively (which includes unpretentiously) Amerikan pieces of music heard since "Mystery Train" or Roy Acuff's "Night Train to Memphis," both of which it's intrinsically related to not only as new ragweed-continent Train litercheer but also as musical construction. You bet it's an obvious song; why didn't you think of it? Just like you should have thought of "Not Fade Away" and "Lay Lady Lay" and lots of other inevitable, indestructible songs that when suddenly they're there it seems like they always were or shoulda been because they roll off the spool as natural as life itself and where they now set there was before a void which you just never noticed, because if you had, and been a genius-type void-filler like ol' Louie Reed, why then you woulda had all the glory.

It's ridiculously late in the course of the Collective Listening Habits of the Western World to mention this now but take special note of that spiffily splintered steel-and-wire guitar counterpoint which underlays this little folk dittywahditty; telegraphic chatter counterpointing the golden flanks of the lunging Super Chief lead guitar. And that vocal and those words! What a voice; the raggedy epiglottis denim jacket personification of wild Amerikid, like Neal Cassidy almost, loose and wild as the promise of a continent that's gone and was going when Jack Kerouac traversed it. Jack Kerouac would like this song, I'm sure, because it doesn't pander to the by now lethally banal idea of the jacket-flapping vagabond in Amerika—we've come all the way from *Route 66* to *Easy Rider* in just a decade, but if you look at it from another angle we've come from Kerouac to "Train Round the Bend." And if that seems ludicrous to you, just reflect that both are true to the eternal often-trampled vision which comes out of a fierce crazy love of America and everything it represents or could or did.

This fine song is also a hoot at the current fad for gettin' back to the land just like what Sterling said, come to think about it: "Train round the bend / Takin' me way from the country / I'm sick of the trees / Take me to the city. . . . Wind in the country yer much too raw / Tryin' to be a farmer / But nothin' I planted ever seemed to grow. / . . . I am just a city boy / don't mean to knock the country life / I miss the city streets and the neon lights / Ah see the train comin' round the bend." Yazoo! Lyrics of the Year. Oughta enshrine 'em in the Smithsonian Institution and play 'em for visiting furriners to show 'em what we *are*—better yet, play 'em the whole album.

What's more, and this is the real trick, they manage, in a day and age when it's all but impossible, to bring off a "folksy" thing like this with next to no hint of self-consciousness; and self-consciousness is probably the number one affliction steeping the wild frame of American music today—just look at the Band for an example of a fine, dedicated group so mired in self-consciousness that it even touches their pinnacles like their second album.

And that is the level of self-consciousness behind their warm, earthy playing and singing. Even Creedence suffers tangibly from this, though not nearly as much. But "Train Round the Bend" is folklore and rock 'n' roll of the highest order and in fulfilling both functions it pulls off a deft one you don't often see in these dog days. And, as if that wasn't enough, it also was apparently just a quick flash from the Muse, what they used to call a "head" arrangement. Sez Lou, "And 'Train Round the Bend,' which is about the Long Island Railway, was conceived and worked out entirely in the studio."

"Sweet Jane" is the most immediately striking, memorable song on the album. An arrhythmic wash of high keening pastel notes, then the perennial guitars-as-rhythm-section pushing on and on with their own easy momentum. You want it to go on forever, or at least as long as it might have; Lou said that a whole middle instrumental section was somehow excised in the studio. And once again he sings with such smooth, joyous insolence, why, it's almost Negroid, folkses. The man is a sure master now of the voice we thought he was trying to train in '68.

Once again the lyrics are right out of a young-old American Dream, Main Street this time, an easy time warp between our rockroll prince slouching on that corner dreaming of his hometide girl and how it was all maybe so much realer back when, Jane and Jack down by the fire before Fenders rang, just crisp in the laps of each other while the old radio plays on to no particular frenzy: "The March of the Wooden Soldiers," for "all you protest kids." Uncle Lou may not wave gratuitous peace fingers and fishy fists your way like Mickey Jagger but he still loves ya almost as much as he loves Jack and Jane in their oldtime lovers' Shangri-La. Or, as the author himself says: "'Sweet Jane' sort of refers back to the 20s, and a romance—'Jane is in her corset, Jack is in his vest.'" Posing the musical question, what's it like to fall in love?, and since "Hard" is only one word we have a little world realized, taking up where "Beginning to See the Light" left off. And maybe the next album will carry it to the next level, where lovesongs fear to tread.

Though Sweet Jane sounds like a girl, indeed; I wouldn't turn around and break it, nossir! And oh, those heart-bracing philosophizings: "Some people they like to go out dancing / And other peoples they have to work—just watch me now— / And there's even some evil mothahs (heh heh) / Who'll tell you that life is jeessst *dirt* / You know that women never really faint / And villains always blink their eyes / And children are the only ones who blush / And life is—just to—die! / But anyone who had a heart / They wouldn't turn round and hate it. . . . " Ah, Lou, Lou, you wise old fart you, how does your benign countenance breathe such beatific verities so effortlessly? Elton John me *this* music, you students of Pedant Rock, and tell me whose wisdom's heartiest!

"Rock and Roll," of course, is simply the most definitive personification of the phrase in a year when fraud and antique quackery are loose in the land. Rather than subject us to yet another tacky period piece, the Velvets sing of our traditions in the context of a gleaming Jetstream arrangement that represents some sort of evolutionary pinnacle for them. The words are a perfect distillation of race memory—recall the first song you ever heard that jived your buns right there in the car, when Elvis and the Drifters sent out that vibrato-rumble you could feel right up through the cushions that made you want to leap and shout even as a child. And "Rock and Roll" not only tells you, it shows you. They should make it the theme song of the Voice of America—the Cold War would be won, finished in a single blast of fine, fine music that would have all of Eastern Europe dancing in the streets for sheer joy. Because if America has a gift to give, this is it: "Their lives were saved by—*Rock an' Roll.*"

"Head Held High" is another slice of unpretentious contemporary folklore, universal memory of those endless injunctions to stand up

straight, keep your shoulders back, met not with self-righteous postur-
ing but Lou's hoot of sanity: "Just like I figured / They always *disfigured*
with they heads held up high!" Another history-making line—in fact,
if there's been a rock 'n' roll album in the last decade with more classic
lines per capita than *Loaded*, I haven't heard it. And the arrangement
and delivery here are energy music personified: easy, unstrained thunder, rushing ahead in wild glee with the feeling that even greater
power is held in reserve. You want it to roar on for the whole side, and
dancing to it must have been one of the alltime workouts.

The rest of the songs are almost as fine, if not nearly so archetypal, as
I don't need to tell you since you probably already know them by heart
anyway. It's been a might dreary season musically, but *Loaded* just seems
to go on and on, getting better and better the more thoroughly it's di-
gested. It ain't no overnight sensation, and I'm confident we'll still be
listening to it in ten years, right along with *Highway 61 Revisited* and
Moondance. And there may never be another Velvet Underground album—the last I heard, the group (still sans Reed), was purportedly
playing at some ski-lodge in Vermont—but you can bet that this music
will go on, as surely as nothing could cut off that mighty guitar solo in
"Oh! Sweet Nuthin'" at the height of its hurtling course. There will be
more Lou Reed albums, make no mistake, just like there will be more
John Lennon albums. Negotiations are, I think, being made with Atlantic right now. Corporations may dissolve. But despite all the amputations, the core rocks on.

U2's IRISH HOMECOMING

CREEM

$2.50 • $2.95 Canada
NOVEMBER 1987

EXCLUSIVE INTERVIEWS
20 YEARS WITH

LOU REED & THE VELVET UNDERGROUND
THE FINAL TRUTH!

SIMPLE MINDS
UNDERSTAND THIS MAGAZINE

ECHO & THE BUNNYMEN
HIP-HOP IS *BACK!*

THE MONKEES
FAB PIX & FAX!

ROGER WATERS
STEVE EARLE
CRUZADOS

AMERICA'S ONLY ROCK 'N' ROLL MAGAZINE

GALA SABIAN CYMBAL GIVEAWAY—DETAILS INSIDE

A silver Millar pillow floats solemnly from the pale hands
of Andy Warhol,
thru the Factory window, across the grainy New York skyline,
and the sound embodying that unhurled work of art was perhaps
a work of art itself—
The Velvet Underground.
They were the stark, elusive balloon that burst upon a
deflated scene,
injecting that scene with a radiance that connected poetry,
the avant-garde and rock & roll.
They were a band of opposites, shooting freely from pole to pole,
without apology, with dissonant beauty,
trampling the flowers of peacemakers,
treading the blond depths,
black in a white world, white in a black world.
They opened wounds worth opening,
with brutal innocence, without apology,
cutting across the grain, gritty, urbanic.
And in their search for the kingdom, for laughter, for salvation,
they explored the darkest areas of the psyche.
And they reemerged. And they delivered up.
All of these things can be deemed romantic, but one aspect
can be truly romanticized:
their work ethic.
And the body they delivered up.
They are the Velvet Underground and their work is the
clipper ship.
They are the Velvet Underground and we salute them.

—Patti Smith, belatedly inducting the Velvets into the
Rock and Roll Hall of Fame, January 1996

THE SONGS OF
THE VELVET UNDERGROUND,
1965-1970

THIS PURPORTS TO BE A COMPLETE LISTING OF ALL SONGS KNOWN TO HAVE BEEN done by the band in the five years it existed as a creative entity with its leader Lou in tow. It is a remarkable body of work, and one that Reed himself resolutely plundered throughout the seventies as his solo career began to hit its stride. Indeed, his first three solo albums—which include the classics, *Transformer* and *Berlin*—feature thirteen songs in total dating from those halcyon days.

I have also attempted to reference every known recording of the band herein, whether in the studio, in their loft, or out on the road—where the songs usually needed to be played to achieve their full potential. With the cancellation of a scheduled bootleg series by Universal, a number of the most important Velvets recordings are likely to remain unreleased, including mono soundboard tapes from the Gymnasium in April 1967, their last shows in New York for over three years. However, there are few "lost songs." Those that remain resolutely "underground" are included here, with some basis for their provenance, in the hope that remaining dusty archives may yet spill their goods.

∿∿∿

Each song title is divided into five categories of recording as follows:

1. **Official studio recordings:**
   VU&N—*The Velvet Underground and Nico* (1967)
   CG—*Chelsea Girl* (1967)
   WLWH—*White Light/White Heat* (1968)
   TVU—*The Velvet Underground* (1969); CM (closet mix) or VM (Valentin mix)

LO—*Loaded* (1970)
FLO—*Loaded: Fully Loaded Edition* (1997)
VU—*VU* (1985)
AV—*Another View* (1986)
WGO—*What Goes On* (1993)
PS&S—*Peel Slowly and See* (1995)

2. Demo and rehearsal recordings:
These can be found on the boxed sets WGO and PS&S.

The dates relate to the following venues/recordings:

July 1965, Ludlow Street
January 3, 1966, the Factory
January 1966, the Factory
Winter 1967, Ludlow Street
Fall 1969, unknown, possibly Atlantic demos (generally known as "The
    Countess of Hong Kong" demos)
April 15 and 16, 1970, *Loaded* demos, Atlantic Recording studios, New York
July 1970, Max's rehearsal, New York

3. Official live recordings:
LAM—*Live at Max's* (1972)
LAM+—Live at Max's (Expanded ed.) (2004)
1969—*1969* (1974)
WGO—*What Goes On* (1993)
PS&S—*Peel Slowly and See* (1995)
TQT—*The Quine Tapes* (2001)

The dates relate to the following venues/recordings:

May 11, 1969, Washington University, St. Louis (TQT)
October 19, 1969, End of Cole Avenue, Dallas (1969)
November 7–9, 1969, Family Dog, San Francisco (1969)
November 12–December 3, 1969, the Matrix, San Francisco (TQT)
July 26, 1970, Max's Kansas City, New York (LAM) (LAM+)*
August 23, 1970, Max's Kansas City, New York (LAM) (LAM+)

---

* Though the recent expanded Rhino release of *Live at Max's* credits both shows to August 23, 1970, I continue to subscribe to the two separate nights theory, and have dated the "early set" to the usually attributed date in late July.

4. Unofficial live recordings:
The dates of these currently extant, unreleased live recordings relate to the following venues/recordings:

> June 23, 1966, Poor Richard's, Chicago
> November 4, 1966, Valleydale Ballroom, Columbus, Ohio
> April 30, 1967, the Gymnasium, New York
> April 28, 1968, La Cave, Cleveland
> October 4–6, 1968, La Cave, Cleveland
> November 1968(?), Cleveland
> December 12, 1968, Tea Party, Boston
> January 10, 1969, Tea Party, Boston
> January 31, 1969(?), Tea Party, Boston
> March 13, 1969, Tea Party, Boston
> March 15, 1969, Tea Party, Boston
> July 11, 1969, Tea Party, Boston
> August 2, 1969, Hilltop Festival, Rindge, New Hampshire
> October 18, 1969, End of Cole Avenue, Dallas
> October 19, 1969, End of Cole Avenue, Dallas
> January 3, 1970, Second Fret, Philadelphia
> April 17, 1970, the Paramount, Springfield, Massachusetts
> May 1970, Second Fret, Philadelphia

5. Rumored recordings and performances:
Any songs rumored to have been recorded and/or performed by the band, along with a general description of the sources of information.

THE SONGS

1. *Afterhours*
   Official studio recording: TVU
   Official live recordings: November 8, 1969 (TQT); August 23, 1970 (LAM)
   Unofficial live recordings: October 18, 1969; October 19, 1969

2. *All Tomorrow's Parties*
   Official studio recordings: VU&N; VU&N CD (alternate mix); PS&S (45)
   Demo/rehearsal recording: July 1965 (PS&S)
   Unofficial live recording: November 4, 1966

3. *Andy's Chest*
Official studio recording: VU

4. *Beginning to See the Light*
Official studio recording: TVU
Official live recordings: November 12–December 3, 1969 (1969); July 26, 1970 (LAM)
Unofficial live recordings: October 4–6, 1968; December 12, 1968; January 10, 1969; March 13, 1969; March 15, 1969; July 11, 1969; October 18, 1969; October 19, 1969; April 17, 1970

5. *The Black Angel's Death Song*
Official studio recording: VU&N
Official live recording: November 23, 1969 (TQT)
Unofficial live recording: November 4, 1966

6. *Blue Velvet Jazz Jam*
Unofficial live recording: October 19, 1969 (an informal jam at the end of the band's second night at the End of Cole Avenue recorded by the person responsible for taping both nights)

7. *Booker T*
Official live recording: April 30, 1967 (PS&S) (The instrumental part of "The Gift," this track can also be heard in its studio incarnation by isolating the right-hand channel of the stereo mix. Indeed, it was issued as a bootleg single in this form.)

8. *Candy Says*
Official studio recording: TVU
Official live recording: August 23, 1970 (LAM+)
Unofficial live recordings: December 12, 1968; January 10, 1969; March 13, 1969; March 15, 1969; July 11, 1969; October 18, 1969; April 17, 1970; May 1970; August 23

9. *Chelsea Girls*
Official studio recording: CG

10. *Coney Island Steeplechase*
Official studio recording: AV

11. Cool It Down
Official studio recordings: LO; FLO (early version)
Demo/rehearsal recording: July 1970
Unofficial live recording: May 1970

12. The Countess of Hong Kong
Demo/rehearsal recording: F69 (PS&S)

13. End of Cole Avenue Jam
Unofficial live recording: October 19, 1969 (another informal jam at the end
of the band's second night at the End of Cole Avenue, recorded by the
person responsible for taping both nights)

14. European Son (to Delmore Schwarz)
Official studio recording: VU&N

15. Femme Fatale
Official studio recording: VU&N
Official live recordings: October 19, 1969 (1969); November 7, 1969
(TQT); August 23, 1970 (LAM)
Unofficial live recordings: November 4, 1966; October 18, 1969

16. Ferryboat Bill
Official studio recording: AV
Unofficial live recordings: March 13, 1969; March 15, 1969

17. Foggy Notion
Official studio recording: VU
Official live recording: November 8, 1969 (TQT)
Unofficial live recordings: October 4–6, 1968; December 12, 1968; January
3, 1970; April 17, 1970

18. Follow the Leader
Official live recording: November 27, 1969 (TQT)

19. Get It on Time
Rumored recordings/performances: Copyrighted on April 22, 1966, the only
known recording is from an as-yet-uncirculated rehearsal tape at the Factory on March 7, 1966.

20. *The Gift*
Official studio recording: WLWH

21. *Guess I'm Falling in Love*
Official studio recording: AV (backing track only)
Official live recording: April 30, 1967 (PS&S)

22. *Head Held High*
Official studio recordings: LO; FLO (alternate mix); FLO (early version)
Demo/rehearsal recording: July 1970
Unofficial live recording: May 1970

23. *Here She Comes Now*
Official studio recording: WLWH
Demo/rehearsal recording: winter 1967—two takes (PS&S, take 1)

24. *Heroin*
Official studio recording: VU&N
Demo/rehearsal recording: July 1965 (PS&S)
Official live recordings: November 12–December 3, 1969 (1969; 1969 CD);
    November 23, 1969 (TQT)
Unofficial live recordings: June 23, 1966; November 4, 1966; April 28, 1968;
    October 4–6, 1968; November 1968(?); December 12, 1968; January 10,
    1969; March 13, 1969; March 15, 1969; August 2, 1969; October 18,
    1969; October 19, 1969; April 17, 1970

25. *Hey Mr. Rain*
Official studio recording: AV (two takes)
Rumored recordings/performances: April 28, 1968 (This song was certainly
    performed live in 1968. According to legend, it preceded the perfor-
    mance of "Sweet Sister Ray" at La Cave in April, but was accidentally
    erased at a later date.)

26. *I Can't Stand It*
Official studio recording: VU
Official live recordings: November 12–December 3, 1969 (1969 CD); No-
    vember 8, 1969 (TQT)
Unofficial live recordings: October 4–6, 1968; January 10, 1969; March 13,
    1969; March 15, 1969; October 18, 1969

27. If I Tell You

Rumored recordings/performances: Mentioned in a 1973 VU retrospective in
Phonogram Records by Richard Cromelin, "If I Tell You" apparently included the following lyric:

> If I tell you all the pretty things
> And if I give you what tomorrow brings
> Would you stop being mean to you
> Stop those things that hurt only you.

28. I Found a Reason

Official studio recording: LO
Demo/rehearsal recordings: F69 (FLO); July 1970
Unofficial live recording: October 18, 1969

29. I Heard Her Call My Name

Official studio recording: WLWH

30. I'll Be Your Mirror

Official studio recording: VU&N
Official live recordings: October 19, 1969 (1969); August 23, 1970 (LAM)
Unofficial live recording: October 18, 1969

31. I Love You

Official studio recording: FLO
Demo/rehearsal recording: April 16, 1970 (PS&S)

32. I'm Gonna Move Right In

Official studio recording: AV
Unofficial live recordings: October 4–6, 1968; December 12, 1968; January
10, 1969

33. I'm Not a Young Man Anymore

Unofficial live recording: April 30, 1967 (Part of the Gymnasium performances in April 1967, this seven-minute blast-out has the simplest of
lyrics and a nagging, insistent riff.)

34. I'm Not Too Sorry (Now That You're Gone)

Demo/rehearsal recording: Winter 1967 (PS&S)

35. I'm Set Free
Official studio recording: TVU
Official live recording: July 26, 1970 (LAM+)
Unofficial live recordings: November 1968(?); December 12, 1968; January
    10, 1969; March 13, 1969; March 15, 1969; July 11, 1969; October 18,
    1969; October 19, 1969

36. I'm Sticking with You
Official studio recordings: FLO; VU
Official live recording: November 8, 1969 (TQT)
Unofficial live recording: October 19, 1969

37. I'm Waiting for the Man
Official studio recording: VU&N
Demo/rehearsal recordings: July 1965 (PS&S); July 1970
Official live recordings: October 19, 1969 (1969); November 8, 1969
    (TQT); November 27, 1969 (TQT); July 26, 1970 (LAM)
Unofficial live recordings: November 4, 1966; April 30, 1967; October 4–6,
    1968; November 1968(?); December 12, 1968; January 10, 1969; January
    31, 1969(?); March 13, 1969; March 15, 1969; July 11, 1969; August 2,
    1969; October 18, 1969; April 17, 1970; May 1970

38. Index
Official studio recording: WGO

39. It's Alright (the Way That You Live)
Demo/rehearsal recording: winter 1967 (PS&S)

40. It's Just Too Much
Demo/rehearsal recording: July 1970
Official live recordings: October 19, 1969 (PS&S; WGO); November
    12–December 3, 1969 (1969); November 8, 1969 (TQT)
Unofficial live recording: October 18, 1969

41. It Was a Pleasure Then
Official studio recording: CG

42. Jesus
Official studio recording: TVU
Unofficial live recordings: October 4–6, 1968; December 12, 1968; March
    13, 1969; March 15, 1969; July 11, 1969; October 18, 1969

43. Kill Your Sons
  Rumored recordings/performances: This has generally been credited, by both
    Reed and other writers, to the Velvets era (or possibly earlier), though no
    VU recording is known. However, it *is* one of the seventeen songs demoed
    by Reed for his first RCA album in late October 1971, even though it
    would have to wait until 1974 for inclusion on *Sally Can't Dance.*

44. Lady Godiva's Operation
  Official studio recording: WLWH

45. Lisa Says
  Official studio recording: VU
  Official live recording: November 12–December 3, 1969 (1969)
  Unofficial live recordings: October 19, 1969; April 17, 1970

46. Little Sister
  Official studio recording: CG

47. Lonely Saturday Night
  Rumored recordings/performances: According to reviewer Aral Sezen, an
    early version of "Lonely Saturday Night," was performed at the Avalon
    Ballroom in San Francisco on November 8, 1969.

48. Lonesome Cowboy Bill
  Official studio recordings: LO; FLO (early version)
  Official live recordings: July 26, 1970 (LAM); August 23, 1970 (LAM+)

49. Loop
  Official studio recording: *Aspen #3* (a multimedia magazine published by
    Warhol)

50. Love Makes You Feel Ten Feet Tall
  Demo/rehearsal recording: FLO

51. Melody Laughter
  Official live recording: November 4, 1966 (PS&S, edit; WGO, alternate edit)

52. Men of Good Fortune
  Rumored recordings/performances: Performed at the January 3, 1966. Fac-
    tory rehearsal, this song did not emerge until Lou Reed's fabled second
    solo album, *Transformer.*

53. Miss Joanie Lee

Demo/rehearsal recordings: January 3, 1966 (Scheduled for inclusion on the deluxe two-CD version of *Velvet Underground and Nico*, "Miss Joanie Lee" was pulled at the last minute when members of the band began to demand a renegotiation of their contract [thus scuppering further volumes of their own official bootleg series into the bargain!]. However, the song, which is an eleven-minute assault on one's frontal lobes, has subsequently circulated, presumably from a pre-release dub. As Olivier Landemaine puts it on his fabulous VU website, "It really is an unbelievable song/jam similar in sonic spirit to 'European Son' but with lots of Bo Diddley thrown in for fun.")

54. The Murder Mystery

Official studio recording: TVU
Unofficial live recording: included in "Sister Ray" performance from Boston Tea Party, January 28, 1969

55. Never Get Emotionally Involved with Man, Woman, Beast, or Child

Rumored recordings/performances: This legendary title was mentioned by Sterling Morrison as one of the songs worked up in the summer of 1965 in their Ludlow Street loft. Moe Tucker has confirmed that such a song did exist.

56. New Age

Official studio recordings: LO (edit); PS&S (long version); FLO (full version)
Demo/rehearsal recording: July 1970
Official live recordings: November 12–December 3, 1969 (1969); November 24, 1969 (TQT); July 26, 1970 (LAM)
Unofficial live recordings: April 17, 1970; May 1970

57. Noise (see Index)

58. The Nothing Song

Unofficial live recording: November 4, 1966 (One of two long instrumentals that the band played at the Exploding Plastic Inevitable shows [the other being "Melody Laughter"], this title was the one given it by the band.)

59. Ocean (Here Come the Waves)

Official studio recordings: VU; FLO

Demo/rehearsal recordings: April 16, 1970, number one (PS&S); April 16, 1970, number two (FLO)
Official live recording: November 12–December 3, 1969 (1969)
Unofficial live recordings: October 18, 1969; October 19, 1969

60. Oh Gin (later Oh Jim)
Official studio recording: April 16, 1970 (PS&S)
Demo/rehearsal recording: April 17, 1970

61. Oh Sweet Nuthin'
Official studio recordings: LO; FLO (early version)
Unofficial live recording: May 1970

62. One of These Days
Official studio recording: VU
Unofficial live recording: October 19, 1969

63. The Ostrich
Official studio recordings: The Primitives 45 (Pickwick 1001).
Rumored recordings/performances: Though the original recording of this Pickwick 45 featured a prototype Velvets, no documented Velvet recording of it has ever emerged, and surprisingly enough the original 45 has never been re-released officially.

64. Over You
Official live recordings: November 12–December 3, 1969 (1969); November 25, 1969 (TQT)
Unofficial live recording: January 3, 1970

65. Pale Blue Eyes
Official studio recording: TVU
Official live recordings: October 19, 1969 (1969); August 23, 1970 (LAM)
Unofficial live recordings: October 4–6, 1968; November 1968(?); December 12, 1968; January 10, 1969; January 31, 1969(?); July 11, 1969; August 2, 1969; October 18, 1969

66. Prominent Men
Demo/rehearsal recording: July 1965 (PS&S)

67. Ride into the Sun
Official studio recording: AV (backing track only)
Demo/rehearsal recordings: F69 (WGO); April 16, 1970 (PS&S)
Official live recording: November 24, 1969 (TQT)

68. Rock and Roll
Official studio recordings: AV; LO; FLO (alternate mix)
Demo/rehearsal recording: April 15, 1970 (FLO)
Official live recording: November 25, 1969 (1969; TQT, same performance, different recording)
Unofficial live recordings: October 19, 1969; May 1970

69. Run Run Run
Official studio recording: VU&N
Unofficial live recordings: November 4, 1966; April 30, 1967; January 10, 1969; July 11, 1969; August 2, 1969

70. Sad Song
Demo/rehearsal recording: April 16, 1970 (PS&S)

71. Satellite of Love
Demo/rehearsal recordings: April 15, 1970, number one (PS&S); April 15, 1970, number two (FLO)

72. Sheltered Life
Demo/rehearsal recording: winter 1967, two takes (PS&S, take two)

73. She's My Best Friend
Official studio recording: VU

74. Sister Ray
Official studio recording: WLWH
Official live recordings: November 11, 1969 (TQT); November 7, 1969 (TQT); December 3, 1969 (TQT)
Unofficial live recordings: April 30, 1967; October 4–6, 1968; November 1968(?); December 12, 1968; January 10, 1969; January 31, 1969(?); March 13, 1969; March 15, 1969; July 11, 1969; October 18, 1969; October 19, 1969; January 3, 1970

75. *Sister Ray, Part Three*
Rumored recordings/performances: According to Cale, in his autobiography *What's Welsh For Zen?*, this was a specific, extended version of "Sister Ray" that the Velvets performed as an encore on occasions. They would "start way off left of field, with something totally chaotic, and gradually work our way back to the version on the record. Very long, very intense, with Lou becoming a Southern preacher man, telling stories and just inventing these fantastic characters."

76. *Some Kinda Love*
Official studio recordings: TVU (CM); TVU (VM)
Official live recordings: November 8, 1969 (TQT); November 12–December 3, 1969 (1969); August 23, 1970 (PS&S)
Unofficial live recordings: October 19, 1969; April 17, 1970; May 1970

77. *Stephanie Says*
Official studio recording: VU

78. *Sunday Morning*
Official studio recording: VU&N
Official live recordings: November 9, 1969 (TQT); August 23, 1970 (LAM)
Unofficial live recording: October 18, 1969

79. *Sweet and Twenty*
Rumored recordings/performances: A song copyrighted by Lou Reed (music) and William Shakespeare (words) on June 10, 1969. The title comes from *Twelfth Night*, act 2, scene 3, part of a two-verse snatch from a love song of sorts:

> *In delay there lies no plenty,*
> *Then come kiss me, sweet and twenty,*
> *Youth's a stuff will not endure.*

80. *Sweet Bonnie Brown*
Official live recording: November 12–December 3, 1969 (1969)

81. *Sweet Jane*
Official studio recording: LO (edit); PS&S (full version); FLO (early version)
Official live recordings: November 12–December 3, 1969 (1969); July 26, 1970 (LAM+); August 23, 1970 (LAM)
Unofficial live recording: January 3, 1970; April 17, 1970; May 1970

82. Sweet Rock and Roll *aka* Sister Ray, Part Two

Rumored recordings/performances: In his article "Dead Lie the Velvets, Underground," Lester Bangs refers to just such a song being performed in San Diego in July 1968. Robert Gold's contemporary review of a show at the Shrine confirms that it was also performed there. According to Sterling Morrison, a recording was made of the Shrine performance, but it has never emerged. He remembered the refrain—"Sweet rock and roll, it'll cleanse your soul"—and the fact that it was used "as a preamble to 'Sister Ray.' It kind of just goes along and then hits the chords, which were very heavy. . . . Cale played keyboard on 'Sweet Rock and Roll,' and that was really what carried it. Good keyboards."

83. Sweet Sister Ray

Unofficial live recordings: April 28, 1968 (An extraordinary thirty-nine-minute jam that prefaced "Sister Ray" at this time, this may well have evolved into "Sweet Rock and Roll" [see above].)

84. A Symphony of Sound

Demo/rehearsal recording: January 1966 (A twenty-six-minute jam at the Factory that was filmed by Warhol, it concludes with the arrival of policemen.)

85. Temptation Inside Your Heart

Official studio recording: VU

86. That's the Story of My Life

Official studio recording: TVU

Unofficial live recordings: October 4–6, 1968; March 13, 1969; October 18, 1969

87. There Is No Reason

Demo/rehearsal recording: winter 1967 (PS&S)

88. There She Goes Again

Official studio recording: VU&N

89. Train Round the Bend

Official studio recordings: LO; FLO (alternate mix)

Unofficial live recording: May 1970

90. *Venus in Furs*
Official studio recording: VU&N
Demo/rehearsal recording: July 1965 (PS&S)
Official live recording: December 1, 1969 (TQT)
Unofficial live recordings: June 23, 1966; November 4, 1966; April 30, 1967; October 4–6, 1968; October 18, 1969

91. *Walk Alone*
Demo/rehearsal recording: One of the songs (co-)written by Lou during his time at Pickwick, "Walk Alone" appears to have survived the transition into the Velvets. It is featured on the Factory rehearsal from January 3, 1966.

92. *Walk and Talk (It)*
Demo/rehearsal recordings: April 16, 1970 (PS&S; FLO); July 1970

93. *We're Gonna Have a Real Good Time Together*
Official studio recording: AV
Demo/rehearsal recording: F69
Official live recording: November 12–December 3, 1969 (1969)

94. *What Goes On*
Official studio recording: TVU
Demo/rehearsal recording: July 1970
Official live recordings: 1968(?) with Cale (1969); October 4–6, 1968 (PS&S); November 8, 1969 (TQT)
Unofficial live recordings: October 4–6, 1968, two versions; November 1968(?); January 10, 1969; January 31, 1969(?); March 13, 1969; March 15, 1969; August 2, 1969; October 18, 1969; October 19, 1969; May 1970

95. *White Light/White Heat*
Official studio recording: WLWH
Demo/rehearsal recording: July 1970
Official live recordings: November 12–December 3, 1969 (1969); December 1, 1969 (TQT); July 26, 1970 (LAM+)
Unofficial live recordings: December 12, 1968; January 10, 1969; March 13, 1969; March 15, 1969; July 11, 1969; January 3, 1970

96. Who Loves the Sun
Official studio recordings: LO; FLO (alternate mix)
Demo/rehearsal recording: July 1970
Official live recording: August 23, 1970 (LAM+)

97. Wild Child
Demo/rehearsal recording: July 1970

98. Winter Song
Official studio recording: CG

99. Wrap Your Troubles in Dreams
Official studio recording: CG
Demo/rehearsal recording: July 1965 (PS&S)

CREDITS

"Ronald Nameth's Exploding Plastic Inevitable" by Richard Whitehall. First published in *L.A. Free Press*, May 1, 1968.

"Verve press release," Verve Records, April 1968.

"The Above-Ground Sound of the Velvet Underground." First published in *Hullabaloo* Vol. 3, #4, May/June 1968.

"Round Velvet Underground" by Sandy Pearlman. First published in *Crawdaddy*, #16, June 1968. Copyright © 1968 by Sandy Pearlman.

"The Velvets at the Shrine" by Robert Gold. First published in *L.A. Free Press* July 26, 1968.

"The Boston Sound" by Wayne McGuire. First published in *Crawdaddy*, #17, August 1968.

"The Day the Velvets Met the Dead: Two Reviews" by F. D. Williams and Joe Anderson. First published in *The Pittsburgh Point*, August 2, 1969.

"Problems in Urban Living" by Robert Somma. First published in *Fusion*, April 14, 1969.

"Review of *The Velvet Underground*" by Lester Bangs from *Rolling Stone*, May 17, 1969. Copyright © 1969 *Rolling Stone* L.L.C. All rights reserved. Reprinted by permission.

"I'm Beginning to See the Light" by Paul Williams. First published in *Planet*, May 15, 1969. Copyright © 1969 Paul Williams.

"Review of *The Velvet Underground*" by Adrian Ribola. First published in *Oz*, May 1969.

"Lou Reed Interview" by Ramblin' Jim Martin. First published in *Open City*, #78.

"It's a Shame That Nobody Listens" by Richard Williams. First published in *Melody Maker*, October 25, 1969. Copyright © 1969 IPC.

"A Rock Band Can Be a Form of Yoga" by Lita Eliscu. First published in *Crawdaddy*, vol. 4, #4, January 1970.

"C/o The Velvet Underground, New York" by Robert Greenfield. First published in *Fusion*, #8, March 6, 1970. Copyright © 1970 Robert Greenfield.

"Sterling Morrison Interview" by Greg Barrios. First published in *Fusion*, #8, March 6, 1970.

"The Velvet Underground" by Lenny Kaye. First published in *New Times*, April 20, 1970. Copyright © 1970 Lenny Kaye.

"Musique and Mystique Unveiled" by Phil Morris. First published in *Circus*, vol. 4, #7, June 1970.

"No Pale Imitation" by Richard Nusser. First published in the *Village Voice*, July 2, 1970. Copyright © 1970 the *Village Voice*.

"Review of the Velvet Underground at Max's Kansas City" by Mike Jahn. First published in the *New York Times*, July 4, 1970. Copyright © 1970 the *New York Times*.

INDEX

Page numbers in boldface refer to illustrations.